# S. A. Cunningham & the Confederate Heritage

# S. A. Cunningham

## &

## THE CONFEDERATE HERITAGE

## John A. Simpson

*The University of Georgia Press  Athens & London*

© 1994 by the
University of Georgia Press
Athens, Georgia 30602
All rights reserved
The paper in this book meets the
guidelines for permanence and
durability of the Committee on
Production Guidelines for Book
Longevity of the Council on Library
Resources.

Printed in the United States of
America

98 97 96 95 94 C 5 4 3 2 1

British Library Cataloging in
Publication Data available

FRONTISPIECE:
S. A. Cunningham in 1912, when he
was elected president of the Tennessee
division of the United Confederate
Veterans. From the *Confederate
Veteran* 22 (January 1914).

Library of Congress
Cataloging in Publication Data
Simpson, John A., 1949–
    S.A. Cunningham and the
Confederate heritage / John A.
Simpson.
        p.   cm.
    Includes bibliographical references
(p.) and index.
    ISBN 0–8203–1570–2 (alk. paper)
    1. Cunningham, Sumner Archibald,
1843–1913.   2. Journalists—Southern
States—Biography.   3. Confederate
States of America—Historiography.
I. Title.
PN4874.C93S56   1994
070′ .92—dc20
[B]                         93–9956
                                CIP

*To Shirley,*

*Jamie, Annie, & Craig*

*Let no man who has never*

*been a soldier judge him who has.*

*William Ripley*

*Medal of Honor recipient*

*Contents*
————

# Acknowledgments

Many people from all walks of life are responsible for this book's becoming a reality.

My father, James P. Simpson, was a proud Scotsman who encouraged us by example to be interested in our family and national heritage. Little did he realize that the weekend we spent in Gettysburg in the summer of 1961 would spark my interest in the American Civil War—a cause that has consumed my attention for the past thirty-three years.

My first exposure to the ranks of professional historians occurred at Western Washington State College. There scholars such as R. L. DeLorme, August Radke, and Keith Murray inspired in me a dedication to the subject that will never be eradicated. At the University of Arkansas, W. David Baird and Timothy P. Donovan started with their guidance the long and necessarily painful process of turning an enthusiastic student with rudimentary writing skills into a journeyman-scholar. As a graduate teaching fellow at the University of Oregon I enjoyed infinitely expanded exposure to the world of books, research, and writing under the tutelage of Richard Maxwell Brown. But it is to my mentor, Jack P. Maddex, Jr., that I owe an incalculable debt. His patience, wit, immense intellect, and constructive criticism were indispensable to me through the process of writing my dissertation on Cunningham. Special thanks go to Herman Hattaway at the University of Missouri at Kansas City for offering criticism on the dissertation, articles, and book. His commentaries are always right on the mark. I am professionally and personally appreciative of these fine scholars.

I am also grateful to many reference people for their support and encouragement. Genella Olker, reference librarian at the Tennessee State

Library and Archive, has been invaluable in her determination to turn up every shred of information on Cunningham. Karina McDaniel provided fine photographic reproductions. Virtually every Southern historical society and state archive conducted material searches. Special mention should be made of several libraries and librarians: Richard Schrader, Wilson Library, University of North Carolina; William Richter, Barker Library, University of Texas; Middleton Library, Louisiana State University; Perkins Library, Duke University; Baker Library, Harvard University; the Huntington Library, San Marino, California; and the Howard-Tilton Memorial Library, Tulane University. Private organizations also proved helpful, including the United Daughters of the Confederacy Library in Richmond, Virginia. Archivists at the *Chattanooga Times* and *Nashville Tennessean* also offered assistance. Finally, I would like to acknowledge the National Society of Colonial Dames for a scholarship that allowed me to conduct research for one summer in Nashville.

I have enjoyed my association with Malcolm Call, director of the University of Georgia Press, throughout all phases of this project. I give special thanks to his staff.

To my family I extend the deepest thank-you. Mom and Jimmy have always been right there. My children, Jamie, Annie, and Craig, played catch without me while I spent long hours at the computer. For my wife, Shirley, I reserve the ultimate appreciation. Her unwavering support is largely responsible for the completion of this book.

The accolades now return full circle to the early 1960s. A warm hand of friendship is extended to my two junior high school history teachers, George Yount and Bud Creighton. It is from these two men that I learned a valuable lesson—that studying history can be fun. Their influence, in no small part, has led me to a career in teaching history to ninth-graders.

Thank you, one and all!

S. A. Cunningham & the Confederate Heritage

# Prologue

A spring shower threatened from a darkening sky as a light breeze swept across the southwest lawn of the state capitol grounds in Nashville. A crowd of five thousand people spilled out onto adjoining streets. Latecomers hung from trees and out of nearby office windows. They had been assembling for more than three hours to witness the unveiling of a monument to Confederate soldier Samuel Davis. Important dignitaries from Tennessee mingled among the audience, including three former governors, the entire General Assembly, and members of the local United Confederate Veterans and Daughters of the Confederacy. Governor Malcolm Patterson, the orator, sat on the podium alongside the master of ceremonies, E. C. Lewis, and Sumner Archibald Cunningham, owner and editor of the *Confederate Veteran* magazine.

Cunningham's prominent position was a reward for his many years of labor on behalf of the Davis monument. The editor's mood was one of exhilaration as the crowd hushed to listen to Patterson's remarks. To everyone's satisfaction, the governor gave a superlative account of the gallant exploits of Tennessee's "boy hero."[1] The speech especially pleased S. A. Cunningham.

As the hour-long ceremony drew to a close, Lewis singled Cunningham out for special recognition. It was, after all, the energetic journalist who had commanded every phase of the monument, from conception through construction. Dr. J. H. McNeilly, an acquaintance standing nearby, noticed how Cunningham's "face shone and his eyes kept filling with tears of joy and gratitude." One insightful observer perceived that the new monument was as much a tribute to Cunningham as it was to Davis. By the editor's own admission, the commemoration marked a "crowning glory" in his life.[2] As the audience drifted away on that sultry afternoon in April 1909, the fulfilled editor of sixty-six years returned to his office on the city square.

On a cold December morning four years later, Cunningham hunched over his desk at the *Veteran*, deeply engrossed in yet another memorial endeavor. He scribbled some notes about the granite shaft proposed as a memorial to Daniel Decatur Emmett, the author of "Dixie." That morning a $25 contribution arrived from his minstrel friend Al G. Fields.[3] Suddenly Cunningham collapsed to the floor, a steady stream of blood flowing from his nose. His diligent secretary of twenty years, Edith D. Pope, worked in an adjoining room, unaware of his problem. Cunningham lay motionless for an undetermined length of time until visitors discovered his condition. Pope summoned an ambulance, which rushed its unconscious patient to St. Thomas Hospital. Physicians packed Cunningham's nose but were only partially successful in controlling the bleeding. He regained consciousness, but intermittent hemorrhaging continued over the next forty-eight hours. The doctor's prognosis was that Cunningham had "hardly a chance for recovery." Cunningham, too, sensed the terminal nature of the attack. Although weakened from the substantial loss of blood, he calmly began making funeral arrangements. His sister, along with several nieces and nephews, were present on the evening of 20 December 1913 when S.A. Cunningham "crossed the river" to be with his Confederate comrades.[4]

The public was stunned when the press announced Cunningham's demise. One front-page headline proclaimed that the "HERO OF A 100 BATTLES" had gone to his final reward. William E. Mickle, adjutant general of the United Confederate Veterans Association, lamented that Cunningham's passing was a "disastrous blow" to veterans everywhere. In Nashville, Frank B. Cheatham Bivouac spoke of the loss of one of the Veterans Association's "leading and most influential members."[5]

Respecting Cunningham's wishes, the renowned theologian James I. Vance officiated at the memorial service in First (Presbyterian) Church, Nashville. A large throng was present, including relatives, business associates, former comrades-in-arms and the social and civic elite of the city. Vance emphasized Cunningham's "amiable temperament, exceedingly courteous manner, and ready facility for making acquaintances." He lauded the editor as a kind, soft-spoken gentleman who was utterly devoid of malice. "No man," he concluded, "whom Nashville has counted as one of her citizens will be more missed than Mr. Cunningham. And none has carried with him into the beyond more universal and unmixed esteem."[6]

Later Cunningham's associates in Cheatham Bivouac sponsored their own service, at which UCV Commander Bennett H. Young spoke eloquently. Cunningham's casket was draped with the worn battle flag of the Twelfth Tennessee, and two aged comrades held up the Stars and Bars in the background. At the conclusion of the ceremony, the gray-clad attendants stood at attention with bowed heads as one veteran blew taps over the remains of S. A. Cunningham.[7]

E. C. Lewis offered his private railcar to transport the funeral cortege to the interment site, located forty miles south of Nashville. The generosity of Cunningham's friend included a free meal at the local hotel to every veteran in attendance. Seventy frail comrades accepted the invitation, which compelled Lewis to add an extra car to the procession. When the train pulled into Shelbyville station the modest middle Tennessee community buckled under the onslaught of mourners. Cunningham's cousin, Sarah Buchanan Robinson, recalled that the funeral and grave-side service was one of the largest ever attended in Willow Mount Cemetery. "When the first buggies arrived at the cemetery," she noted, "there were some still on the town square."[8] Family and friends had given Cunningham a send-off befitting a Confederate hero. Seven years later a beautiful eight-foot shaft marked his resting place.

The popular acclaim Cunningham won for exonerating Southern actions of 1861–1865 is measured partly by the display of affection paid to him at his death. For Cunningham, as for other Southern men of his generation, the defining life experience was involvement in the Confederate military. That experience so traumatized Cunningham that it drove him to expound the merits of the Confederate heritage over a forty-two-year career in journalism. Beyond any doubt, the man and the war were inextricably bound together.

# Chapter 1 Family Ties

The settlement of Bedford County, Tennessee, dated from the 1780s. The first pioneers came mostly from North Carolina to set up farms on several thousand acres of land reserved for veterans of the Continental army. S. A. Cunningham's grandparents—Humphrey and Margaret Patton Cunningham—descended from Scotch-Irish immigrants. They were married in North Carolina in 1801 and eleven years later moved to the most populous district in Bedford County.[1] Shortly thereafter, on 27 March 1812, their sixth child, John Washington Campbell Cunningham, was born.[2]

Into early adulthood, J. W. C. Cunningham worked as an agricultural laborer. He married Sarah E. Couch in 1835 and purchased a fifty-acre homestead for six hundred dollars from his recently widowed mother.[3] The property, located in the nineteenth civil district along Sinking Creek, was bordered by that of affluent relatives, and the family cemetery. Fishing Ford Road cut through the neighborhood and provided easy access to Shelbyville, eight miles to the northeast. The bustling town of Richmond was even closer—four miles to the south.[4] J. W. C. Cunningham made no substantial improvements to the farm over the next few years. The loss of his wife and one infant to the cholera epidemic in 1837 testified to the hardships of frontier living.[5]

The fortune of J. W. C. Cunningham changed on 13 September 1842, when he married Mary Buchanan, a widow from nearby Lincoln County. Mary was the twelfth child of Samuel and Rachel Greenfield Buchanan, Kentuckians who had moved to Tennessee in 1812. The Buchanan clan were devout Cumberland Presbyterians, and Mary Buchanan Cunningham contributed an unquenchable Christian zeal to the marriage. One admirer later claimed that Mary was "universally esteemed because of Christian virtues and loveliness of character."[6] The marriage of J. W. C. Cunningham and Mary Buchanan set the stage for the birth of Sumner Archibald Cunningham on 21 July 1843.

Sumner Archibald Cunningham attended the Phillipi School, near Richmond, and received there a solid education in reading, writing, and arithmetic.[7] The Cunninghams' ability to send their children to private schools rather than public ones, which had the reputation of being inefficient, dramatized the family's status in the community. The opportunity to receive an academy education was available to only the most affluent families. Thus S. A. Cunningham belonged to an elite group of middle Tennessee children who received private instruction.[8]

Cunningham also acquired religious training as a youth. Most denominations established churches in the county, including the Methodists, Baptists, and Presbyterians, and revivals occurred with frequency. Cunningham's immediate family, following the Buchanans' lead, were staunch Cumberland Presbyterians. They resided in the Elk Presbytery, pastored by the Reverend Isaac Shook, and attended Sunday services at Flat Creek, a mile from their home. S. A. Cunningham's private schooling and religious training had a great impact on the development of his personality.[9]

The wooded section of Bedford County where Cunningham grew up contained all of the topographical features common to the Great Central Basin of Tennessee—a fertile basin trimmed by a hilly outer rim and surrounded by rugged highlands. Many creeks sliced the landscape, and all of them flowed into Duck River, the largest waterway in the region. Clover, wheat, oats, sweet potatoes, and corn grew in abundance in the rich humus. This region was sometimes referred to as the Southern breadbasket and "one of the richest areas in the entire Confederacy."[10] A recent study by Stephen Ash labeled the thirteen central counties in middle Tennessee an "agricultural cornucopia."[11] As farm production gradually increased and Bedford County became an area of commercial, rather than subsistence, agriculture, land values soared.

S. A. Cunningham claimed that he grew up "among a plain but fairly well-to-do people."[12] Initially, the Cunninghams were neither gentry nor landless. Rather, they were proud, hard-working, ambitious people. It was the gradual introduction of slavery into Bedford County that raised their economic status. By the time S. A. Cunningham was seven years old, more slaves toiled in middle Tennessee than in any other section of the state. Bedford County typified the trend; its slave population exceeded one-third of the total number of county residents.[13] Owning no slaves in 1840, J. W. C. Cunningham registered five slaves ten years later and added three child laborers in the 1850s.[14] By 1860 Negroes worked on slightly more than half of the seventeen hundred farms in Bedford County, but the vast majority of households owned only one or two slaves. The number of slaves the Cunninghams owned demonstrated their substantial economic status within the neighborhood. They belonged to a class of farmers whose future prosperity depended upon the continuation of slavery.[15] It is probable, however, that the entire Cunningham family worked alongside their slaves in the fields.

The farm on which S. A. Cunningham resided increased in value tenfold in the 1850s while the typical middle Tennessee farm increased only twofold. The average property value in the state ($3,300) was well below that of the typical Bedford County farm. If landless families in the nineteenth district were discounted, the average property value soared to $8,200. The Cunningham farm surpassed the latter figure by $3,200. Every economic indicator documents that the Cunninghams belonged to the upper one-sixth of Bedford households.[16]

The agricultural census also substantiates that the Cunninghams belonged to a prospering upwardly mobile class. A comparison of agricultural expansion from 1850 to 1860 illustrates this point (see Table 1). By every measure the Cunningham farm sustained steady economic growth in the 1850s. Although the amount of improved acreage remained within the mainstream of most Bedfordites (25 percent growth), property values skyrocketed by 535 percent. In comparison with their county neighbors, the overall value of the Cunningham property was three times greater. While the number of livestock actually decreased, its overall value leaped significantly (335 percent) despite relatively stable unit numbers. Outstanding growth occurred in many produce categories, including wheat (2,900 percent) and corn (82 percent). These startling figures point strongly to a transformation from subsistence to commercial agriculture. The Cunningham family used a portion of their new prosperity to invest in additional real estate. In 1854 J. W. C. Cunningham purchased three parcels of land and within three years owned approximately five hundred acres.[17]

The future appeared bright during S. A. Cunningham's early adoles-

## Table 1
### Agricultural Production on the Cunningham Farm

|  | 1850 | 1860 |
|---|---|---|
| Acres of land |  |  |
| improved | 80 | 100 |
| unimproved | 73 | 76 |
| Cash value of farm | $1,800 | $11,400 |
| Value of farm tools | $ 20 | $ 70 |
| Livestock |  |  |
| horses | 11 | 8 |
| mules | 11 | 11 |
| milch cows | 7 | 10 |
| oxen | 11 | 2 |
| other cattle | 10 | 9 |
| sheep | 25 | 9 |
| swine | 100 | 60 |
| Value of livestock | $ 716 | $ 3,112 |
| Value of slaughtered livestock | $ 100 | $ 236 |
| Produce |  |  |
| wheat (bushels) | 11 | 330 |
| rye (bushels) | 11 | 0 |
| corn (bushels) | 1,000 | 1,820 |
| oats (bushels) | 380 | 0 |
| Irish potatoes (bushels) | 5 | 10 |
| sweet potatoes (bushels) | 0 | 10 |
| wool (pounds) | 70 | 20 |
| butter (pounds) | 0 | 100 |
| beeswax (pounds) | 11 | 0 |
| hay (tons) | 0 | 9 |

cence until catastrophe struck—his father died in October 1855. The grieving family laid J. W. C. Cunningham to rest beside his first wife in a graveyard near Wartrace.[18] Widowed for the second time, Mary Cunningham faced the responsibility of raising three children alone. Relatives in Bedford County lent a helpful hand. Mary's brother-in-law, Joseph Cunningham, executed the estate. He assured Mary that all of the family's needs would be met, and future real estate transactions indicate that he honored this commitment.[19]

The loss of his father deeply affected S. A. Cunningham. The suddenness of the death may have given rise to the nervous anxiety and chronic insecurity that became trademarks of Cunningham's personality. The fact that the future journalist never publicly recorded one single word about his father strongly suggests repression. Moreover, Cunningham was without an immediate male role model. He eventually transferred the role of authoritarian to his older half-brother. Joseph "had been as a father," Cunningham later boasted, "a man of spotless integrity."[20] But Joseph soon married and moved away.

Mary Cunningham was an invaluable source of comfort and support to the child, who was, after Joseph's departure, the oldest male living in the household. New responsibilities thrust upon mother and son fostered a close relationship, and the boy identified keenly with his mother. A family acquaintance observed that it was the careful guidance of Mary Cunningham that shaped S. A. Cunningham's character.[21]

The death of J. W. C. Cunningham, which turned out to be the pivotal experience in S. A. Cunningham's adolescent life, brought to light character traits in the son. "Granted that the seeds of personality flaws and defects are implanted quite early in life," explains C. Vann Woodward, "and may always be latently present, their manifestations in behavior can take many and wildly contrasting forms."[22] Paradoxical behaviors became more clearly visible when Cunningham served in the Civil War, an experience that tested the values he had absorbed from his family and community.

# Chapter 2
## The Civil War Approaches

S. A. Cunningham was acutely aware of the growing crisis that gripped the United States in the decade preceding the Civil War. Family discussions centering on the Whig party line and opinions of a respected neighbor in national politics appraised him about the worsening political situation.[1]

In the aftermath of the Compromise of 1850 an affluent uncle, George Washington Cunningham, was selected to represent Bedford County at the Nashville Convention.[2] This honor was a demonstration of the high esteem in which the public held the family. It was also a testament to the political conservatism that enveloped middle Tennessee.

The gravity of the sectional rift in the United States came home to seventeen-year-old Cunningham after the Federal attack on Fort Sumter. However, on the secession referendum, Bedford County recorded the third-largest negative vote. "When the war came," announced one Shelbyville resident, "there was still much division."[3] Profound anxiety existed in the Cunningham household—a family lukewarm to secessionism.

When Governor Isham Harris called for volunteers to fight for the Confederacy, Cunningham reacted cautiously. His age did not meet the legal requirement for induction into military service, and the family's uncertainties about secession clouded his thinking. The most influential person in Cunningham's life at this moment proved to be a neighbor, Meredith Poindexter Gentry,[4] whom he described as "the most gifted man in America."[5] Cunningham's veneration for Gentry's principles indicated that the young man had assimilated the family's political values on Whiggery and their opposition to secession.

In October 1861 Cunningham attended a highly charged community meeting at a tiny church in Richmond, Tennessee, where a debate was held between Meredith P. Gentry and Edmund Cooper on the key issues of the day. Here Gentry revealed his conversion to the Confederacy.[6] Cooper, a Unionist from Shelbyville, came specifically to refute Gentry's remarks. As the two men argued, Gentry's eloquence rose above the noisy audience and fell upon the attentive ears of S. A. Cunningham. Gentry was, Cunningham later recalled, "the greatest man I ever knew."[7]

In a wave of volunteerism, young men across Tennessee organized into local home guards. As a member of Cunningham's neighborhood later remembered,

> The seething atmosphere and war madness which then prevailed throughout this country, could hardly be erased from the memory of anyone who passed through it. Reason and moderation vanished before the presence of the approaching war storm. It was impossible to escape taking sides. Neutrality was out of the question.[8]

One Shelbyville newspaper trumpeted the latest appeal for volunteers: "Many it is true, did not at first respond to the call of patriotism, but now they SEE and FEEL the NECESSITY and DUTY devolving upon them as loyal citizens of the South."[9] Caught by the spirit of volunteerism, Cunningham enlisted in the local home guard, the Richmond Gentrys, with many of his friends and neighbors.[10]

The first Confederate regiments in Tennessee were formed from similar county-based units. The Confederate government in Richmond quickly put a halt to the madcap volunteerism and ordered Governor Harris to begin numbering the new Tennessee regiments with the number forty-one.[11] Cunningham was destined to play a role in the first newly formed regiment.

Mary Cunningham disapproved of her son's decision to sign up. But she reasoned that the induction officer would reject him because of his short stature; he stood only five feet seven inches tall. In turn, the boy fretted over his mother's financial condition at a time when he might march off to war. The problem was solved when Mary Cunningham received the deed to the family farm in October 1861. She now owned outright the comfortable farmhouse and 40 acres of land and had a large cash reserve from the sale of 115 acres.[12] The only obstacle to Cunningham's enlistment had been removed.

Cunningham answered Governor Harris's call to arms and joined the service of the Confederacy on 28 October 1861. He described the occasion of the guard's departure to Nashville as the "most eventful day in Shelby-ville history." It appeared as though the entire county had crammed into the town square to send their young men off. Excitement permeated the scene as the soldiers, including Cunningham, posed for photographs in their homespun uniforms. Cunningham fondly remembered the gift of a girl's belt buckle to adorn his standing collar.[13] Perhaps he had already decided to keep a diary in which to recount his military experience.

The men said their warm good-byes at the Shelbyville station and boarded a train. They spent a cold night sleeping in an open freight car and arrived the next morning, tired and hungry, at the training cen-ter, Camp Trousdale. There they were promptly issued tents and cooking utensils; by the end of the week they were all sworn into the service of the Confederate States of America for one year. At the end of October the Richmond Gentrys were reassigned to Company B, 41st Tennessee Infantry Regiment.[14]

Exactly how Cunningham felt about the political and military situation of the day remains a mystery. But his refusal to volunteer during the first call-up in the spring of 1861 reflects a mood of vacillation he shared with other Bedford County enlistees. The persuasiveness of Meredith P. Gentry encouraged Cunningham's enlistment more than any other single factor. The family's political persuasion played a part in his tardiness in enlisting, and it was an inescapable fact that his future financial security was deeply tied to the preservation of slavery. Undoubtedly his decision to join the army was influenced by the emotional fervor surrounding vol-unteerism and the community sentiment that would be likely to label as a traitor anyone who refused to enlist. Thus participation in the war offered Cunningham several incentives, not the least being a quick rite of pas-sage from adolescence to adulthood.[15] Whatever Cunningham's rationale for joining up, the excitement quickly wore off, because he never clearly articulated his war aims.[16] As armed conflict loomed ever closer, the chal-lenge would test Cunningham's courage, honor, and dedication to duty.

# Chapter 3 — *The Experience Begins*

S. A. Cunningham experienced the hardships of camp life common to the Confederate foot soldier: boredom, training, disease, substandard food, and unsanitary living conditions. Without adequate preparation, he embarked on a three-year adventure in a bloody war that would severely test his character.

At Camp Trousdale, the 41st Tennessee trained to become soldiers. One commander bragged that the regiment numbered a thousand men, but in reality it never exceeded six hundred.[1] In keeping with Confederate army regulations that enlisted men select their own commanders, the unit picked Robert Farquaharson. Colonel Farquaharson was a veteran of the Mexican War and remained a popular choice during his tenure with the 41st Tennessee.[2] While in training, Cunningham received a promotion from private to the rank of sergeant, probably because of his literacy and family status. Indeed, military rank and civilian social status were highly correlated in the Army of Tennessee.[3]

Several problems appeared in the first month at Camp Trousdale. There was a measles epidemic, then an acute shortage of weapons. The state arsenal stored only eight thousand flintlock muskets, some of which had been manufactured in 1808. These "Tower of London" models had last seen action in the War of 1812. They proved to be useless in wet weather, and none were of standard caliber. Morale in the regiment wavered as the impatient soldiers drilled with sticks. A riot nearly erupted when the troops learned that rifles would not be quickly procured.[4]

Cunningham shared the common soldier's contempt for military discipline. A casual atmosphere existed in camp, in large part because of the independent spirit of the trainees. Most units, including Cunningham's

Company B, were comprised of young men from the same neighborhood, and they brought from home an awareness of class distinction that contributed to considerable laxity between the enlisted men and the officers. This condition did not change until the 41st Tennessee bivouacked far away from home.[5]

While Cunningham the recruit prepared for war, General Albert S. Johnston worked assiduously on a defensive plan for the Confederate heartland.[6] An enemy force under generals Ulysses S. Grant and Don Carlos Buell presently consolidated in central and western Kentucky. In response to the Union threat, Cunningham's regiment received marching orders for Bowling Green, Kentucky, in December. Colonel William E. Baldwin assigned his new charges to patrol the Barren River area, but there was still a shortage of weapons.[7] While the 41st camped at Mitchellville (near the Kentucky line), a saloonkeeper sold whiskey to some of the men, and a melee ensued.[8]

The Bowling Green locale was inhospitable; heavy rains and cold temperatures caused many cases of pneumonia and influenza. Soldiers from rural Tennessee continued to suffer from devastating attacks of measles. Inexperienced recruits gave little consideration to sanitary camp habits, frequently urinating wherever it was convenient. As a result, water contamination and pestilence, or "Bragg's Bodyguards," abounded. Leading the list of deadly diseases at Bowling Green were diarrhea, malaria, typhoid, and pneumonia.[9]

The Confederate command near Fort Donelson realized their untenable position. General Simon B. Buckner ordered Cunningham's unit to patrol a vital railroad line to Nashville at Russellville for three weeks.[10] Buckner agreed with General Joseph E. Johnston that Fort Donelson was a trap and offered an alternative plan: to concentrate all Confederate forces fifteen miles upstream. General John B. Floyd concurred and ordered the 41st Tennessee, along with the bulk of Buckner's command, to Cumberland City after the fall of Fort Henry.[11]

Meanwhile, General Gideon Pillow lodged a vigorous protest from his command at Fort Donelson and convinced his reluctant subordinates to consolidate at the beleaguered post on the Cumberland River. Cunningham remained behind at Cumberland City with a small contingent of troops as the argument continued over troop displacement.[12]

On 12 February Pillow ordered Colonel Baldwin to rush the last three regiments from Cumberland City to Fort Donelson. These instructions included the 41st Tennessee.[13] When Baldwin's first regiment arrived at

1 A.M. on 13 February, Pillow dispatched it immediately to the extreme left wing, under the command of General Bushrod Johnson. Cunningham accompanied the last Confederate unit to unload at the Dover landing, at 10:30 A.M. Buckner hastily assigned the 41st Tennessee to his position on the extreme right flank under the temporary command of Colonel John C. Brown.[14]

Colonel Farquaharson struggled to organize his men, but the regiment's baggage cluttered the narrow streets of Dover. Fledgling soldiers were often loaded down with excessive gear in the opening year of the war, and the 41st Tennessee was no exception.[15] The scene grew frantic as the Federal gunboat *Carondelet* opened fire on Confederate positions, signaling the beginning of the battle. Cunningham and his comrades, forgetting their equipment, sought protection behind a fence. The whistling projectiles frightened Cunningham and other soldiers as they marched down shell-pocked streets.[16] During one intense fusillade, Cunningham witnessed Captain T. N. McNorton panic and rush off in the direction of the fighting. Later the 41st filed past his dismembered corpse. The ugly spectacle impressed Cunningham profoundly on the "terribleness of war." The impact of his baptism of fire was a dominant sensation and caused him extreme anxiety. The regiment double quicked to its position, but not before many men had thrown down their knapsacks. Cunningham dropped into a trench for protection from shrapnel, artillery, and sharpshooter fire.[17]

In the evening, inclement weather complicated the battle for Fort Donelson. Mild temperatures prevailed before the Federal attack, but after dark on the thirteenth, a cold sleet began to fall and an icy, northern gale blew. By morning three inches of fresh snow lay on the ground, and the thermometer dipped to ten degrees. Cunningham found it impossible to walk on the slippery surface. No one dared to build a fire for warmth because of constant Union sharpshooter activity. Cunningham complained bitterly about his discomfort.[18] His misery, directly attributed to fighting in frigid conditions, negatively impacted his will to fight.

For most of the next day, the enemy kept a shivering and fatigued Cunningham pinned down in a trench. Disdaining the thought of spending a second night exposed to the frigid elements, he retired to a tent belonging to a friend in the 32nd Tennessee[19] and was absent when Buckner gave marching orders at 3 A.M. When he awoke two hours later, he fell in with the 14th Mississippi. His adopted unit broke camp to form the rear guard for Buckner's movement. The detachment trudged cautiously over the slick terrain, and Cunningham rejoined his outfit by 8 A.M.

---

Meanwhile the Confederates had launched an assault at 5 A.M., and fierce fighting continued for three hours. Buckner was disheartened by the lackluster deployment of his division. What little military discipline existed soon crumbled. Regiments fell into total disarray, and the Southern force fought in one uncoordinated mass.[20] Buckner kept the two largest units—the 2nd Kentucky and 41st Tennessee—out of the fray. He intended to use them as the nucleus of a rear guard in anticipation of a retreat to Nashville. Cunningham waited nervously in reserve, and when confusion ruled supreme, he strayed along Wynn's Ferry Road with hundreds of other frightened soldiers.[21]

At the crucial moment when the Confederate assault hung in the balance, Buckner ordered the 41st Tennessee to prepare for action. However, General Pillow countermanded the order after conversing with Colonel Farquaharson; the former surmised that the 41st was poorly led, inadequately armed, and in low spirits. On his fateful decision hinged the outcome of the battle.[22] Cunningham, the wandering reservist, joined dejected Confederates returning to the trenches. But before he managed to reach the safe confines of the earthworks, the Federals launched a ferocious counterattack bent on crushing Buckner's division in transit. From his perspective, Cunningham described the ensuing two-hour fight as "one of the most persistent infantry engagements of the war."[23] Only darkness halted the Union charge.

In the evening, the Confederate commanders met at the Dover Inn to discuss their limited options. As they bickered, a cold and hungry Cunningham curled up on a pile of guns to stay off of the snow. Then news of impending surrender shot through the Confederate ranks. Too miserable to sleep, Cunningham searched for his tenting partner of the previous night and stumbled across Buckner sitting in front of a fire. Cunningham sympathized with his commander, who he thought looked "pale" and "sad."[24] Later that night, the sergeant of Company B received orders directing his unit to stack its weapons. On the following morning, the Federals marched into Fort Donelson to the strains of "Yankee Doodle." One of the fourteen-thousand Confederates taken into custody was Cunningham.[25]

The initial combat experience of S. A. Cunningham was hardly glorifying. Indeed, the stressful experience at Fort Donelson so deeply impacted him that personal accounts of that combat remained vivid many years later. Despite the impressive size of Cunningham's regiment, it earned at Fort Donelson a reputation for lack of aggressiveness. Never did the 41st

Tennessee play more than a perfunctory role in planned engagements. In fact, the unit seldom performed with corporate bravado except when ambushed. Only with great reluctance did future corps commanders press it into service, because they recognized that it lacked the collective will to fight.[26]

Cunningham shared the apprehensions of fellow Bedford County enlistees. There is little question that his regiment was poorly led. It had received limited military training at Camp Trousdale; necessity rushed the men into action before they were adequately prepared. Besides, these raw recruits had neither the time nor the inclination to learn military discipline. Camp life and military protocol mirrored the class system that operated in civilian life. Cunningham's first taste of combat at Fort Donelson was hardly glorifying and more than discomfiting—it resulted in a six-month stay in a prisoner-of-war camp. This incarceration kept Cunningham and his comrades from developing any kind of combat-related esprit de corps.

The Fort Donelson experience implanted a deep and lasting psychological scar on Cunningham. It unnerved him to view the corpse of Captain McNorton, and sobering thoughts about the realities of war made him painfully aware of his own endangerment. The idea of self-preservation plagued Cunningham; he later admitted that fear of dying preoccupied his thinking throughout the war.[27] It challenged his manhood and strained his commitment to the Confederate struggle for independence. But, for the present, Cunningham resided in a prison camp, far from shot and shell. This experience tested his commitment to the Confederate cause too, but in a different manner.

# Chapter 4 Camp Morton

The victorious Federals did not allow their rebel prisoners an opportunity to lounge around Fort Donelson. On the morning following the surrender, Cunningham was promptly marched to the steamboat landing. Standing in formation in ankle-deep mud for several hours, he waited while Federal guards searched every prisoner for concealed weapons.[1] One soldier wrapped the regimental colors of the 41st Tennessee beneath his shirt to keep them from falling into enemy hands. When ordered to do so, Cunningham boarded the steamboat *Empress*, destined for a prison camp somewhere in the North.[2] The condition of the old and poorly maintained boat added to Cunningham's anxiety.

Hungry prisoners huddled together on one side of the deck and caused the vessel to list dangerously. "Our suffering had made us careless in life," explained Cunningham.[3] The weather remained cold, and he marveled at ice patches hundreds of feet square floating down the Mississippi.[4] In St. Louis the Federals transferred the enlisted men to railroad cars for the next leg of the journey.

Cunningham, like his comrades, was in ragged condition. Quite weak, he noted in his diary the generosity of some Quaker women who ran alongside the slowly moving train tossing fritters to the half-starved men. The twenty-two boxcars pulled into Indianapolis with their human cargo on February 22. Sitting in one of the cars, a despondent Cunningham acknowledged the first anniversary of the Confederate government.[5]

When the prisoners detrained at the Indianapolis station, they marched a mile in single file to Camp Morton, which was to be their home for the next six months.[6] "With hardly life sufficient to march we moved with firm step, head erect," boasted Cunningham, "and a determination to make no compromise of Southern honor." A comrade expressed "deep humiliation." A local newspaper reported that the Fort Donelson prisoners "presented a most shabby and forlorn appearance." Their disparate dress, irregular step, and generally poor demeanor showed them to be entirely unworthy to be called soldiers. Some prisoners in the 41st Tennessee publicly expressed the belief that the Union would soon be restored.[7]

Camp Morton, constructed in 1860, housed the Indiana state fair. When war broke out, Captain James A. Ekin prepared the thirty-six-acre enclosure for human occupants. He built wooden bunks in the animal stalls to accommodate four men per stall. Work crews turned the large display halls into barracks and placed stoves at twenty-foot intervals.[8] Cunningham was assigned to Division Nine; he bunked beside one of the stoves on the center aisle, which he later recalled as a "snug" spot.[9] Several wells dotted the grounds, and prisoners bathed in a stream dubbed the Potomac. Whitewashed palisades with raised walkways enclosed the compound. Unsanitary conditions arose when camp latrines overflowed because of poor soil drainage.

Colonel Richard Owen commanded the 60th Indiana, the guardians of Camp Morton. The commandant, noted for fair discipline and sympathy, exhibited a strong but gentle character. Cunningham described him as a "kind-hearted gentleman."[10] Owen allowed the prisoners a degree of self-government within the camp. He established a post office and encouraged his Confederate charges to mail home personal daguerreotypes taken by a local merchant. In mid-March two visitors arrived from Shelbyville with letters and money from home. Cunningham felt "great consolation" in hearing from his mother. Owen also permitted the distribution of books and periodicals. He encouraged development of the arts through the formation of a drama troupe, glee club, and band. Prisoners constructed a camp bakery and enjoyed playing baseball when the weather permitted. But whittling was the most popular form of recreation.[11]

The uneventful pace of life at Camp Morton was ruinous to Confederate morale. Cunningham observed that new arrivals were always hungry and often ate their daily ration in a single sitting. Owen offered the prisoners a choice between cornbread or wheat bread. Coffee was rationed, and sugar was mixed with dirt so that the supply would last longer. Many prisoners complained about fatty bacon. Continuous rainfall throughout the spring turned the compound into a muddy bog. The captives rarely exercised, and frequently quarreled and fought.

Poor weather and unsanitary conditions exacerbated the health-care situation at Camp Morton. The first arrivals suffered from a combination of maladies including exposure, malnutrition, and diarrhea and dysentery. Within the first week, hundreds of men were placed on sick call.[12] Federal health authorities established hospitals throughout Indianapolis to deal with the mounting crisis. Private citizens opened their homes to convalescing soldiers. Ironically, Colonel Owen denied permission to the Sisters of Charity to aid ailing prisoners.[13] Cunningham's affliction was unspecified, but it led to his name's being erroneously placed on the camp's death list.[14] Not until late spring did health conditions improve noticeably.

As the local community accepted more sick prisoners into its care, escape attempts increased. The earliest took place in hospitals where security was loose.[15] But the most severe breaches of discipline occurred in four separate incidents in April and July. In early April, two Tennessee Unionists, William G. Brownlow and Edmund S. Cooper, arrived in camp to persuade the prisoners to sign the newly adopted oath of allegiance. They enjoyed a measure of success, much to the relief of the overburdened health authorities. But Cunningham remembered that many prisoners became angry when Brownlow said, "Jeff Davis is about out of soap." The unruly audience shouted back, "Traitor." The visitors exited quickly, and two Federal companies rushed into the compound to restore order.[16]

Less than a week later, a scandal rocked the Camp Morton administration. On the evening of 15 April a group of prisoners was returning to camp from a visit with friends in a town hospital. Foolishly, the escort allowed the prisoners to enter a saloon, where they became inebriated. As they approached the gate on their return to Camp Morton, someone threw rocks at the guards stationed atop the palisades. In the ensuing melee, the angry guards wounded four prisoners and fired a blank artillery cartridge into the compound. The Federals restored order and promptly suspended all hospital visitations.[17]

The biggest threat to camp order and discipline took place during a boisterous Fourth of July celebration. The day before, a rumor circulated around Indianapolis that General George B. McClellan had routed General Robert E. Lee in Virginia. Patriotic ardor overwhelmed the local citizenry, and hundreds of cheering people gathered outside the prison walls to taunt the incarcerated Confederates. The guards added to the demonstration with rounds of cannon fire. Cunningham charged that the Federals became overly excited and behaved in a threatening manner toward the prisoners.[18]

On 4 July the crowd outside Camp Morton grew to ominous proportions. The prisoners tightened ranks inside and prepared to defend themselves. When the story of McClellan's triumph proved to be unfounded, the mob of citizens disbanded. The Confederates took delight in the reversal of the rumor. They lit candle stubs and placed them conspicuously around the compound in a silent vigil. The men extinguished the candles when the lights-out order was given, but, as the camp darkened, cheers for Jefferson Davis echoed from stall to stall.[19] For several days following the candle demonstration, Owen would not allow prisoners to congregate in groups. Tensions ran high on both sides. On the rainy evening of 14 July, twenty-five Confederates escaped through an opening in the northeast corner wall. The Federals retrieved all but one escapee.[20]

Just as the situation appeared to stabilize, rumor of a prisoner exchange circulated at Camp Morton. Indeed, negotiators had completed plans for removing prisoners beginning on 22 August. Choosing not to return to Confederate service, three hundred Tennesseans signed the oath of allegiance immediately. Cunningham's "pride of honor" prevented him from signing the document despite the fact that the "temptation to return to home and loved ones was very great, while to return to the service had a gloomy prospect of either comfort or life."[21] As Federal officials administered the oath outside the prison, loyal Confederates inside the compound "hooted, yelled, threw stones and old shoes." One demonstrative prisoner climbed to the top of the palisade and refused to get down; he was shot by a guard. The case paralleled an incident in which Cunningham was once the target of a careless guard.[22] He lodged a complaint with the new post commandant, Colonel D. G. Rose, who showed little compassion. He informed Cunningham, "You don't deserve any better."[23]

Cunningham was among the first contingent of Confederate prisoners to be exchanged. At the Indianapolis station these men boarded a freight train that took them to Cairo, where they were transferred to the steamboat Fanny Bullitt, which lay anchored in the Ohio River for more than two weeks waiting for the arrival of other prisoners. Finally, in early September, they headed south in a flotilla of eight vessels and two gunboats.[24]

Meanwhile Confederate officials in Mississippi were instructed to assign the men to their original regiments as soon as possible. When the small armada arrived in Vicksburg, the soldiers to be exchanged formed two single-file lines, the Confederates facing south and the Federals facing north. Then one by one, a man from each line, equal in rank, passed through a checkpoint on the dock until the exchange was complete.

Through this tedious process, Cunningham was restored to active duty along with 596 of his comrades.

As a prisoner of war, Cunningham reacted fearfully to taunts and harassment from citizens and guards. He suffered from nostalgia when visitors and letters arrived from home. He endured hunger and suffered physical discomforts brought on by inclement weather. Unsanitary conditions prevailed, and disease forced him to make frequent visits to the infirmary. For Cunningham, being a prisoner proved to be nearly as deadly as serving in combat.[25] Given his weakened physical and mental condition, it is remarkable that Cunningham declined to take the oath of allegiance and return to Bedford County. Certainly the conditions he had endured clouded his mental outlook, but it is to his credit that he refused to sacrifice personal honor for the comforts of home.

Yet, his remaining twenty-seven months of active service in the Army of Tennessee would be marred by repeated malingering, illness, and mental duress. Specifically, his commitment to the Confederacy wavered.

# Chapter 5 Reluctant Warrior

When the 41st Tennessee reassembled in Clinton, Mississippi, Sergeant S.A. Cunningham, though lacking in enthusiasm, was present for duty.[1] As the commanders worked to reestablish military discipline, he acknowledged the pitiful condition of the troops. "Many of our fellows who had survived the prison life," he pointed out, "were so ill and nearly exhausted that death claimed them soon after their arrival for exchange [at Vicksburg]."[2] In October the regiment took a major conditioning march to Holly Springs. They encamped on a tributary of the Coldwater River and honed their military skills, but morale plummeted. Some men refused to train unless they were paid. At the end of a week, the regiment drew two months' back pay, an issue of clothing and new Enfield rifles— a distinct improvement in weaponry.[3] Cunningham found it necessary to shorten the barrel of his rifle for easier handling. When many Tennesseans were discharged because their one-year enlistments had terminated, Cunningham elected to stay with the regiment. On 1 November the freshly paid, clad, equipped, and reenlisted army marched in grand review for its commander, General John C. Pemberton.

On the same day, General Grant initiated a Federal movement directed at Holly Springs. The Confederates stationed in the area consolidated and began an orderly withdrawal southward. The twenty-mile route crossed swampy terrain, and some of the marchers became feverish during the fifteen-hour ordeal. Poorly conditioned soldiers dropped out of the march from fatigue. The army "partly reorganized" following a three-hour rest, but then the trek continued. Cunningham observed much straggling, and when the army crossed the Tallahatchie River, he collapsed from exhaustion. A companion dragged him to a fire for warmth.[4]

While the 41st Tennessee rested behind prepared breastworks, a new brigadier, General John Gregg, assumed command.[5] When the three-thousand-man unit pulled out it promptly fell into a Federal ambush south of Oxford. The 41st Tennessee fell back in "bad order," recalled Cunningham, in his first combat since Fort Donelson.[6] Three days later the regiment dug in safely behind the Grenada line. The troops remained inactive at that location until Christmas Day.[7]

Grant had demonstrated before Grenada, but only as a diversion to free General William T. Sherman to launch an amphibious assault above Vicksburg. Because of the precarious nature of the Confederate defense, Gregg's brigade was ordered from its strong position to the mouth of the Yazoo River. En route, Cunningham's regiment passed through Jackson, where he felt exhilaration after an inspection by General Joseph E. Johnston and President Jefferson Davis.[8] Gregg's troops arrived at the Yazoo on a rainy December afternoon and promptly felled trees and dug breastworks. Although three days of vicious fighting followed, the 41st Tennessee stood in active reserve. The Federals withdrew, but Cunningham was miserable from the fierce rainshowers that fell continuously.

After this fight, Gregg's brigade was promptly ordered to fortify a weak spot on the Mississippi River. The 41st Tennessee boarded the steamboat *Charm* and set out downriver to its new assignment. Port Hudson sat on an eighty-foot bluff overlooking the Mississippi about thirty miles north of Baton Rouge, Louisiana.[9] The natural stronghold held a commanding view of the river, and its ten thousand defenders made it a formidable installation. But Cunningham and his fellow Tennesseans took an immediate dislike to the inhospitable environment, which posed as threats heavy rainfall and numerous rattlesnakes, lizards, and bugs.[10] Port Hudson turned out to be home for the regiment for the next five months. A French-speaking unit, the 30th Louisiana, bivouacked beside the 41st Tennessee.[11]

In mid-January the popular Colonel Farquaharson returned to the regiment five months after his exchange. His arrival cheered the spirits of the Tennesseans, but it coincided with bad news of a Confederate defeat at Murfreesboro. Many of Cunningham's fellow soldiers, disturbed by the setback, threatened to leave Louisiana and return to defend their homeland. One Confederate inspector reported that "lack of discipline and instruction among the troops" at Port Hudson was a matter of official concern.[12]

Shortly after the 41st Tennessee arrived in Louisiana, some of the men contracted smallpox. The commander immediately quarantined the regiment four miles away "in the midst of a magnolia forest." Other maladies, such as diarrhea, flu, and measles, also beset the regiment. Cunningham complained about the damp quarters and charged that the men had "camped out to die."[13] These adverse conditions, coupled with Braxton Bragg's defeat at Murfreesboro, led some of the men to take French leave. During the regiment's twenty-five-day isolation, eight deserted; all of them, however, were rounded up and punished. The unit did not return to its line position in Port Hudson until early February.[14]

A month later the Federals launched an amphibious assault on Port Hudson. The 41st Tennessee occupied trenches close to the river and prepared to repulse an expected landing. Enemy gunboats initiated a bombardment, and land-based mortars dropped shells at two-minute intervals. Cunningham huddled in his trench as the enemy fleet made a night run past the Confederate batteries.[15] One regimental officer of the 41st Tennessee remembered the vivid scene:

> The thunder of cannon, the sharp notes of steam-whistles, the hoarse hissing of broken and punctured pipes, were terrific to the ear, the bursting of shell and the blazing of fuses high in air were beautiful to the eye, but not a man was killed and the Forty-First Regiment never afterward seemed to have any fear of cannon on land or water.[16]

The high cost of the naval operation convinced the Federals that the troops at Port Hudson could not be reduced from the river side. They halted their attack to regroup.[17]

The ensuing months at Port Hudson were arduous for Cunningham and his colleagues. Rations were cut in half, and hungry soldiers supplemented their diet with fish and sweet potatoes.[18] During the interlude, the Confederates resumed training, and wishful rumors surfaced that the regiment would be transferred back to Tennessee. Such stories seemed plausible when Gregg marched the command seventy-five miles cross-country to Osyka. They proceeded north along the railbed and secured transportation into Jackson.[19] On the trek eastward, the division visited the garrison's hospital at Clinton, Louisiana. The marchers welcomed the respite from the hot and dusty lanes, beside which stagnant water collected in filthy pools. "Each succeeding day," recorded one Tennessean, "we suffered an increase in these hardships; our feet became so sore that we could hardly put them to the ground, and many of us threw away our shoes and surplus clothing."[20] At one point a combination of heat, thirst, and fatigue overcame Cunningham, and he collapsed. A Bedford County neighbor, William S. Gambill, tended to his needs. Once the marchers reached the rail line, Gregg turned his brigade northward and secured transportation, much to Cunningham's relief. On the evening of 9 May the travel-weary men arrived in the Mississippi capital.[21]

The Confederate high command suggested stationing a lookout in Raymond, a small village twelve miles southwest of Jackson. From that vantage point Federal troops in the greater Vicksburg area could be closely monitored. Pemberton selected Gregg's brigade for the Raymond line, but he warned against any attack. Rather, he cautioned, the troops should be prepared to fall back to Jackson. Above all, said Pemberton, "Be careful that you do not lose your command."[22] These instructions found the men of the 41st Tennessee relaxing in camp. Some soldiers were swimming in the Pearl River. When Gregg arrived, the seven regiments of the brigade rapidly fell into formation. With the 41st Tennessee in the lead, they marched off to the strains of "The Girl I Left Behind Me." On 11 May the brigade set up camp two miles south of Raymond.[23] Unknown to the Confederates, an enemy corps lay only nine miles away.

The next morning, Federal cannon drove in Gregg's pickets, and he opted to dislodge the artillery. The noontime advance stirred up great clouds of dust; Confederates found it difficult to see the enemy. It turned out that the Confederate brigade had unwittingly attacked a Federal corps led by General William J. McPherson. At the beginning of the fracas, the 41st Tennessee had been stacking knapsacks in the Raymond graveyard. Gregg instructed the regiment to assume its traditional reserve position. The brigadier planned to use it to bolster his center later in the struggle. But when the enemy counterattacked along both flanks, he wheeled the 41st around to the extreme left wing. Cunningham marched at the front of Company B as the 41st Tennessee deployed through dense woods. He boasted that Gregg's maneuver at Raymond was "as tactful as ever was known in military affairs."[24]

The Confederates charged into battle four abreast, and Cunningham noted in his diary how the dust flew like giant raindrops when the regiment was hit by enemy rifle fire. The regiment held its sector for less than half an hour. "Raymond!" exclaimed Cunningham, "Who of those old veterans now living does not remember Raymond?"[25] Like many foot soldiers unaware of the overall fight, he often employed overstatement in describing such skirmishes.[26]

The rapidly mounting number of casualties convinced Gregg that he faced an opponent of great strength. The Raymond engagement, which lasted a total of two hours, mangled his brigade. As the Confederates withdrew northward, he ordered the 41st Tennessee to cover the rear. The unit fought off several aggressive charges supported by heavy shelling. A steady rain complicated the retreat and turned the road into a quagmire. When the tattered brigade limped to a halt, the soldiers had only blankets for shelter.[27]

On an otherwise soggy and depressing evening, Cunningham was excited to learn of the arrival of "that great man" General Joseph E. Johnston, who correctly surmised that the Federals outnumbered his own forces. He urged all Confederate forces to consolidate at Clinton. Cunningham's regiment maintained its position in the rear and skirmished with the advancing enemy.[28]

The Confederates began to destroy military stores and evacuate Jackson during a particularly heavy downpour. Colonel Farquaharson temporarily commanded the brigade as Gregg assisted Johnston with overall operations. The Confederate army moved slowly to the west but shifted northward after meeting stiff resistance.[29] Disorderly soldiers in the rear guard discarded clothing and personal belongings in the mud as military discipline deteriorated. Describing the scene in his diary, Cunningham wrote, " 'What next?', thought we, while it [the Confederate army] seemed to be striving against hope."[30]

Cunningham had chosen to return to the ranks in the autumn of 1862 under considerable physical and mental duress, and his sense of honor was challenged by his weak physical constitution. As his condition deteriorated, he lost all inspiration to continue the good fight. But however much his physical infirmity inhibited his active participation, at least he was present when the regiment withstood fierce attacks at Port Hudson and Raymond. Such would not be the case in the next phase of his military service.

# Chapter 6 *Year of Decision—1863*

The year 1863 evolved into a pivotal one in the military life of S. A. Cunningham. The recurring illness that afflicted him was nothing new; what changed was that he made calculated decisions to be absent from the ranks on the eves of impending battles to an extent that approached desertion. While Cunningham lacked the will to join in combat, however, he did not, like some of his dispirited comrades, refuse to return to active service; he dutifully returned to the regiment once all signs of danger had abated. As 1863 drew to a close, Cunningham expressed strong feelings of homesickness.

After the skirmish at Raymond and the brigade's subsequent retreat from Jackson, General Johnston shocked the 41st Tennessee by reassigning it to a Georgia division commanded by General W. H. T. Walker.[1] The displeased regiment dug in behind muddy breastworks near Vernon and awaited the inevitable surrender of Vicksburg. The high desertion rate in some Mississippi regiments encouraged disgruntled soldiers in other units to follow suit.[2] General Johnston dealt sternly with the mounting crisis. He personally conducted the court-martial of Private James F. Cresow, Company A, 41st Tennessee, a man charged with cowardice at Raymond. The court found the defendant guilty and sentenced him to receive thirty-nine lashes, wear an eighteen-pound ball and chain while working his eight-hour shift, and receive no pay for six months. Johnston demonstrated a no-nonsense approach in meting out military discipline to the 41st Tennessee. When the army relocated to Yazoo City at the end of May, two stragglers from the regiment were disciplined by having their heads half-shaved.[3]

On the hot and dusty march to Yazoo City, Cunningham and his regiment complained vociferously about the lack of drinking water. Indeed, the triangle of land between Vicksburg, Jackson, and Yazoo City was noted for its unhealthy environment. At one point Cunningham had a sudden attack of chills and fever and fell to the rear. Companions helped him into a wagon, which delivered him to a roadside hospital, where it was determined that he was suffering from malaria. For the next ten days two local women nursed him back to health. During his convalescence, he hocked personal items to a local merchant for cash.[4]

Though he was still feeble, Cunningham returned to the regiment just in time to countermarch to the former entrenchments near Vernon. Along the way, General Johnston and his staff nearly rode over the sluggish Tennessean. But the sight of the general picked up his spirits, and he continued to march. On 4 July Cunningham's unit moved again and dug new trenches at Edward's Station. Something was obviously wrong, however—Cunningham could hear no cannon fire from the direction of Vicksburg.[5] Then disastrous news spread about the fall of the city. As the Confederate army dropped back to Jackson, heavy skirmishing broke out almost immediately. Cunningham saw homes burning in the Mississippi capital and vividly recalled the bitterness of local residents who had refused to offer water to the thirsty soldiers.[6]

Cunningham volunteered with fifty comrades to form an advance skirmish line in his sector. He spent several days at the outpost slumped against his weapon. Federal artillery, sounding every five minutes around the clock, added to his discomfort. General Johnston recognized his precarious position in Jackson and made plans to abandon the capital for the second time in less than a month. Cunningham's detachment provided picket fire all night, repelling a particularly aggressive night assault, as the army secretly withdrew. An unidentified officer assigned Cunningham the job of informing each company of the 41st Tennessee when to move out. He executed the instructions by crawling on his stomach from company to company. At daybreak Cunningham accompanied the last regiments to leave Jackson. They crossed a burning bridge, the last one standing across the Pearl River. He felt sympathy for the frightened citizens who trailed the army away from the city.[7]

As the army marched eastward, desertion increased with each passing mile. During a one-month respite at Morton, one foot soldier estimated that some regiments lost more than half of their members.[8] The countryside swarmed with renegades, who constituted a new danger to the army.

Now the Confederate high command feared an enemy attack at Enterprise, Alabama, as part of a larger campaign aimed at Mobile.[9] As the 41st Tennessee waited in the Meridian station yard for transportation to Enterprise, Cunningham recorded with disgust the arrival of a trainload of drunken paroled soldiers from Vicksburg. The inebriated Confederates bullied the depot guards and helped themselves to stores of sugar stacked on the platform. When one zealous guard resisted the mob, an unruly officer in the crowd shot him in the head. Temptation weakened the resolve of some men in the 41st Tennessee as they joined in the melee and filled their haversacks with supplies. Cunningham concluded, "We had more sugar than coffee for some time."[10]

As he awaited the expected attack at Enterprise, Cunningham suffered another bout of malaria. He was sent to a local infirmary for treatment. Meanwhile, local Indian women came into camp daily to sell fruit; one officer of the 41st Tennessee recalled "feasting on peaches done in every style." Some men idled the time playing poker. Others responded to the first wave of religious revivalism to sweep through the regiment.[11]

While the 41st Tennessee guarded eastern Mississippi, a larger consolidation was occurring around Chattanooga. Many units in Mississippi, including Gregg's brigade, received emergency orders to report to General Bragg in Tennessee.[12] These instructions came while Cunningham was hospitalized, so when the 41st Tennessee pulled out on 7 September, he remained behind. He boarded a train the next day, however, motivated partially by the prospect of returning to his home state. The circuitous route, via Mobile, Montgomery, and Atlanta, nearly proved fatal for Cunningham. Poor ventilation, the jerking motions of the train, and a lack of water made the trip extremely uncomfortable for the feverish soldier.[13] When the train pulled into the Alabama capital, an attendant helped him into a wagon bound for the Ladies Hospital, where he stayed until 18 September. Meanwhile the regiment completed its journey and participated in a surprise attack, which was foiled, at Dug Gap near Resaca. On the morning of Cunningham's release from the hospital in Montgomery, the 41st Tennessee assembled under the temporary division command of General Bushrod Johnson. It arrived on the field just in time to participate in the most momentous engagement in the history of the regiment.[14]

As daylight broke on the frosty morning of 20 September, the 41st Tennessee held a crucial salient along at the Confederate center at Chickamauga. On the previous day they had cut through thick underbrush and met stiff resistance.[15] They retreated only after the temporary field commander, Colonel James D. Tillman, feared that the enemy had flanked their position. Cunningham knew Tillman personally.[16]

Severely bloodied, the 41st Tennessee fought with determination in the famous breakthrough at Brotherton Farm. They groped toward the summit of Snodgrass Hill and halted at nightfall, out of ammunition and field commanders.[17] The 41st Tennessee captured nine artillery pieces. But the regiment paid a dear price. While they suffered less than any other regiment in the brigade, many of their bravest soldiers died on the field at Chickamauga.[18]

The horror of the battle did not end with the cessation of hostilities. After the fighting, the parched woods caught fire, and many wounded soldiers who lay unattended on the field burned to death. In another quarter, wild hogs scavenged among piles of amputated limbs.[19] Cunningham arrived on the battlefield in time to witness these revolting scenes. He wandered aimlessly in search of the 41st Tennessee. The tardy sergeant described the grisly landscape of death:

> Going over a battlefield, without the animation and excitement of the fight, is rather like a citizen's contemplation of battle. A sort of timid feeling is excited in viewing the butchered dead, but more especially by the groans of the dying. There were piles of artillery horses as they were shot down by sixes, and dead men in almost every conceivable position.[20]

That evening Cunningham spent an unpleasant night slumbering among the dead.

Upon Cunningham's reunion with his comrades, the regiment received orders to board trains bound for Mobile. These instructions caused severe consternation among the Tennesseans. They wanted to follow up on the great victory at Chickamauga and liberate their state. Cunningham overheard some men in the regiment vow not to fight again unless someone countermanded the orders. As they marched against their will to the depot, a new directive ordered them to report to Chattanooga. "When the good news came," Cunningham rejoiced, "such a yell was never heard perhaps from the soldiers and 'marching' officers of the 41st Tennessee Regiment."[21] By the end of the week, the regiment bivouacked on high ground surrounding the east Tennessee city.

Meanwhile, the Confederate command was in no mood for celebration.

In fact, the leaders of the Army of Tennessee neared a state of mutiny. These high-level disagreements were apparent to the common foot soldiers. Political dissatisfaction with Bragg's leadership led to a major military realignment involving no fewer than eighteen commands and placing Cunningham's regiment back in a Tennessee brigade led by General George E. Maney.[22] The 41st Tennessee bivouacked in the vicinity of Graysville, patrolled the Chattanooga Valley, and protected the supply line between Lookout Mountain and Missionary Ridge.[23]

The drudgery of the Chattanooga campaign tested Cunningham's endurance, as it did that of thousands of other chronically ill soldiers. Once again the Tennessean suffered a relapse of fevers aggravated by heavy rain and cold temperatures. This time he was dispatched to a wayside hospital in Barnesville, Georgia, and then transferred to Forsyth.[24] As he passed through Atlanta, he saw the arrival of President Davis on his way to a confrontation with Bragg's rebellious staff.

While convalescing in Forsyth, Cunningham visited a comrade recuperating at the home of William B. Davis, a distant relative of Jefferson Davis.[25] There he met and became enamored of Davis's fifteen-year-old daughter, Laura. He spent several unauthorized weeks on the Davis plantation, returning to his unit the first week of November.[26]

When Cunningham returned, Colonel Tillman promoted him to the rank of sergeant-major, a curious development in light of the former's absences from combat.[27] Tillman and others may have been able to believe that Cunningham's brand of feigned illnesses at crucial times were real medical crises rather than cowardice. Cunningham did have a history of malaria, and at this time there was a great deal of sickness in the Confederate army.[28] Tillman also trusted Cunningham; he was a reliable friend in all instances save combat, and this flaw could be overlooked because Cunningham provided vital services to the regiment. After all, Cunningham was a literate individual capable of filling out commissary orders for a regiment seriously depleted of personnel.

When the 41st Tennessee relocated to a support position near Missionary Ridge, the anemic Cunningham ostensibly became ill again on the eve of a major battle. This behavior pattern—an ability to anticipate an impending battle and subsequent reporting to the surgeon's tent, was becoming monotonously routine. In his absence, Cunningham's comrades provided vital assistance around Tunnel Hill. In the wild Confederate retreat from Missionary Ridge to Chickamauga Station, Company B of the

41st Tennessee detached to support an exposed artillery battery. Pursuing Federals exerted tremendous pressure and ambushed Company B a mile north of Graysville, killing four men.[29]

Many Confederates straggled in the aftermath of battle. The retreating army destroyed huge stores while hungry soldiers helped themselves to food. "It was a laughable looking rear guard," commented one soldier.

> Every one of us had cut open the end of a corn sack, emptied out the corn, and filled it with hard-tack, and every one of us had a side of bacon hung to our bayonets on our guns. Our canteens, and clothes, and faces and hair were all gummed up with molasses.[30]

The frightened mob finally stopped running at Dalton, Georgia, where the Confederates went into winter quarters. Cunningham safely returned to his regiment a short time later.

Frequent marching and recurring illnesses commonly associated with nineteenth-century warfare had substantially weakened Cunningham by the end of 1863. A more significant hazard, combat on an unprecedented and horrific scale, deeply bothered him.[31] After the Chickamauga experience, his chief concern was to achieve his own survival.

It is important to understand that Cunningham's medical experience was not atypical. Over the course of the war he fell victim to malaria, pneumonia, and sciatica. His name appeared on the regiment's sick roll six times, which was an average figure for Civil War soldiers. But it is disconcerting from a modern perspective to think that he spent more than one-fourth of his tour of duty on medical leave. And the timing of his illnesses is suspicious. However, his regimental comrades fared little better. Of the 193 fatalities in the 41st Tennessee over the course of the war, seventy-eight percent were caused by illness. The regiment's overall mortality rate, thirty-two percent, was average, but it was exceedingly high for a regiment that saw relatively little combat.[32]

It is clear from Cunningham's record that personal honor played a deciding factor in his decision to stay in the army. While the evidence suggests that he feigned illness in order to avoid combat, it is to his credit that he did not, like so many others, become an outright deserter. His traits of loyalty and obedience to some extent were inculcated from his childhood and adolescent training; thus the influence of home had some bearing on his decision.[33] But the strongest factor was his overriding concern for comradeship. Soldiering offered a unique camaraderie that civilians were incapable of understanding. As the war dragged on, Company B became a substitute family to Cunningham. His willingness to return to the ranks—fostered by what Reid Mitchell terms "small unit cohesion"—was understandable. Cunningham could no more repudiate his comrades through desertion than he could abandon his own loved ones in Shelbyville.[34] Furthermore, any decision to desert outright would have betrayed Cunningham's masculine sense of honor. While his behavior demonstrated distaste for battle, his attitude showed unswerving loyalty to the Southern cause. As Mitchell explains, desertion did not signify that Confederates had repudiated their cause; rather, their initial commitment to the Confederacy was weak.[35] Thus, Cunningham exemplified the growing awareness of defeat that permeated the entire Army of Tennessee.

# Chapter 7 Hopelessness

Despondent, Cunningham settled into winter quarters near Dalton. From his vantage point the war seemed to drag on endlessly. Boredom, pessimism, and defeatism filled Cunningham as well as the army in general. He personified the deteriorating spirit; during introspective moments, he questioned his value to and future in the service. His morale was laced with self-doubt. As signs of military disintegration became more acute, nothing short of returning to Tennessee would placate him.

When Cunningham rejoined the 41st Tennessee, the overall strength of the western army had dipped below 30,000 men. Straggling, desertion, and other forms of absenteeism were chiefly to blame. With only 226 men present for duty, the 41st Tennessee typified the manpower shortage. Cunningham recognized that many of the best fighting men in the regiment either had been killed or had taken unapproved leaves that winter.[1] Another Tennessee soldier noted:

> The men were deserting by tens and hundreds, and I might say by thousands. The morale of the army was gone. The spirit of the soldiers was crushed, there [sic] hope gone. The future was dark and gloomy. They would not answer at roll call. Discipline had gone. A feeling of mistrust pervaded the whole army.[2]

Shortages of food, blankets, and rifles tested the loyalty of every Confederate. As his unit's commissary officer, Cunningham sometimes foraged twenty miles afield for supplies. Camp "sins" such as drinking, gambling, thievery, and sexual indulgence prevailed. The sergeant-major listed theft as the single most serious offense amongst the 41st Tennessee. The regimental surgeon disagreed, stating flatly that drunkenness was appalling.

Sedentary camp life definitely contributed to deteriorating morale.[3]

Cunningham shared in the physical and mental strains of camp life. Bivouacked three miles east of Dalton, his regiment continued to suffer through bad weather. The skies were gloomy, and temperatures frequently dropped below freezing in January. One day the thermometer plunged to three degrees below zero. The officers of the 41st Tennessee purchased fence planks from a private vendor for their men to use as firewood.[4]

General Johnston implemented several reforms to mellow the mood of the army and restore faith in his leadership. The first tangible improvement in spirit occurred in mid-January when one Tennessee brigade released a statement:

> That we . . . do this day agree to enlist for the duration of the war, determined never to lay down our arms until our homes are rescued from the enemy and the Confederacy permanently established among the nations of the earth.[5]

Enthusiasm generated by the resolution spread to other Tennessee units. Within six weeks Cunningham and four-fifths of the army had reenlisted.[6]

The 41st Tennessee had experienced a significant religious awakening at Enterprise; now entire brigades came under the influence of evangelism. Many regiments, most without chaplains, held nightly prayer meetings beginning in February. Roving missionaries distributed Bibles, religious tracts, and denominational newspapers. On average, fifty men, including officers, were baptized daily at the height of the revival.[7]

Cunningham's own religious rebirth occurred when a converted friend from Shelbyville urged him to attend a prayer meeting in one of the makeshift wilderness chapels. After the service concluded, Cunningham went into the woods alone "in an agony of prayer."[8] His friend remained with others at the chapel altar to discuss the sermon. Suddenly a burned-out tree fell upon the congregation and killed ten men from the 4th Tennessee, Cunningham's friend among them. During the memorial service for the men, the eulogist looked directly at Cunningham and said that "it was only necessary for him to give himself up as a guilty, worthless worm of the dust, and look to the Cross for redemption."[9] At the grave of his friend, Cunningham took an oath to enter into Christian fellowship. It is significant that the revival stressed virtues that Cunningham had accepted long ago: sacrifice, commitment, obedience, discipline, and patience.

Until relatively recent times, it has been argued that religious revivalism had improved army morale. Gardner H. Shattuck, Jr., brings a fresh interpretation, suggesting that neither military nor religious goals were served. The bizarre burning tree episode, laden with otherworldly symbolism, probably inspired Cunningham because of emotional ties to a fallen comrade. In the long run, it probably did little to bolster his enthusiasm for either combat or military service.[10]

Granting furloughs proved to be the most effective method to improve army morale at Dalton. General William Hardee initiated a scheme that authorized every thirtieth man a one-month pass. Johnston relaxed the requirement and approved leaves to every tenth soldier who reenlisted. Under this arrangement, Cunningham drew a "tenth man leave" in early March.[11] He used the time to tour the Carolinas, Virginia, and east Tennessee. He did not venture home because a Federal army occupied Bedford County. Cunningham printed the letters TENN on his hat so that strangers would know his home state.[12] His wandering around the Confederacy suggests a rootlessness of sorts. It is regrettable that his journey carried him away from two important morale-building events—the snowball combat in March and the mock battle and dress parade in April.[13]

Cunningham's regiment had not heard of its impending reassignment to Cheatham's Tennessee brigade when orders arrived in mid-February to debark for Alabama. The shocking announcement displeased most Tennessee troops. At the Atlanta depot, Cunningham observed with disgust as men from his unit broke into a supply train and stole sixty sacks of goobers—peanuts—and four barrels of whiskey. He later learned that a telegram preceded their arrival in Montgomery and warned that the "meanest men in the Confederacy" were on their way.[14]

The regiment progressed slowly from Mobile to Demopolis, having to rely on irregular steamboat runs. Cunningham stayed at the latter location under directions from General Benjamin F. Cheatham to gather up deserters. Given a captain's sword and charge over two companies, Cunningham went about his assignment with gusto. He made several arrests and reported personally to Cheatham on the success of his mission. Apparently Cheatham, like Tillman, had acquired a tolerance for Cunningham's conspicuous absences, which would surely have brought condemnation earlier in the war.[15]

Cunningham rejoined his unit on patrol in the Dug Gap sector of northern Georgia. Then, on 4 May, a large Federal force drove in Confederate pickets near Ringgold. The Atlanta campaign had begun. Only Federal timidity and Johnston's rapid deployment of troops prevented a disaster at Resaca.[16] There well-positioned Confederates fought fiercely along a three-mile arc. Desperate skirmishing erupted along Cheatham's line, and the commander used the 41st Tennessee in reserve at several places. From a trench, Cunningham observed that some Confederates ran to the Federal line and willingly surrendered. In one heated repulse, the young Tennessean narrowly escaped capture. The numerical superiority of the enemy forced the Confederates to retreat from Resaca after dark. Cunningham, with typical postwar bravado, asserted that Johnston's retreating tactics were "near flawless."[17]

Meanwhile Johnston devised an ingenious plan to ambush the Federals twelve miles to the south at Cassville. "There was an eagerness for the fight," confided Cunningham, "seldom witnessed during the war."[18] At Cassville Johnston set the tone for impending battle by issuing a general order that brigade commanders read to the troops.[19]

All stood in readiness for the attack, but the Confederates lost the initiative when General John B. Hood suspected that there were Federal troops at his rear. In the controversial retreat from the strong position at Cassville, Cunningham and the 41st Tennessee disappeared into the larger operation of Cheatham's division. Although no record survives to document their precise movement, the regiment undoubtedly joined the debate over the "Cassville incident." The retreat affected the entire army badly; in the following month desertions averaged more than 140 men a day. Seventeen consecutive days of heavy rain also contributed to the soldiers' dreary attitude.[20]

The lost opportunity at Cassville disturbed the young sergeant-major with the checkered combat record. He evaluated his commander in bittersweet terms: "General Johnston, whose sagacity in conducting a retreat is too well known to require mention, met and foiled every effort to cut us off but we were kept on the move almost constantly, day and night until we became desperate."[21] Constant retreating lowered morale still further in the Atlanta campaign, and while the army outwardly carried on its function of soldiering, inwardly it suffered from war-weariness. Dense underbrush and severe thunderstorms hampered the Confederate retreat, and Cunningham explained tongue-in-cheek how he lived from day to day with a spade in his hands.[22]

The disgruntled army continued its strategic retreat to Lost Mountain in early June, and Cunningham expressed physical discomfort. When a freak artillery shell struck down the popular general Leonidas Polk, it was another blow to his sagging spirit; Cunningham reported "much sadness and gloom" upon hearing the news. Desertion in the Confederate ranks reached its wartime peak on that day.[23]

Cunningham witnessed a shocking death similar to Polk's four days later as the 41st Tennessee bivouacked in reserve. The day was unusually calm except for occasional sharpshooter fire. Sergeant John T. Patrick was reading a captured Yankee newspaper aloud to his messmates. Cunningham stood directly in front of the reader when, without warning, a bullet pierced Patrick's skull, killing him instantly. Visibly shaken, Cunningham volunteered his blanket to wrap his dead comrade for burial.[24] Later the same day Cunningham forded several streams in the area to draw rations for the company. He slept that evening in wet clothing, and when he awakened the next morning, he suffered from symptoms later diagnosed as sciatica.[25] Considering his continuous exposure to wetness over the previous two-week period and his history of fever-related illnesses, it is likely that he did suffer from the rheumatic ailment. It is also conceivable that he suffered a psychosomatic complaint brought on by the traumatic death of Patrick.[26]

On 19 June Cunningham was taken by ambulance to a hospital in Marietta. A surgeon administered a dose of morphine and ordered his transfer to a larger facility in Atlanta, the Fairgrounds Hospital. After several days there, Cunningham was issued crutches and granted a thirty-day furlough.[27] He traveled by rail to Montgomery to visit a sick friend while the Army of Tennessee fought a furious battle at Kennesaw Mountain. Once again poor health kept Cunningham from participating in a major battle. His regiment suffered minimal casualties and probably kept its customary distance in reserve. When the Confederates fell back to trenches along the north bank of the Chattahoochee River, soldiers were reported to be deserting by the company.[28]

When Cunningham returned to the 41st Tennessee on 8 July, the command had relocated to a new line south of the Chattahoochee, where soldiers from the two enemy armies exchanged coffee and tobacco. Such fraternization chagrined Cunningham, but he welcomed a recent command reorganization that sent the 41st Tennessee to General Otho Strahl's brigade. At this time too the elderly Colonel Farquaharson, whose irregular presence was a matter of general concern, finally retired. Colonel James D. Tillman, the de facto commander, succeeded Farquaharson and led the regiment until its surrender in 1865.[29]

Cunningham reported back to the regiment still in weak condition prior to the expiration of his medical leave. Since his furlough had not expired, the regimental officers asked him to travel to Augusta to purchase new clothing. Cunningham complied and thus missed the fierce battles around Atlanta on 20 June to 22 June. Returning by way of Macon, he bought a treat for the regiment—several bushels of onions at a cost of seventy-nine dollars.[30] It is probable that he stopped at the Davis plantation near Forsyth to visit his sweetheart, Laura Davis.

While Cunningham was on this trip, President Davis relieved General Johnston and put General John B. Hood in his place. Hood engaged his forces immediately in several poorly conceived maneuvers, and the Confederates lost heavily. The new commander withdrew his army; the forty-day siege of Atlanta had begun.[31]

Cunningham returned from his furlough shortly after the battle of Peachtree Creek and located the 41st Tennessee on the extreme right flank of the Confederate army near Decatur. Fortunately for Cunningham and his comrades, they did not participate in the senseless assault at Ezra Church. But he felt hopeless nevertheless. He wrote to a friend:

> In the engagements during my absence some of our truest soldiers, and my near and dear friends, gave their lives for their country. Of all that were killed in my regiment I fear that neither one was prepared to die. How strange that men will go blindly into eternity, when a light is offered that will show them the way.[32]

While the letter reaffirmed Cunningham's devotion to Christian principles, it also expressed his disillusionment over the loss of comrades. The Decatur sector stayed relatively peaceful, although light skirmishing did occur throughout August.

The closing chapter in the defense of Atlanta transpired on 26 August when Hood lost contact with the Federal army. It took four days to ascertain the true objective of the enemy—the rail line at Jonesboro. A quick night march to that location tired Cunningham appreciably. Immediately upon its arrival on the morning of the 31st, the 41st Tennessee was pressed into combat. In the halfhearted attack that followed, the Confederates tallied many casualties. During the assault Cunningham heard for the first time the roar of Spencer repeating rifles—a racket "hardly known before." He also experienced firsthand the futility of assaulting strong entrenchments. "At no time previous," he concluded, "were we more convinced of the enemy's superior strength."[33] Troopers refused to advance, and the woods filled with stragglers and deserters. Cunningham referred contemptuously to these marauding parties on both sides. In expected

fashion, he performed as a battlefield nurse at Jonesboro. Although men who functioned in such capacities were generally recognized as stragglers, most regimental commanders were satisfied that they engaged in useful acts.[34]

The battered Army of Tennessee withdrew six miles south to Lovejoy Station and effectively brought on the evacuation of Atlanta. The common soldier comprehended the significance of this loss. Atlanta was the transportation hub of the western theater.[35] Almost immediately the commanding general reported cases of near mutiny in the ranks. Tennesseans refused to march any farther south, and straggling and desertion multiplied. Enlisted men like Cunningham were acutely aware of comrades who had recently died or deserted. For many weary Confederates, including Cunningham, the war had acquired a sense of hopelessness.[36] Licking its wounds, the remnant Confederate army shifted to Palmetto in mid-September.

In the autumn of 1864 Cunningham and his Tennessee comrades were in a rebellious mental state. Most foot soldiers, like Cunningham, had been pushed beyond the limits of physical and mental endurance. Although quasi-desertion was an acceptable code of conduct to Cunningham, most like-minded soldiers opted for outright desertion.

Cunningham and countless thousands of other Tennesseans who remained in the ranks had not been home for several years. Their collective mood in Palmetto verged on the suicidal—either to liberate their home state or to die in the attempt. In this Cunningham mirrored the go-for-broke philosophy of his comrades.

*Chapter* **8** *Going Home*

The Army of Tennessee, disintegrating from within, had lost its ability to rebound from military setbacks. The struggle against internal hardships had become more important than the need to defeat the enemy.[1] Supply shortages compounded the suffering, and the officers who remained employed thousands of men to forage so that the troops could survive. An acute shortage also existed in the officer corps, and Cunningham was granted authorization to sign regimental requisitions and vouchers.[2] Fortunate units, such as Cunningham's own Company B, received two issues of clothing—a testimony to their shabby apparel.

When President Davis inspected the disconsolate army on 28 September, some soldiers shouted defiantly, "Give us back General Johnston."[3] That evening Cunningham walked three miles to an open field and listened to the president deliver a stirring speech. He focused on a speaking platform erected in a stand of pine trees. In the forefront, a huge bonfire emitted a tremendous glow. A regimental band struck up patriotic melodies as tattered battle flags snapped in the breeze. Cunningham described the scene as "unlike anything we had ever known."[4] Governor Isham Harris of Tennessee electrified the audience of soldiers when he revealed that they would soon march northward. All eyes were riveted on President Davis as he stood up to speak. "We must march into Tennessee," he commanded, "and push the enemy back to the banks of the Ohio."[5] The Tennessee troops erupted into spontaneous cheers.

General Hood devised a preliminary plan to hamper enemy communications between Atlanta and Dalton. As the army inched northward, Cunningham assisted in ripping up railroad tracks, burning ties, and bending rails around trees. He participated in the capture of a Federal garrison defended by Negro troops and worried about the possibility of being killed by ex-slaves. Though he thought the fortification was "impregnable," the Confederates proved victorious and immediately impressed the Negro soldiers into work breaking up more tracks.[6]

Foodstuffs ran dangerously low as the army operated without a clear line of supply. Cunningham remembered great privations in the ranks; four men were forced to share one ear of corn as the daily ration. The resourceful Tennessean supplemented his diet by roasting wild acorns and apples. Few men possessed appropriate cooking utensils, especially kettles, pans, and skillets.[7] The commencement of the rainy season dampened the spirits of the hungry army. Cunningham counted himself fortunate because he was able to secure a cow stall for one evening, which he said he would have made "his home through life, rather than endure further and worse hardships."[8]

After a soggy nine-day march, the Confederate army tramped into the northern Alabama town of Tuscumbia in search of provisions. The high waters of the Tennessee River prohibited a quick crossing, so the army halted to construct pontoon bridges but were impeded when their portable walkways kept submerging. Cunningham's unit waited anxiously for two weeks before crossing the swollen river. Meanwhile, Hood reassigned Strahl's brigade, which included Cunningham's unit, to the division of General John C. Brown.[9]

On 21 November, thirty thousand wet, hungry, and weary Confederates marched northward, most of them for the last time. Bitter wind and snow announced one of the harshest winters of the nineteenth century. Muddy wagon ruts froze solid and then thawed into slick mudholes. Supply trains were covered with mud up to the hubs. Strahl detached the 41st Tennessee to cut log skids to lay across a particularly treacherous stretch of road. The regiment conducted the task with reckless abandon, and several men died in an accident caused by carelessness. The men of the regiment had become callous to death.[10]

The Confederates averaged fewer than ten miles a day. Heavy precipitation extinguished their campfires and added to their misery. Many soldiers lacked hats, coats, and shoes. Overcome with nostalgia, Cunningham reminisced about the Bedford County home he had not seen for three years. He fretted about the renegade bands that roved the countryside and posed a threat to his mother.[11]

As dawn broke on 29 November, Hood hoped to block the Federals at Spring Hill, but his army encountered delays in crossing Rutherford

Creek just three miles below the middle Tennessee community. General Brown's division did not arrive until an hour before sunset.[12] Mysteriously, Brown held his troops out of the fight. Cunningham later gave a reason for the reluctance to attack:

> While we thought the opportunity for victory the very best ever known, we felt no special eagerness to charge this line, heavy as it was, with their glittering cannons ready to pour into our ranks the "shrapnel" grape and canister.[13]

On the one hand, Cunningham had hoped to liberate his home state. But he was not eager for the fight that might accomplish it. Most Confederates recognized their superior tactical advantage on the field at Spring Hill, but the troops lacked the will to execute their orders. Cunningham, always charitable to his superiors, absolved the Tennessee commanders of blame for the Spring Hill fiasco:

> There were grave mistakes made, but the ability and the faithfulness of Confederate generals are a source of pride and gratitude to which we should cling for all time. Even at Spring Hill, where the greatest of misfortunes occurred, I have no word of reproach.[14]

Cunningham also exonerated the common soldier for lack of aggressiveness that day.

After dark, the disjointed Confederate army settled in for the night. Meanwhile, the Federal army sneaked past them along an unguarded road. When Hood discovered that the enemy had slipped away, he could not contain his rage. As his army pursued the Federals, a mood of almost suicidal passion swept the ranks. Cunningham sensed that the men displayed an unprecedented determination "to conquer or die."[15]

The Federals planned to continue northward, but they were well protected behind heavily fortified earthworks at Franklin and could easily make a stand there if attacked. Before they executed their escape, the Confederates arrived on the Columbia Pike. Eager to attack, Hood ordered a frontal assault against the entrenched Federals. An entire corps and the artillery had not even arrived on the field when nineteen thousand Confederates deployed in battle formation at 3 P.M.[16]

The Columbia Pike divided the field of operation in half. Brown's division, arranged in two lines, touched the road with its right flank. Cunningham stood in the second row nearest to the pike. Tennessee units cheered enthusiastically in anticipation of the battle.[17]

An unseasonably balmy breeze blew in the faces of the Confederates as they awaited the order to charge. The Federals waited patiently across the open field, two miles distant. Cunningham captured the full drama of the moment in the sad expression etched on Strahl's face. Moments before the attack sounded, Strahl turned to his brigade and said, "Boys, this will be short but desperate." At 4 P.M., Hood gave the nod to attack. The Confederate soldiers moved out in orderly array, led by the entire officer corps. Cunningham noticed that Strahl chose to go into battle on foot rather than on horseback.[18] An enemy officer wrote about the Confederate approach:

> Bands were playing, general and staff officers were riding in front of and between the lines, a hundred battle-flags waving in the smoke of battle, and bursting shells were wreathing the air in great circles of smoke, while twenty-thousand brave men were marching in perfect order against the foe.[19]

The most memorable charge in the history of the Army of Tennessee was underway. It earned the distinction of being the last great Confederate charge of the Civil War.[20]

Cunningham was the right guide for the regiment and stood nearly atop the Columbia Pike. As the Confederates advanced up the gentle slope, he turned to his left and viewed a gray column a mile long. The enemy had placed a powerful skirmish line approximately half a mile in front of the Carter House. The skirmishers, equipped with repeating rifles and supported by artillery from Fort Granger, created gaping holes in the assault line. Some Confederates pulled their hats down over their faces for protection against the intense hail-like fire coming from the Federal position.[21]

The Confederates opened fire within a hundred yards of the outpost. As the Federals withdrew to the inner earthworks, the Confederates bellowed the rebel yell and broke into a sprint. The defenders along the inner ring could not fire on the charge because soldiers from both sides were intermingling. Cunningham climbed over the chevaux-de-frise with great difficulty but was able to help push the Federals out of their advance position. The Confederates' momentum carried them inside the earthworks, where vicious hand-to-hand fighting took place. Some attackers actually penetrated fifty yards inside the Federal line. Only the arrival of reinforcements stemmed the ferocious assault. The Confederates fell back to the outer parapet.[22]

At this point the battle flag of the 41st Tennessee—the emblem of home—fell across the trench; it would lie on the ground there until the following morning.[23] The combatants huddled in lines only sixty-five yards apart. Retreat for either side was ill-advised. Federal sharpshooters in the Carter House and in a salient in front of the cotton gin a hundred yards to the east kept the 41st Tennessee pinned down. From the latter vantage point, Cunningham saw the Federals literally firing down the Confederate line. The Tennessean looked with mounting concern as the ditch filled with dead comrades. Men fell in grotesque, upright positions, and in some places bodies were stacked seven deep. It was reported that the trenches ran red with blood. One Federal observer counted thirteen desperate Confederate charges from this precarious location.[24]

Brown's division controlled approximately seventy-five yards along the outer parapet, but it never fought as a coordinated unit. Men at the base of the ditch loaded weapons and passed them forward to soldiers at the top of the works. Cunningham busied himself with the former task until the forward ranks became so depleted that General Strahl personally ordered the sergeant-major to scale the wall and continue firing. Cunningham stepped over several corpses and began firing as Strahl loaded spare guns.[25] Perhaps, for the first time in the entire war, combat exhilaration overcame Cunningham. Surely the desperate nature of the situation played a part in overpowering his usual instinctual reaction of self-preservation.

Confederate units, many without line officers, fought with fanatic desperation as men of rank fell indiscriminately with enlisted personnel. Near twilight someone close to Cunningham suggested retreat, but Strahl replied, "Keep firing!" A moment later the brigade commander lay on the ground mortally wounded. The death of Strahl, whose model character in battle had inspired many men, unnerved Cunningham. He slid down to the base of the ditch and resumed loading weapons for others.[26]

Darkness enveloped the battlefield less than an hour after the attack had begun, and Confederates resorted to firing at the flash of Federal guns. A dazed Cunningham crawled up the line and stumbled across a relative who had lost an eye, Captain William E. Cunningham.[27] Panic overcame the sergeant-major. He reasoned that the corps commanders probably were ignorant of the plight of the men in the trench, so he took it upon himself to run to the rear and search for General Cheatham.[28] Failing to locate anyone of sufficient rank, Cunningham collapsed exhausted beneath a tree to rest. From his vantage point, he witnessed the arrival of General Stephen D. Lee's corps. He drifted off to sleep with the noise of sporadic gunfire in the background. The Federals silently withdrew to Nashville after midnight.

Confederate losses at Franklin were staggering. The Army of Tennessee was, in effect, destroyed. The heaviest blow fell on the officer corps, of which sixty-six regimental commanders were either killed or wounded. One private described the confusion:

> Where were our generals? Alas! there were none. Not a single general out of Cheatham's division was left—not one. Nearly all our captains and colonels were gone. Companies mingled with companies, regiments with regiments, and brigades with brigades.[29]

Hood assigned Strahl's brigade, during the emergency reorganization that followed, to Colonel Andrew Kellar under the division command of General Mark P. Lowry. The 41st Tennessee was consolidated with the 19th and 24th Tennessee. Captain Daniel A. Kennedy commanded the new unit. Many of these new and inexperienced field officers did not hold the confidence of the enlisted men. The troops were completely disconsolate.[30]

Cunningham awakened the next morning and returned to the battlefield. He sought to retrieve his gun, which had been left behind during the melee the previous night. He located the weapon at the bottom of a trench, partially submerged in blood. Cunningham remained in Franklin with his realigned regiment to assist in burying the dead as the shattered army pulled out for Nashville.[31] Hood reasoned that retreat would work against the morale of his army. "We were willing to go anywhere, or follow anyone who would lead us," lamented one veteran of many battles. "We were anxious to flee, fight or fortify. I have never seen an array so confused and demoralized . . . and every private soldier in the whole army knew the situation of affairs."[32]

The shattered Army of Tennessee arrived on the outskirts of Nashville two days later and deployed along an uneven line. The hungry and poorly clad Confederates were tormented further by snow and freezing rain five days later. The temperature plunged to ten degrees and stayed at that point for six consecutive days.[33]

In the meantime, Cunningham and the consolidated 41st Tennessee rejoined its division on the extreme right flank near the Nolensville Pike. A heavy fog lifted on the morning of 14 December, and a thaw turned the fields into a sea of mud. The weather break coincided with increased activity along the Federal line. An attack appeared imminent, so Confederate officers awakened their men at 4 A.M. on the fifteenth. Thus they were prepared when the first blow fell two hours later along Cheatham's line. The Federals held a decided edge in manpower and weaponry, and Confederate resistance crumbled. Only the shadows of evening prevented a complete rout.[34]

That evening Captain Kellar ordered Cunningham to deliver an order for the removal of all infirmary and supply wagons on the right flank. Before returning to the regiment, the emissary stopped at the home of a friend and warmed himself by the fire. After dark, Hood retreated half a mile and dug new emplacements. Drowsy and reluctant, Cunningham returned to the regiment's new position atop Shy's Hill shortly before dawn because he feared capture by the Federals.[35]

In their fatigue and haste to dig in, the Confederates entrenched too far back from the brow of Shy's Hill. The error limited their vision to only twenty yards; they could not see the base of the hill. The enemy advanced cautiously to within six hundred yards. The crucial spot for the Confederates proved to be the salient atop Shy's Hill. The 41st Tennessee occupied a ravine only a hundred yards from the summit.[36]

Shy's Hill took a tremendous battering. Federal sharpshooters fired from three sides and kept Cunningham and other defenders pinned down.[37] A cold drizzle began at noon and added to the Confederates' difficulties. At 3 P.M. Hood made a critical miscalculation and removed three brigades from Shy's Hill to reinforce the right flank. This fateful miscalculation set the stage for the final encounter.

At 4 P.M. a Federal skirmish line approached Shy's Hill to test the defenses. This small fraction of Federal strength equaled the total number of Confederates on the entire field. The assault crushed the defensive salient "like a nutcracker." Terrified Confederates threw their weapons down and ran for the rear. The Confederate army resembled a mob as panic spread down the line. Cunningham watched many of the "best soldiers" surrender rather than run across the open field.[38] He elected to join the muddy uphill sprint to the Granny White Pike. "It was a perilous run for a long distance," he later recalled. "It was a real 'stam-pede.'" An officer ran in front of the fleet-footed Tennessean and was hit in the skull. Blood and brain matter splattered on Cunningham.[39]

The first Confederates arrived in Franklin while the rear guard engaged in desperate hand-to-hand combat with the enemy. Cunningham caught up with the 41st Tennessee, but to his chagrin, only thirty men were present. Rumors circulated that officers in the 42nd and 48th Tennessee instructed their men to "go home." "What few men were left," decided

Cunningham, "seemed incapable of any important service."[40] First in retreat, Cunningham marched at the head of the Confederate army with the remnants of the 41st Tennessee. At Spring Hill he asked for and received a ten-day furlough.[41] Continuing to travel southward, word quickly spread that only wounded troops would be permitted to cross the Duck River. So Cunningham procured a crutch and a mule and befriended a wounded Kentuckian named Grant. A bridge sentry allowed both men to cross, but the mule tossed Cunningham into the cold stream. A poor swimmer, he struggled to reach the opposite bank. Together the two men pushed on to Columbia, where they spent the night in a cottage and slept snugly on a pile of harvested cotton.[42]

Cunningham made his way back to Bedford County in time to spend Christmas with his family—his first visit home in four years. He made only a half-hearted attempt to return to the army. There were too many Federal troops between Shelbyville and what remained of the Confederate army. He barely escaped detection by one Federal patrol, but he declined to take the new oath of allegiance before the local provost marshall. In his own words, he chose to stay at home "becoming a school boy again until the final surrender."[43] He could rationalize his desertion, in a sense, by believing that he was answering a higher calling to duty—to protect his home and family.[44] Indeed, war weariness alone does not adequately explain Cunningham's ultimate decision to terminate his military career. Since early in the war, his home county was subject to enemy occupation, acts of renegade violence, and political instability. Such a tumultuous climate undoubtedly caused concern in Cunningham for the safety of his mother. When the Tennessee campaign failed, removing any hope of terminating Federal occupation, his eventual decision to desert was not too difficult.[45]

The Army of Tennessee existed in name only when Cunningham decided to desert. The regimental commander of the 41st Tennessee indicated that, during the war, the regiment "lost more men on picket duty than in battle." Servicemen from Bedford County registered the highest desertion rate west of the Appalachian Mountains. When Southern disillusionment heightened in late 1864, his calculated decision to leave did not place Cunningham in exclusive company. By the time the last of the Confederate army surrendered, three-fifths of all surviving soldiers had already gone home.[46] In light of this fact, it is amazing that Cunningham maintained a quasi-participant status for so long.

Cunningham's Civil War experience cannot be seen entirely as negative. In fact, it gave rise to several positive events that had a lasting effect on his life. Foremost, the war enabled him to meet his future bride. Second, the life-threatening nature of war guided him into a commitment to Christianity that he maintained for the rest of his life. Third, he was tendered a measure of responsibility, as evidenced by his field promotion to sergeant-major. Fourth, Cunningham did not avoid combat entirely: he was present at Fort Donelson and Port Hudson; he participated sporadically in the Atlanta campaign; and he fought, albeit grudgingly, at Raymond and Nashville. The valor he exhibited at Franklin is remarkable, considering his overall performance. That one fierce hour of bravado entitled him to a legitimate share of the Confederate heritage, complete with all of its future mythological trappings. More important, it allowed Cunningham full membership in the postwar association of Confederate veterans.

Cunningham's participation in the Civil War sheds light on the particular brand of "Lost Cause" journalism that he practiced later. In the decades that followed the war, he was sensitive about his Confederate service, as were many Southerners of his generation for whom the war became the central life event.[47] Cunningham spent a large portion of his life coming to grips not only with Confederate defeat but also with guilt feelings associated with his lackluster military performance. In later years he confided to a disbelieving friend that he "carried a gun and was insignificant in the service." On another occasion he stated modestly that he "was badly frightened from the day of his enlistment to the close of the war."[48] He never uttered more honest words. Over time, he came to exemplify a coterie of comrades who sought to overcome feelings that they had behaved dishonorably in the war.[49]

# Chapter 9 *Adjusting to Peacetime*

Christmas 1864 found Cunningham relatively safe at home "within the [enemy] lines."[1] But ever-present Federal patrols and ex-Confederate guerilla bands posed a constant threat in Bedford County. To avoid detection, family members secreted the former sergeant-major in one hideout after another. Once he narrowly avoided capture by the local provost marshal.

The family farm, like the surrounding community, had fallen into disarray. "It will perhaps never be the case again," Cunningham lamented, "that Shelbyville will exceed its ante-bellum prosperity."[2] No immediate plans were made for spring planting.

The closing months of the war and first few years of Reconstruction forced Cunningham and his fellow Tennesseans to deal with a vast assortment of social, political, and economic changes. Of immediate interest to Cunningham was the discussion over franchise restriction. Legally he was still a rebel. The General Assembly drafted a suffrage oath that virtually excluded all former Confederate soldiers. Cunningham loathed the terms of this "Brownlow oath" and was incensed that it compromised his honor. Thus he waited until the final surrender of the 41st Tennessee and the last Confederate holdouts in Texas. On 27 May 1865 he traveled to the Federal military magistrate in Nashville and received the general amnesty oath.[3]

In August an election was held to select federal representatives; its results cast a long shadow over Tennessee politics. In the contest, the new Conservative party campaigned actively, and its successes in middle Tennessee shocked Radical Republicans in Washington, D.C. The Radicals required the General Assembly to adopt the Fourteenth Amendment as the new criterion for full statewide enfranchisement.[4] Many people in the Volunteer State were embittered over the harsh and partisan decision.

Violence erupted in Bedford County over implementation of universal manhood suffrage. Carrying the state election in 1867, the victorious Conservatives mounted acts of terrorism against Negroes. The hooded vigilantes, or Ku Klux Klan, intimidated Radical Republican officials in Bedford County who attempted to enforce government programs. Governor William G. Brownlow assigned a detective named Seymour Barmore to infiltrate the local organization. The agent promptly disappeared, only to turn up six weeks later in the Duck River.[5] Radical officials in Shelbyville pleaded with Governor Brownlow to send in the militia. The governor responded by dispersing twenty-one companies across Tennessee. Cunningham's former regimental commander, Robert Farquaharson, was captain of one detachment in middle Tennessee.[6]

No evidence exists to indicate whether Cunningham belonged to or supported the Klan. But the terrorist organization was known to be active in Bedford County that summer. Meetings were held in Shelbyville at the old academy near Brandy Wine Warehouse. Cunningham knew several prominent Klan members, either as wartime comrades or through contact at postwar Confederate reunions.[7] He had witnessed firsthand the methods of the Klan in the famous Dunlap incident. John Dunlap, a teacher from Ohio who had opened a Freedmen's Bureau school in Shelbyville, had received several threatening demands from the KKK to stop teaching racial equality. He refused these and a similar Klan order to leave town. On the evening of 4 July 1868, approximately fifty night riders escorted Dunlap to the outskirts of town and whipped him. Two hundred lashes and a burned down schoolhouse did not discourage the teacher from returning to his post. Six months later, the hooded terrorists returned to the town square and shouted belligerently for "Dunlap and fried nigger meat." An unidentified group of blacks fired at the Klansmen, killing one and injuring several others.[8]

Cunningham was subpoenaed in September 1868 by a congressional investigation committee to answer questions on the Dunlap matter. Speaking before that group, he publicly condemned the violent methods of the Klan and intimated that he knew nothing about the secret organization. He stated in conclusion that "such conduct [by the Klan] would destroy the peace and harmony of the country." His remarks were printed in the *Congressional Record*.[9]

Cunningham voiced mainstream Southern thought on the leading issues of reconstruction in Tennessee in stating that "the camp followers [carpet-baggers] maintained a reign in our devastated land that cannot be compared to anything short of the torment described with four letters, the first of which is 'h.'"[10] In 1869 the gubernatorial victory of the moderate Republican DeWitt C. Senter marked the end of Radical Reconstruction in Tennessee. Cunningham's commander at Fort Donelson and Spring Hill, John C. Brown, presided over Tennessee's constitutional convention. The first election held under the new system resulted in a clean sweep at the polls for Brown and the Conservatives, a party dominated by former Confederates. Political restoration in Tennessee was then complete, and Cunningham welcomed the return of home rule.[11]

Cunningham's family life in these postwar years contrasted sharply with the tumult in community politics. In August 1866, Mrs. Cunningham had shared with her son the prewar profits from the sale of acreage.[12] This allotment provided young Cunningham with the financial independence necessary to marry his Georgia sweetheart on 27 November 1866. The newlyweds moved into quarters on the west side of Shelbyville's town square. On their third anniversary Laura gave birth to Paul Davis Cunningham at her parents' estate near Forsyth. The Cunninghams' son bore a striking physical resemblance to his mother. Laura recorded Paul's childhood antics in a diary, its pages "filled with the sweet, simple incidents of pure home life." Cunningham observed that mother and son were "two congenial associates."[13]

Cunningham's decision to start afresh in Shelbyville was not unusual for a newlywed with middle-class aspirations; it reflected a general shift that was taking place in Tennessee from rural to urban living. Several status groups, whose leadership showed remarkable continuity with antebellum society, worked to redefine the local power structure. They included old families, new fraternal organizations, new professionals, political parties, church members, and new entrepreneurs.[14] Once the twenty-three-year-old Cunningham left the farm, he became a part of this dynamic phenomenon, personifying a class of professional men in the South who strived for a career with status.[15]

In 1867 Cunningham invested his savings and formed a partnership to operate Reeves and Cunningham Dry Goods Store, where he spent the next few years as a small-town merchant.[16] The store contained large stocks of wallpaper, window shades and thousands of miscellaneous books. He recognized, as did many enterprising young men, the economic advantage of owning a store. National manufacturers and wholesale houses were seeking to open new markets in the postwar South. Many of the new Southern businessmen were young former Confederates who accepted the view that clerking was a gentlemanly profession. Cunningham's store met other needs besides that for merchandising; its location on the town square across from the county courthouse made it an ideal community clearing-house for gossip and credit.[17] Agents for R. G. Dun, a leading commercial information firm, described the mercantilist as "a young man of good char-acter . . . a clever, honest nice little man [sic]."[18] The local newspaper praised him: "Cunningham is untiring in his efforts to please the tastes and serve the wants of the reading public." He took special interest in the book section of the store. Yet the prospect of achieving financial success through a bookstore in Shelbyville was slim, according to Dun agents.[19] Cunningham's fondness for books was unusual among storekeepers, who generally concentrated on dry good sales. He made credit available based on crop lien, but this system was inefficient. Cunningham repeatedly im-plored customers through the local press to pay their debts. Reeves and Cunningham failed to turn a profit in Cunningham's three-year association with the company, despite a large inventory.[20]

Cunningham worked hard at the mercantile trade, but he concealed another ambition—to write. Journalism, like the dry goods business, was regarded as a "highly desirable profession."[21] In November 1870 Cunning-ham took advantage of an opportunity to purchase the troubled *Shelbyville Commercial.* Its owner required a modest down payment and Cunning-ham offset the cost by taking a partner, T. S. Steele. He leased Reeves and Cunningham to a younger relative, Cyrus W. Cunningham.[22]

Cunningham suffered one disadvantage when he assumed ownership of the *Commercial:* he was untried in journalism. Acquiring the newspaper had been easy, but maintaining it would be more difficult. He competed against two established weeklies in Shelbyville, the *Bulletin* and the *Res-cue.* Three newspapers saturated the modest local market. This was not an uncommon occurrence in Southern journalism, however. Indeed, short-lived journals flourished in postwar Tennessee. But Cunningham was not totally unqualified to run a newspaper. The social side of operating the dry goods business had brought him into daily contact with the public, and he understood many of the sociopolitical issues concerning postwar Bedfordites. Besides, Cunningham boasted a high school education, a fact that many editors could not match.[23]

As owner and editor of a paper, Cunningham enjoyed the luxury of speaking out on contemporary issues. He trumpted the biases of Shelby-ville's conservative persuasion, including a deep distrust of Republican-ism.[24] He became sole owner of the *Commercial* in less than three months and took bold steps to purchase the floundering *Rescue* in 1873.[25]

Cunningham became embroiled in a feud with the *Pulaski Citizen*, owned by the infamous klansman Frank O. McCord. The latter wrote that Shelbyville merchants had profited during the war by selling supplies to the enemy. Cunningham defended the majority of local businessmen against these accusations. The two editors debated the issue hotly for several months, but Cunningham benefited most from the squabble; it attracted readers who were proud of his defense of local entrepreneurs.

Cunningham contributed surprisingly little to the editorial page and relied heavily on "readyprint" supplied by the recently formed Western Newspaper Union.[26] This news service permitted the *Commercial* and other Southern papers to rise above strictly parochial stories. But Cun-ningham never shunned local tidbits; even the most insignificant event found its way into the *Commercial*.

Cunningham's single greatest accomplishment as manager of the *Com-mercial* was to print his *Reminiscences of the 41st Tennessee Regiment*. He drafted the forty-three-page memoir in 1872 from his wartime diary and cranked out three hundred copies. Strangely, he made none avail-able for sale, but sent copies to the Tennessee State Library and General Marcus J. Wright, the Tennessean responsible for collecting Confeder-ate military records in Washington, D.C.[27] The document is remarkable in that it anticipated, by a full decade, the plethora of war sketches that were to become so popular with American readers. It also avoided the trappings of future accounts that generally glossed over daily military routines in favor of more adventurous or dramatic events. Cunningham's *Reminiscences* boldly put into print a mundane, but highly typical, nar-rative that the common foot soldier could identify with. Its significance lies in the fact that its author garnered immense satisfaction in belong-ing to the more successful corporate bodies—the 41st Tennessee and the Army of Tennessee. Indeed, the military experience became a powerful postwar symbol for those men who remained loyal to the sacrifices made by former comrades.[28] For S. A. Cunningham, sharing his recollection of the apocalyptic event of his life elevated the quality of his individual wartime performance.

Cunningham made his intentions clear in the introduction to the *Remi-niscences:*

The writer having been a common soldier could not procure much that is valuable to the general public and these pages will only interest specially [sic] members of the regiment with, perhaps, their immediate friends.[29]

The narrative supplied valuable accounts of regimental history, but some sections read like a personal apologia. Cunningham's self-consciousness about its contents was evident in a correspondence with John P. Nicholson, editor of *The History of the Civil War in America*. "Pardon my curiosity," Cunningham asked, "to inquire how you happen to know of the pamphlet. It is a poor record and poorly gotten up."[30] Today the account is viewed as a rare volume in Tennessee's Confederate regimental histories.

Cunningham struggled both financially and stylistically at the helm of the *Commercial*. His lack of experience in journalism, the intense local competition, and spiraling financial losses took their toll. The editor relied on a small core of faithful subscribers, but many patrons did not pay their accounts regularly. Cunningham even sued the county for delinquent payments for advertising the sale of public land.[31]

Cunningham encountered serious financial problems beginning in mid-1872. In July he borrowed $500 from William H. Driver to keep the press in operation. Six months later he used his house on the town square as collateral to borrow $1,500 from Richard P. Stevenson. Two wealthy relatives, John H. Cunningham and Thomas W. Buchanan, cosigned the note as trustees. Cunningham reinvested the funds in improvements for the *Commercial*, but his battle to keep the newspaper solvent ended when he leased the publishing rights to his principal rival, Robert Russ.[32]

The financial panic that gripped the nation in 1873 also contributed to Cunningham's problems. The unemployed Tennessean turned over the *Commercial* building to Stevenson and six months later sold the newspaper outright to Russ. To meet other financial obligations, he sold controlling interest in Reeves and Cunningham for only $2,100. With this capital he mysteriously purchased a plot of land in Texas. Perhaps he planned to relocate his young family and escape his financial problems in Shelbyville.[33]

Despite the large real estate liquidations, Cunningham was still indebted to Driver and Stevenson. Nevertheless, he foolishly obtained another loan, this one from William Jett, that permitted him to draw $1,500 in farm supplies from the W. G. and O. Cowan Store. Three months later he purchased twenty-five acres of land in the twenty-third civil district of

Bedford County, having abandoned any notion he may have had of moving to Texas.

Unfortunately, Cunningham did not use these transactions to extricate himself from debt. Instead he became more deeply encumbered. By mid-1875 a series of circuit court injunctions ordered him to repay the loans to Driver, Stevenson, and Jett. He did so by liquidating all properties in Texas and Bedford County, but he emerged impoverished.[34] Added to his professional dilemma was a personal tragedy. A second child, Mary, had been born to the Cunninghams on 15 March 1873. She died in October 1875.[35]

By this time Cunningham was in financial and professional ruin. A fresh start in a new city—perhaps a young and booming city like Chattanooga—might clear the air.

# Chapter 10 Fiasco in Chattanooga

By late 1875 Cunningham was on the staff of the *Nashville Rural Sun*, a tabloid devoted to regional farm news and edited by a man he deeply respected, Ben M. Hord.[1] Reviewing Hord's sheet in 1872, he had stated, "The *Rural Sun*, one of the neatest printed papers in the country, and the best Weekly Agricultural paper published South of the Ohio river, should find a friend and subscriber in every farmer in Tennessee."[2] In tune with the paper's agricultural focus, Cunningham's first piece for the *Sun* was entitled "Jersey and Holstein Cattle." He worked at the *Rural Sun* for less than a year but boasted proudly about its high quality.[3]

Meanwhile Cunningham learned about the impending sale of the *Chattanooga Times*. This paper showed promise, but like Cunningham's *Commercial*, it struggled against formidable opposition. Its owner, Z. C. Patten, worked diligently and had increased the subscription list to almost seven hundred. Still, Patten was more interested in manufacturing medicine.[4] Representing two prospective buyers from Nashville, Cunningham traveled to Chattanooga to inquire into the terms of the sale. He negotiated a fair deal from Patten, but when he returned to his clients with the news, they backed away from the proposal.

Cunningham returned to Chattanooga to explain the embarrassing situation to Patten. Instead of being angry, Patten countered by offering to sell the *Times* to Cunningham on credit and without collateral. "I told him," recounted a stunned Cunningham, "I couldn't buy anything. He replied, 'You can buy the Chattanooga *Times*.'"[5] Cunningham promptly signed a promissory note totaling $1,500. "It was a strange courage that induced me to move into Chattanooga," he admitted.[6] Fate had delivered a second editorship to him, but this time in an unfamiliar metropolitan setting.

Cunningham urgently needed cash to move his family to Chattanooga. He turned to his mother, who still resided in the same farmhouse in Bedford County. She loaned him $75. When his family came to their new home, Cunningham had only $20 in his pocket, but that was sufficient to pay the Associated Press charges for the first week.[7]

Cunningham immediately found an associate in W. I. Crandall, but their partnership dissolved after an argument on the first evening. Their quarrel typified a succession of such arguments Cunningham had with other associates, most of whom left the *Times* within six months. Desperate, Mary Cunningham went to visit her relations and borrowed money. But rather than spend the newly acquired capital to replace outdated equipment like the hoe cylinder press,[8] Cunningham bought out another pair of disgruntled partners.[9] His inability to modernize the *Times* was unfortunate because its poor layout was a major defect. Thick print and poor paper quality contributed to a messy product.

Cunningham's first issue, three pages long, rolled off the press on 1 October 1876. That morning a delegation of prominent Chattanoogans visited the editor's office on the corner of Ninth and Market to wish him well. Cunningham's *Times* was not published on Mondays, and during the first month of operation it often skipped an issue. He devised impractical promotional gimmicks like giving away copies to stimulate interest. Curiously, the editor's name did not appear atop the city page for almost a year. But he did initiate a personal column under the initials SAC, soon to be a familiar byline in Tennessee journalism.[10] The usually clean-shaven editor sported a beard and prepared an engraving that showed both him and his son standing in the doorway of the *Times*. He proudly displayed the photograph in his workplace for the next thirty-seven years.

Before Cunningham's arrival in Chattanooga, the city had been relatively small, poor, and unimportant. It sustained a crippling blow in 1874 when the Chattanooga Railroad failed. At that time a group of Northern investors stepped forward and proposed to build a new line originating in Cincinnati and going to an unspecified Southern terminus. They placed Chattanooga at the top of their list of possibilities. At this auspicious moment Cunningham reopened the *Times*.[11] But inexplicably he wrote a damning editorial entitled "Cincinnati's hatred of the South." His emotional diatribe lambasted the industrial North for its alleged insensitivity to Southern economic needs. This ill-timed pronouncement sealed Cunningham's fate in Chattanooga. Angry citizens wrote letters to the *Times*, and Mayor Tomlinson Fort and twelve businessmen published an official disclaimer asserting that the editorial misrepresented the true spirit of Chattanooga.[12]

Cunningham sorely misread issues that were important to Chattanoogans. He seemed out of place; because of his middle Tennessee background, he ran a disproportionate number of articles on Nashville. Accordingly, business and political leaders cooled to him, and the advertising page dwindled. As subscriptions waned, the editor lashed out at his critics:

> We might as well say that we have no hope of pleasing everybody, either in editing, printing, or delivering the *Times*. He who dreams of freedom from complaint, no matter how hard his struggles to do well, is destined to disappointment. There are persons who live, in one sense, by croacking. We beg our friends to resist for a moment their human disposition of fault-finding and apply a few grains of common sense to the subject of our change.[13]

The *Times* teetered on the brink of insolvency, and Cunningham spent many weary days begging for short-term loans. "It was such a strenuous life," he recalled in better days, "that I felt I might drop dead in the street."[14] Mounting stress took a toll on him.

Although the *Times* originated in an urban community, it relied heavily on patronage from rural folks in northern Georgia and Alabama, where the resurging *Atlanta Constitution* rivaled the *Times* for the market. Initially relations between the two papers had been amiable. Once Cunningham wrote a glowing description of a recent trip to Atlanta. The *Constitution* reciprocated with kindness in referring to the *Times* as "one of the handsomest and liveliest dailies of the State of Tennessee."[15]

But the rivalry over rural readers finally soured the positive relationship between the *Times* and the *Constitution*. In March 1877 the *Constitution* abruptly terminated its policy of exchanging news with Cunningham's paper. The decision coincided with Chattanooga's winning the bid for the Southern terminus of the Cincinnati rail venture instead of Atlanta. Many country weeklies, on whom Cunningham relied greatly for local news, inexplicably stopped their flow of copy. In retaliation, he canceled delivery of complimentary issues of the *Times* to the rebelling editors. It took only six weeks for the *Constitution* to forge new alliances and corner the rural market.[16]

A far more direct challenge to the *Times* occurred two months later when Frank Paul founded the *Chattanooga Dispatch*. The rival paper made rapid inroads into the local market. Having seen this kind of threat before, Cunningham wrote that he regretted "that Chattanooga business- men . . . are to be called on to support two papers."[17] The businessmen concurred—they endorsed the *Dispatch* almost unanimously. Paul offered to buy the *Times*, but when Cunningham proposed a partnership, nego- tiations collapsed.[18]

The struggling editor moved his business twice to more reasonable lodgings. In the process, he misplaced valuable equipment, including the printing type. Then in February 1878 Cunningham could no longer afford the cost of the telegraphic service, and two weeks later he lost exclusive rights to the Associated Press dispatches.[19]

Cunningham blamed Joel Chandler Harris and Henry Grady, associate editors of the *Constitution*, for his recent misfortune in Chattanooga. In an angry editorial, he lashed out:

> If Atlanta had a NEWSPAPER it would be a BLESSING, not only to Georgia, but the entire South. By its monopoly of the associated press dispatches, competition has been kept down until the *Constitution* is now, not only a disgrace to Atlanta and Georgia but to the Southern people.[20]

Cunningham's *Times* reeled under the burden of competion. He suspended publication for three months but resumed the press in mid-March. Re- sourcefully, he picked up a Knoxville newspaper on the morning train. He copied almost every item, even the editorials, but he avoided foreclosure.[21]

Cunningham's political commentaries were not always out of touch with the public. His brand of Bourbonism—fear of New South ideology, North- ern businessmen, Republicanism, and social change—was well within the mainstream of Southern thought. It is interesting that he attended the inauguration of every president from Rutherford B. Hayes to Benjamin Harrison. His coverage of the disputed presidential election of 1876 was a prime example of popular Southern opinion. The editor endorsed the Democratic ticket, headed by Samuel B. Tilden because he believed the New Yorker could most expeditiously restore peace and prosperity to the South. Two days after the election, a joyous headline in the *Times* read, "Tilden Elected. The End of Radical Rule." But two weeks later Con- gress challenged the electoral returns from Louisiana, South Carolina, Florida, and Oregon.[22]

Cunningham embodied conservative thought on the "stolen election," posing the question of whether this was the crucial test of Republican government in America and concluding that the selection of Rutherford B. Hayes was a "climax of villainy," though Cunningham was determined to give him a "fair trial."[23] When Hayes promised to restore home rule in the South, Cunningham rejoiced. "An era of good feeling toward the South has sprung up so suddenly," he wrote, "that the Radical backbone is broken, and we hail the prospect of peace with the sincerest pleasure."[24] When the first Federal troops departed from Southern soil, a *Times* headline declared, "Let the nation rejoice! South Carolina is to be set free today."[25] Cunningham admired the Republican Hayes's bravery in liberating the South. The two men met in Chattanooga a year later, and the president complimented the editor by seeking his views on the "ex-Confederate element in the South." In a flattering and significant endorsement, Hayes also praised the high quality of Cunningham's newspaper.[26]

Only with great difficulty did Cunningham grasp the complex economic issues of the day, but he made an admirable stand on Tennessee's controversial state debt issue. The debt originated in the 1850s when the state provided generous loans to private corporations for construction of railroads. The General Assembly authorized public investment in bonds at high fixed rates of interest. Destruction of Tennessee's economy during the Civil War, combined with ill-advised spending during Reconstruction, brought about bankruptcy. New bonds were issued in a veiled attempt to bring relief, but this tactic caused a wave of speculation and bribery instead. Tennessee's indebtedness exceeded forty million dollars in 1870.[27]

When Cunningham took over the *Times*, the citizens of the Volunteer State were equally divided between assumption (full funding) and repudiation (low tax). The editor aligned with the state credit wing, led by Isham G. Harris, which pushed for full payment. Cunningham did not view the state debt issue as an economic one but rather as a matter of collective obligation and personal honor. "The pride of our people to vindicate State as individual honor, has been manifested throughout the South in a highly creditable degree," claimed the editor. "State credit is jealously guarded as that of individual honor."[28] Cunningham's opinion reflected two central themes of Tennessee Bourbonism—honor and justice. "We will risk our reputation on the assertion that the people of Tennessee are honest," Cunningham stated, "and will prove themselves honest in the end. They will prove themselves honest because it is right."[29] Using an antebellum analogy, Cunningham declared, "We are the bondholders slaves and will remain so until the obligation is canceled. We can't repudiate."[30] In 1878 a state referendum pushed by the Democratic party failed to settle the economic crisis. Four years later, the repudiation wing of the party finally gained control and settled the matter.[31]

Growing agrarian discontent paralleled Cunningham's tenure at the *Times*. But his lack of sympathy for the movement caused a deepening rift between him and his farmer clientele. He printed the platform of the Independent Green-back party of Chattanooga but disagreed with its primary concern, bimetalism. According to the conservative editor, one dollar should contain a dollar's worth of metal. He saw the demonetization of silver as a misguided quick attempt to remedy a complex problem.[32] His endorsement of "hard money" alienated the small farmers who mostly favored "cheap money," and he failed to see the connection between his commentaries and declining rural interest in his newspaper.[33]

Lacking any understanding of how his agrarian views antagonized the farm community and drew heated reactions, Cunningham offered a lame response:

> Our idea of the business of an editor of the daily newspaper may not be correct, but we must adhere to them till otherwise convinced. We do not think that it becomes the editor, to thrust his personalty [*sic*] upon his readers every day in the form of a long-winded article upon subjects which he but half understands.[34]

For a man in his professional position, his confession of ignorance and simplicity on the money question highlights an intellectual weakness.

Unlike his economic thought, Cunningham's social and historical interests were far less controversial. He personified middle-class respectability, validated the Protestant work ethic, and demonstrated gentile, Victorian attitudes. He also nurtured pride in the Confederate heritage. This ingratiated Cunningham to like-minded Southerners who found value in vindicating the Lost Cause.[35] When J. William Jones founded the *Southern Historical Society Papers* to preserve reminiscences of the Confederate elite, Cunningham approved wholeheartedly. "No man," he explained, "who deserves to be well instructed in the history of this great struggle [Civil War] and to judge intelligently the conduct of the respective governments and armies, can afford to neglect this source of information.[36]

Cunningham participated in the first reunion of the 41st Tennessee, held in Shelbyville on 9 June 1877. This gathering was one of many regimental reunions across the South. Cunningham encouraged such activities in a Decoration Day editorial:

Noble sentiments of patriotism nerved those gallant men to face death and drink the cup. Conscientions [*sic*] in the performance of a patriotic duty they performed it. And now let those who survived them ever keep fresh in their hearts the respect due, and once in each year have a reunion to pay the homage due our fellows.[37]

James D. Tillman, the last unit commander, delivered a speech at the reunion Cunningham attended, and his compatriots of the 41st Tennessee agreed to meet on an annual basis. When they chose association officers, Cunningham was named camp historian.[38]

Cunningham actively promoted the construction of monuments and parks in Chattanooga to commemorate the Confederacy, but he did so cautiously, understanding that to bestow honor on a defeated revolution might attract unfavorable criticism from the victors. When national sympathies favored creation of a military park at Chickamauga, Cunningham lobbied assiduously to erect a Confederate memorial there and spurred Chattanoogans to support the project.

All that is needed now is united action. The people of Chattanooga will do their duty to the memory of the Confederate Dead, if the Association [in charge of collections] will only give them the opportunity. Will the Association have faith in our people to do it? Or will they allow the money to lie at interest, while the interest of our people in the object completely dies out?[39]

On the business of constructing war memorials, Cunningham began to build a solid reputation.

He was also intensely interested in tracing in the *Times* the postwar activities of former Confederate leaders. Stories about Jefferson Davis, Alexander Stephens, Joseph E. Johnston, John B. Gordon, Varina Howell Davis, and Mrs. Thomas "Stonewall" Jackson appeared with regularity. Personal interviews with Johnston, Stephens, and William T. Sherman also appeared.[40] Clearly Cunningham revealed his devotion to preserving Southern military history along with encouraging Confederate reunions and promoting the construction of monuments.

It is remarkable that Cunningham kept the *Times* operational for twenty months. However, by mid-1878, his financial resources ran out. The subscription list had declined to fewer than 250 customers. In May the distraught owner reluctantly advertised for a buyer, and twenty-year-old Adolph S. Ochs stepped forward. Ochs had learned the newspaper trade from his immigrant father and had gained valuable work experience with several Chattanooga newspapers, including the *Times*. Cunningham portrayed Ochs as a hustler with "energy and capacity." Cunningham's terms were $800 in cash plus assumption of all outstanding debts. Ochs could muster only $250, so the editor agreed to lease the operation for two years. The final price would be fixed by arbitration. Ochs accepted and took over controlling interest on 28 June 1878.[41]

Behind Ochs's genius, the *Times* reversed its spiraling financial tailspin. His success benefited Cunningham at the arbitration hearing in September 1880, at which Cunningham was awarded an additional $5,500. This brought the final cost to more than ten times the original asking price. Ochs felt duped, but Cunningham had not swindled him. The final settlement probably reflected the poor condition of Cunningham's *Times* at the moment when Ochs took over. Moreover, it illustrated Cunningham's ignorance in not recognizing the full value of the newspaper.

Cunningham eventually realized a handsome cash settlement, but that future transaction was of no immediate value to him in 1878. Even though he drew income from the modest lease, he desperately needed a job.

The fiasco in Chattanooga brought to light characteristics in Cunningham's work that were destined to be repeated. On the negative side, he showed poor understanding of budgetary matters. Furthermore, his relative lack of experience and his learn-as-you-go style of reporting ran afoul of local leaders and workers. Mismanagement was becoming a trademark of SAC.

On the positive side, Cunningham exhibited dogged determination in the field of journalism. He gained valuable experience in operating a daily newspaper. He also demonstrated considerable skill in reporting on Confederate gatherings and memorial activities. On topics of wider scope, Cunningham's editorial commentary regularly echoed the thoughts of conservative Tennesseans.

Cunningham was destitute in 1878, just as he was in 1868 and would be again in 1888. But there were opportunities in journalism. A tragic death in Cunningham's immediate family and a substantial cash settlement from Ochs brought about a radical relocation—this time to New York City.

# Chapter 11 Our Day

Two days after Ochs placed his initial down payment on the *Times*, a notice appeared in the *Chattanooga Weekly Commercial* that the *Cartersville* (Georgia) *Express* had been sold under foreclosure. Although Cunningham never owned the *Express*, he did become its editor in January 1879.[1] He was joined in his personal exodus by thousands of other Chattanoogans who were fleeing the yellow fever epidemic that had crippled the city. The Georgia newspaper's letterhead advertised the growing trend toward urbanization in the region by labelling every city between Chattanooga and Atlanta. A prominent red star located Cartersville in the center of the network.[2] Ironically, the clientele of the *Express* was essentially yeoman farmers, one element Cunningham had alienated in Chattanooga.

Cunningham was probably more comfortable in Cartersville because it resembled Shelbyville, his hometown. The population was under ten thousand; it was in composition agrarian; and had been a center of Unionist activity during the Civil War. But deep political cleavages existed in Cartersville, where vociferous yeomen campaigned against the abuses of "cotton ring rule." Many Georgians considered the *Express* to be an organ of the corrupt ring.[3] Furthermore, Cunningham's conservatism ran against the grain of agrarian radicalism in upcountry politics.

The prospect of Cunningham's remaining at the helm of the *Express* appeared slim. A letter he had written to Tennessee's governor-elect, Albert S. Marks, mailed only two weeks after he departed for Cartersville, underscored his reluctance to remain in Georgia:

Don't consider this [Cartersville] my home—I have no thought of severing my commission with Tennessee. The fact of my having indicated my desire to share in our [unclear word] appointments at your hands is a profound secret known only to my immediate family. And it was quite unexpected to my wife. So if you should favor me I would be truly greatful [*sic*].[4]

The morose tone of the correspondence is compounded by sloppy penmanship, poor punctuation, and unclear phrases—all strong indications of stress.[5]

Cunningham felt ashamed of asking Marks for patronage. Such forwardness not only surprised his wife but also compromised his sense of honor. Under duress, he drafted an apology a week later.

True, I have had hope in that direction and have been ambitious for manifesting af [*sic*] favor from you—But allow me once for all and say that I do not mean to embarrass you, as my friend, in the least.[6]

Humbly, Cunningham attempted to rectify his forwardness by withdrawing his name from consideration for a government position.

In May 1879 Cartersville hosted the Georgia Press Association convention. Cunningham felt uncomfortable among this group. He later commented dryly that "there are more 'Colonels' in the Georgia Press Association than were in Joe Johnston's army."[7] But in his brief stay Cunningham was introduced to two well-known Cartersville men—the humorist Bill Arp and the evangelist Sam Jones.[8] He quickly befriended both men.

Several months after Cunningham began working at the *Express*, the paper hired an associate editor, John W. Akin. This decision signaled that Cunningham was once again on the way out. Whether the restructured *Express* reflected the views of Cunningham or Akin is not clear, but the paper remained hostile toward yeoman radicalism.[9]

Then came the most shattering event in Cunningham's entire life—the unexpected death of Laura Davis Cunningham on 8 October 1879. She passed away on her parents' farm following complications from an ovariectomy.[10] From every available account, Cunningham was crushed. "It was the love of a devoted wife, who was called away from him in early manhood, that most influenced Mr. Cunningham's life," commented a close friend.[11] Twenty-three years after her premature death, Cunningham expressed fond memories of Laura:

As a wife, mother, friend, she was loyal, patient, joyous, grave; possessing a radiant faith in the deeper truths of religion, which illuminated her sympathies with that rare quality of universal charity which made her presence a benediction to all who entered it.[12]

It is possible that Laura was buried in the Davis family cemetery along Tobesofkee Creek south of Forsyth, but there are no records in existence to verify the location of the grave.[13]

The trauma associated with Laura's death hastened Cunningham's departure from Cartersville. First he made arrangements to send his eleven-year-old son to live with Laura's parents. Then he hurriedly completed a pamphlet entitled *The Woman's Health Journal* with R. L. McElree, an associate of Z. C. Patten. He also contributed free-lance pieces to the Tennessee Historical Society. Cunningham's life was temporarily without direction.[14]

The handsome cash settlement for the *Chattanooga Times* in 1880 freed Cunningham to sever his affiliation with the *Express*. It also allowed him to ponder future possibilities with some degree of financial security. He visited New York City in 1881 and so enjoyed it that he spent the entire winter there. Armed with endorsements from the *Nashville American, Banner,* and *Christian Advocate,* Cunningham returned north in November 1882. It is possible that he hoped to secure employment on one of the large dailies as the Southern correspondent, or that his intention all along was to establish an independent magazine.[15]

Cunningham explained in the first issue of *Our Day* that its purpose was to capture "the *spirit of the South*" and "espouse the cause of the Southern people" in New York City. The object of the enterprise, stated Cunningham, "is the good of all men. The North and the South deserve to know each other better."[16] To the unsuspecting reader, Cunningham's journal had a conciliatory tone. The cover indicated that *Our Day* would also serve as a "transient southerner's directory." He hoped to make his business office, located at 234 Broadway, "a headquarters for Southerners when visiting" the city.[17] The editorial page layout that he cut would be used in future enterprises.

*Our Day* received praise from prominent people living in the South as well as from transplanted Southerners living in Manhattan. Bill Arp sent encouragement:

*Our Day* is a right good day—a smart day. I think I see you, friend Cunningham, a digging away, hurrying along with *Our Day*, tired and anxious and ready sometimes to say "Ah, that I had the wings of a dove, that I might fly away and be at rest." But if anybody can stand it you can. If you want to find a man of endurance, who can carry all you can put on him, take one who is stoop shouldered, and has a head covered with coarse, bristly hair. So push ahead, old boy, and keep *Our Day* as bright and cheerful as your own good nature.[18]

The Georgia humorist contributed lighthearted stories to almost every issue. Andrew H. H. Dawson, a noted New York attorney of Southern birth, thanked Cunningham for uniting "all Southern exiles on Northern soil in the strongest bonds of social sympathy."[19]

Not all reactions were favorable. Cunningham took exception to a review appearing in the *New York Sun* which referred to *Our Day* as an "exponent of the spirit of the new South." "We have never accepted the phrase *new* South," the editor argued. "No 'new' South for us."[20] Cunningham never tolerated comments he considered an affront to Old South values and traditions.

The first issue of *Our Day* contained thirty-two pages and sold for the modest annual fee of a dollar. It included a wide assortment of reprinted articles on debt repudiation in Mississippi; a tour of Manhattan; articles by Bill Arp on the "Negro question"; articles on education in the South, military cemeteries in the South, and gallantry toward women; poetry selections; and statistics on immigration, elections, and apple production.[21]

Cunningham's first editorial dealt with a perceived lack of courtesy shown to women on New York ferries. A rival columnist ridiculed his remarks, and the thin-skinned Tennessean challenged him to a duel. "There is much to condemn the practice of dueling and there is perhaps, something to commend," said Cunningham at an earlier time, "but at all events the code has stood the test of time . . . as the best means of chastising insolence and defending honor."[22] Nothing came of the confrontation.

Cunningham took seriously his self-imposed charge to develop Southern themes in *Our Day*. He worried, for instance, that the South had fallen behind the North in its responsibility for maintaining cemeteries and constructing monuments. He proudly supported an effort in Nashville to build a monument to commemorate Confederate soldiers, arguing that

to do less we would be recreant to every sense of honor and fidelity to their noble memories which we hold most dear and sacred. Americans will not respect us if we fail in this manifest duty. Such monuments and parks mark an era of refined civilization and culture of any people.[23]

The time would come, Cunningham prophesied, "when there will be pride in the breast of every American citizen for confederate valor."[24] Cunningham made it a paramount concern to publicize such memorial proposals.

In mid-1883 Cunningham mysteriously scrapped the news and history format and replaced it with Southern letters and poetry. This menu, copied from other sources, appeared at a time when Cunningham made a trip to Tennessee.[25] He might have been homesick for his beloved South, but it is more likely that he was trying to drum up support for *Our Day.* In September, no issue appeared at all. Publication resumed a month later and *Our Day* returned to its traditional focus, but the editor's lax managerial style had resurfaced. Indeed, he missed five publication deadlines in the eighteen-month life of *Our Day.*

Even though Cunningham specialized in writing about traditional themes, he was not uninterested in modern technology. His fascination with industrialization dated from his first visit to New York City, in 1872. He wrote copiously in *Our Day* on such marvels as cable cars, skyscrapers, and steel bridges. He was especially interested in the opening of the Brooklyn Bridge. The hustle and bustle of city life fascinated the observant editor, and he felt particular compassion for young people who "grow into robust manhood in the dismal co-ops."[26] Cunningham's favorite place to go was the southwest corner of the post office on Broadway, where he loved to watch the people. "There was the roar of the vehicles," he noted, "like the ever restless tides of the ocean, and the throng of human beings as incessant in their movements as if great armies were passing towards every point of the compass."[27]

It is a paradox that he criticized Southern cities for their efforts to attract technological expositions. "Another centennial!" he lamented on the Louisville and Atlanta fairs in 1883. "For good reason it will be pardoned for lack of enthusiasm . . . because experience has shown that the *one principal* result . . . has been to impoverish the moderately well-to-do people."[28]

A marvelous example of Cunningham's interest in technology is recorded in the April 1883 issue of *Our Day,* in which he proposed the construction of an underground arcade to link the west side of Broadway with City Hall Park. This arcade—ninety feet in width, framed with iron and glass walls, and lined with shops—would allow people a safe subterranean crossing at a busy intersection. He estimated the cost at roughly $500,000 and even employed an artist to draw a representation of it.[29]

Cunningham received considerable publicity but little financial support for the arcade. The *New York World* and *Tribune* interviewed him, and the *Sun* gave its endorsement. He drafted a prospectus for William G. McAdoo and former mayor Edward Cooper. A millionaire, John H. Inman, offered to promote the venture providing that Cunningham secure a lease from City Hall. This proposed urban renewal project demonstrated an imaginative side of Cunningham's personality, but it remained an unfulfilled dream.[30]

From its inception, *Our Day* fought a losing battle to attract subscribers. Cunningham was offended by acquaintances who gave him verbal encouragement but failed to subscribe. "The stupidity of the Southern people in not being more clannish in behalf of a literature of their own is reproachable," charged the frustrated editor.[31] Cunningham had invested his personal estate in the venture, and it appeared that all might be lost. "Zealous labor has been given," he explained, "and considerable expense incurred in the enterprise."[32] He resorted to a familiar but unsuccessful ploy—donating free copies to prospective clients. In early 1884 he reluctantly moved to more reasonable accommodations.

*Our Day* languished in the unsympathetic surroundings of New York City. Not surprisingly, Cunningham's strongest advocates and largest circulation appeared in Tennessee. As the months wore on, he stuffed unsold copies into bags and heaped them in his office. In a final effort to save the magazine, he shifted to a bimonthly publishing schedule.[33] He acknowledged that publication delays and delivery problems had caused bad temper among some patrons, and he promised to be more diligent in the future.[34]

Cunningham was pressed to shut down *Our Day* when the first public acknowledgment of trouble appeared in December 1883. There, the editor issued a three-page appeal for new subscribers and advertisers. He resented the fact that Southerners had abandoned him and Northerners ignored him.[35] He summoned his handful of supporters to send cash immediately. "In this earnest *plea* there is a degree of humiliation," Cunningham admitted, "but there is so much at stake that pride is sacrificed to duty." In his deepest despair, he admonished, "There is a great fault somewhere." In May 1884 he stumped the South one last time to collect delinquent payments and drum up support.[36]

Shortly before the demise of *Our Day*, Cunningham became embroiled in a controversy over a proposed home in Brooklyn for disabled Confederate soldiers. He supported the plan, but many Southerners objected to it on the grounds that it might rival similar projects currently under way in Richmond and Atlanta. Some critics accused Cunningham of playing politics to save *Our Day*.[37] The editor served on the committee to boost the Brooklyn site and attended a very important gathering on 9 April at Cooper Institute with distinguished veterans from both sides of the war. But not even the presence of John B. Gordon of Georgia and Joseph Tanner of the Grand Army of the Republic (GAR) could stem the cries. Cunningham's association with the Brooklyn home project crowned his misfortune in New York City. *Our Day* folded inconspicuously after the July 1884 issue.[38]

Although the New York hiatus accentuated Cunningham's loneliness, it also helped him to focus more sharply on topics he intended to pursue in the future. And even though he had failed in another business venture, he had at least discovered that the monthly format was the best vehicle for his brand of journalism. Indeed, the most significant breakthrough in *Our Day* was its physical layout. Cunningham had designed for the magazine a cover and editorial page that would reappear in a later periodical. His distinctive writing style had also emerged in *Our Day:* for the rest of his life, Cunningham wrote in the third person and drafted long, cumbersome sentences that were heavily punctuated.

When *Our Day* collapsed, Cunningham returned to familiar surroundings. Once again defeated in every category except spirit, he applied for a position with the *Nashville American*. Perserverance bred success, for within three years SAC introduced a column destined for fame with Nashvillians.

# Chapter 12 *With the* Nashville American

Upon arriving in Nashville, Cunningham took lodgings in the Maxwell House, which would be his residence until his death.[1] The office of the *Nashville American*, the largest daily newspaper in the state, was located across the street. The seven-column sheet had earned an unsavory reputation for yellow journalism, but new ownership promised a change and stability. The "new" *American* supported state credit, segregation, prohibition, railroad regulation, and Bourbon democracy.[2] Cunningham's values aligned perfectly with the editorial policy of the newspaper.[3] Its owner, Duncan B. Cooper, hired Cunningham as a staff correspondent, and he held that position with rising distinction for six years.

Cunningham's first story appeared on 3 October 1885. It carried the soon-to-be-familiar non de plume SAC. Thereafter his colleagues called him Sac Cunningham.[4] His articles usually started at the top of a column, a practice that made it easy for Nashvillians to find them. The earliest pieces were cabled from Chattanooga.

Between 1887 and 1892, three men edited the *American*—A. S. Colyar, John W. Childress, and Edward Ward Carmack. Their broad interests greatly influenced the variety of features assigned to Cunningham. For Colyar, topics relating to industrialization and economic growth topped the priority list. Childress and Carmack favored stories about the Confederate heritage.[5] Cunningham had displayed a knack for reporting on both subjects in prior assignments. Associations to be covered in Nashville included the Tennessee Historical Society, the Hermitage Club, and various church gatherings, all natural assignments for Cunningham. Eventually he belonged to all these organizations. His first series, which appeared in 1886, covered his friend from Cartersville, the traveling evangelist Sam Jones.[6]

The editors of the *American* perceived Cunningham's deep religious nature and had him report routinely on the annual state and regional conventions of the Cumberland Presbyterian Church and the Methodist-Episcopal Church, South.[7] His superb coverage of ecumenical sessions caught the attention of Dr. Henry M. Field, editor of the *New York Evangelist*, who in 1889 engaged Cunningham as "southern representative" for the Presbyterian weekly journal. This second job might explain Cunningham's frequent absences from Nashville that year.

In mid-1886 Cunningham started a column entitled "That Reminds Me!," which featured personal accounts of city life, local geography, biography, and business. These vignettes were especially popular with Nashvillians, though the themes often lacked cohesion and the writing was done in Cunningham's typical rambling style.[8]

Cunningham covered the monthly meetings of several prominent civic organizations. The Tennessee Historical Society gathered on the second Tuesday of each month at the Watkins Institute building. Like many Americans during this period, Cunningham was attracted to associations, and he joined the society in 1880.[9] Membership offered him an inside perspective into its activities, which was helpful to him as a reporter and also allowed him to participate in its meetings, donate items of historical value, and deliver a lecture on his favorite topic, the battle of Franklin.[10] The cultural activities of the prestigious Hermitage Club, founded in 1882, also attracted Cunningham's commentary, as did other city organizations and the local music hall, library, and lyceum. In his biographical pieces he covered such visiting dignitaries as the historian George Bancroft.

Cunningham became an advocate for improving Tennessee's educational facilities, especially for women. In 1890 he wrote an interesting series of articles on a local technical institute and girls' academy. Nashville's "pride is in her schools and culture," he concluded. He sensed that economic improvement in the state was dependent upon increasing educational opportunities.[11]

As the public indulged more and more in leisure activities, Cunningham reported on vacation spots and hotel accommodations in Tennessee, Kentucky, and northern Alabama. He contrived an unhurried, folksy style in his travelogues, one he had first used in *That Reminds Me!* They opened routinely with a dialogue between Cunningham and a citizen on some interesting piece of local geography or history and weaved in descriptions of such natural surroundings as mountains, hot springs, and parks. These social accounts also recorded the guest registers of area hotels. From the comfort of home, the reader was transported to fashionable middle-class retreats. Nashvillians enjoyed these graceful travelogues.[12]

In his business coverage, Cunningham showed great appreciation for technological developments. Editor Colyar owned a large interest in the Tennessee Coal, Iron and Railroad Company and frequently sent Cunningham to report on Alabama's manufacturing triangle between Tuscumbia, Florence, and Sheffield. The correspondent traveled extensively throughout the region in 1886 and 1887. Special letters from Cunningham to the *American* read like propaganda sheets to lure prospective workers to this industrial belt.[13] He interspersed his coverage of heavy industry with stories about Nashville businesses: lumber yards, banks, hardware stores, pharmacies, carriage works, carpet houses, and railroads. He thirsted to educate the public as much as possible about the economic potential of his city. "I wish I had full information about the best business enterprises of Nashville," he stated in an open letter. "I should like to be informed—should like to help inform the public."[14] Cunningham recognized the potential benefits of industrialization. "Ah, the future!" he philosophized. "Of it who can tell?"[15]

On 17 November 1888, Cunningham featured the city of Franklin in his first "Towns of the State" series. Over the next five months he wrote similar accounts of Shelbyville, Columbia, Lawrenceburg, Pulaski, McMinnville, Manchester, and Tullahoma, all familiar sites to the author.[16] Nashvillians eagerly followed this series. One citizen praised Cunningham's column:

> Mr. Cunningham . . . has already made such a reputation for "writing up" the towns and counties of the State. Mr. Cunningham is one of the smoothest writers on THE AMERICAN and his articles are always read with great pleasure and much interest.[17]

A rival editor accurately described Cunningham as a "most versatile and entertaining writer."[18] It is conceivable that he received inspiration from the earlier writings of Joel Chandler Harris.[19] Just as "Roundabout in Georgia" solidified Harris's reputation, so too did the "Towns of the State" series enhance Cunningham's status as a respected journalist.

Cunningham exposed a bias on two volatile issues in Tennessee politics, prohibition and race relations. Prohibition had made great strides in Tennessee since the late 1870s. It took only ten years for the forces of temperance to push for a statewide referendum on the issue.[20] Cunningham abstained from consuming alcohol, in obedience to a strict church mandate, and he cautioned in his writing that people should "be temperate in all things; in this lies the secret of all happiness."[21] He monitored the national temperance movement carefully while he was residing in New York City. He corresponded with Frances E. Willard of the Women's Christian Temperance Union and reprinted her speeches in *Our Day*.[22] Cunningham greatly respected another temperance advocate, Anson Nelson, who was the secretary of the Tennessee Historical Society. In the early 1880s Cunningham reported to Nelson on the Georgia Prohibition Party. He made his personal feelings known when the party swept the Fulton County elections. "Atlanta," he stated, "is proud of the distinction just achieved in the moral effect upon the country."[23] Although editor Carmack often ridiculed prohibition, Cunningham continued to give it his undivided support.[24]

The prohibition movement in Tennessee soon became inundated with white supremacy ideology. Shortly after Carmack arrived at the *American,* he rechanneled attention from Nashville's urban reform, which included temperance, toward segregation.[25] Cunningham agreed with Carmack on this issue of race. He exposed his prejudice by describing the character of the black race as low, cunning, malicious, and cowardly. Negro virtue, he concluded, was "rarer than honesty." He offered this suggestion as a remedy to the "Negro question": "The race problem can be managed very much better by the parties immediately concerned than by others."[26] Without a doubt, the correspondent was the product of a time when white supremacist ideology was overtly disseminated.

At first it appeared to be a professional setback when Cunningham returned to Nashville in 1885, but in retrospect it is evident that the move skyrocketed his career in journalism. His views were compatible with those of his editors, and writing fashionable series earned him considerable notice. In his six-year tenure at the *American,* Cunningham focused on popular themes, and the subject that attracted him most strongly proved to be the activities of ex-Confederates.

# Chapter 13 Associational Ties

Cunningham supported charitable, memorial, social, and historical concerns of ex-Confederates dating from the end of the Civil War. Some of his fellow veterans hesitated to form associations because of political and other considerations.[1] Cunningham, however, participated in the first gathering of the 41st Tennessee, in 1877, and revered the ensuing encounters. "The faithful members of the old regiment," he declared, "are my fondest associates among men."[2] His associational ties with former wartime comrades formed the basis of his reputation as a disseminator of Lost Cause ideology.

In the mid-1880s former regiments consolidated into larger veterans' assemblies in middle Tennessee. Survivors of the 41st Tennessee merged with neighbors belonging to the 17th, 23rd, and 44th Tennessee and the 4th Tennessee Cavalry. Frequently their annual affairs were cloaked in regimental one-upmanship. For instance, Cunningham defended his unit at the 1889 gathering in Wartrace. "The 'Forty-one' was as brave a regiment as fought in the war," he boasted, "except perhaps the Tenth Tennessee (Irish) who by their absolute recklessness were nearly all killed."[3] As mortality rates among veterans increased dramatically at the close of the century, survivors from regiments like the 1st, 3rd, 8th, 16th, and 32nd Tennessee joined the original group of which Cunningham was a member.[4] The fraternal meetings grew in popularity with the public and attracted powerful orators, usually politicians, who held crowds spellbound as they glorified the vanquished Confederacy.

As middle Tennessee regiments bonded, so did ex-Confederates in other states. At first they were not united. "Here then all over the South were men working toward the same end," noted a contemporary, "but with no system nor organization to their work, each locally pursuing an independent course."[5] The initial desire of many veterans, typified by Cunningham, was to foster a closer comradeship and assist needy ex-Confederates. The moment seemed right for hundreds of decentralized ex-Confederate societies to consolidate into a larger association.

When Cunningham returned to Nashville in 1885, the local affiliation of ex-Confederates was Frank B. Cheatham Bivouac #1. This group met in Pythian Hall on a monthly basis to conduct fraternal and memorial activities. For a decade the brotherhood maintained a low profile, and membership lagged. Then, in 1887, a reorganization meeting was called at the Merchants Exchange. The presence of leading civic, business, and former military leaders—Albert Marks, Peter Turney, John W. Childress, John C. Brown, William B. Bate, John P. Hickman, and George Maney—ensured the survival of the Bivouac.[6]

Cheatham Bivouac's membership roll reflected a decidedly middle-class orientation: thirty-one percent were professional or white-collar men, thirty-eight percent were propertied or middle-class, twenty-four percent were skilled craftsmen, and only seven percent were from the unskilled worker class. Gaines Foster is correct in suggesting that the rapid growth of ex-Confederate bodies was largely an urban phenomenon.[7] Without a doubt, the formation of Cheatham Bivouac was linked to the big city associationalism occuring throughout the country.

Cunningham followed the proceedings of Cheatham Bivouac with great interest because of its heavy emphasis on comaraderie. On no other single subject did he write so prolifically or with such care. He became a leading booster and reveled in its mercurial rise over the next five years. Indeed, at its peak in 1902, Cheatham Bivouac registered 345 members and was the largest society of Confederate veterans in Tennessee. By its very size, Cheatham Bivouac experienced a social leveling among its middle-class members: editor stood beside governor, grocer stood beside diplomat. In this climate, Cunningham and his associational comrades enjoyed a pervasive spirit of egalitarianism.[8] Attendance at meetings averaged fifty members through 1904 and posed the problem of finding adequate space. The group moved from hall to hall until Davidson County donated space in the new courthouse for a permanent headquarters.

Cheatham Bivouac lured a wide range of capable public speakers who extolled the virtues of the Confederate experience. Cunningham was present for what was perhaps the most famous address ever given, that of Chief Justice Peter Turney of the Tennessee Supreme Court.[9] Entitled

"The South Justified," Turney's speech contained remarks that mirrored the thoughts of the audience on defending the right of secession, and he challenged the body

> to awake the Southern man and woman to the importance of having their children study our lost cause from constitutional, legal, and historical standpoints, [so] that they be not misled. Our cause was worth all we sacrificed to it. Though lost it deserves vindication.[10]

Turney's remarks inspired Cunningham.

Cunningham solidified his reputation as a professional journalist with his extensive coverage of local Confederate reunions throughout middle Tennessee.[11] A flurry of monument dedications kept him on the road for much of 1887.[12] That year, Cunningham wrote a personal account of the battle of Franklin that was more widely read by contemporaries than his *Reminiscences*. The four-column story met with instant success and reappeared over the next few years in many other Southern newspapers. It established Cunningham as the leading expert on that bloody battle from the Confederate side. However, the immensely popular "Battles and Leaders" series compiled by Johnson and Buel for *Century Magazine* passed over the acclaimed article in favor of those by higher ranking authorities.[13]

In its own right, Cunningham's manuscript on Franklin is a fascinating example of self-justification, a characteristic not unusual in this genre. In *Reminiscences* Cunningham described his desperate predicament in the trench at Franklin shortly after the death of General Strahl:

> An almost helpless handful of us were left, and the writer was satisfied that our condition was not known, so he ran to the rear to report to General Brown, commanding the Division. He met Major Hampton of the Division Staff, who told him that General Brown was wounded, and that General Strahl was in command of the Division. This confirmed his prediction, so having failed to find him for some time, and seeing that relief was being sent, he lay down to rest and sleep. His shoulder was black with bruises from firing, and it seemed that no moisture was left in his system. These personal mentions are all we can give, for it was night, and the writer never knew other than what he saw.[14]

It is irregular, but not unexplainable, that Cunningham's details changed when J. William Jones published an update in the *Southern Historical*

*Society Papers.* In its recast form, originally prepared for presentation to the Tennessee Historical Society, Cunningham altered the ending in an explanation of his inability to sleep that night:

> The battle was over and I could do no more; but animated still with concern for the fate of comrades, returned to the awful spectacle in search of some, who year after year, had been at my side. Ah, the loyalty of faithful comrades in such a struggle! These personal recollections are all that I can give, as the greater part of the battle was fought after nightfall, and once in the midst of it, with but the light of the flashing guns, I could see only what passed directly under my own eyes. True, the moon was shining, but dense smoke and dust so filled the air as to weaken its benefits, like a heavy fog before the rising sun, only there was no promise of the fog disappearing.[15]

The latter writing is significant because it stressed a late Victorian theme vitally important to ex-Confederates in the decade following the 1880s: loyalty to comrades. But the revision contradicted the original account. The fact that Cunningham did not return to the trench until the next morning in the original version but found his way back that night in the revision suggests an alteration of facts to make the account more acceptable to an audience of veterans keenly interested in high morality and symbolism. Most damning is the fact that no moon shone at all on the evening of 30 November 1864.[16] To Cunningham's credit, later published accounts revert to the original version.

As a staff correspondent, Cunningham enjoyed touring Tennessee's battlefields with well-known commanders and recording their impressions in the *American*. At his own initiative, he led an excursion to the Fort Donelson site in 1890 and offered a personal analysis of the fray. Other stories concerning the Confederate past further bolstered the reporter's popularity in Nashville.[17]

Cunningham wrote with equal gusto on the formation of a state association of Confederate veterans. Actually, the concept of establishing a statewide organization preceded the revamping of Cheatham Bivouac by several weeks. When the Association of Confederate Soldiers, Tennessee, filed for incorporation in 1887, it became the first chartered Southern organization of its kind. Its constitution provided for annual meetings on the second Wednesday of every October.[18] The association grandfathered membership to any veteran who qualified for a local bivouac. The numerical strength of the Nashville camp ensured the survival of the state organization. Cunningham reported on these proceedings, but there is no record of his direct participation.

The earliest effort to amalgamate all ex-Confederates into one regional body had failed in the 1870s because local fraternities had not yet become commonplace. In 1888 George Moorman invited former Confederate cavalrymen to attend a reunion in New Orleans. Veterans from thirteen Southern states responded to the Kentuckian's appeal. The men in attendance proclaimed the meeting a resounding success, and Moorman laid plans to make the event an annual one.[19] Cunningham was interested in Moorman's venture but did not attend the gathering.

Cunningham did attend a banquet later that year in New Orleans at which related issues were discussed. Leon Jastremski, a druggist and politician from Baton Rouge, had recently visited the annual reunion of the Grand Army of the Republic (GAR), after which he pondered the notion of organizing a national Confederate society along similar lines. In Chattanooga, J. F. Shipp made a simultaneous appeal for all interested ex-Confederates to attend a banquet in New Orleans. Shipp hoped that such a group would support a plan to secure Chickamauga as the site of the first national military park.[20] He also suggested that those men present should unite in a "loose" association. The veterans who attended represented ex-Confederate organizations from Louisiana, Tennessee, and Mississippi. They established a committee chaired by Jastremski to study the feasibility of Shipp's proposal.[21] Cunningham applauded the committee's efforts and later submitted an account of their findings to Francis Trevelyn Miller's *Photographic History of the Civil War.*[22]

Jastremski and Shipp alerted Cunningham and like-minded veterans to the growing sentiment favoring a regional ex-Confederate association. The exploratory committee appointed Fred S. Washington to mail a circular to every known Confederate group in the South. The document, sent in June 1889, called for

> The formation of an association for such benevolent historical and social purposes, as will enable us to do justice to our country, care for our needy and disabled comrades in their declining years, and assist the needy widows and orphans of our comrades in a spirit of mutual friendship, fraternity and goodwill.[23]

Fifty-two delegates responded to the calling. They represented nine separate veterans' organizations, including Nashville's Cheatham Bivouac.[24]

Cunningham arrived two days after the proceedings had begun, but that did not dampen his enthusiasm. "I rejoice that a general organization too long neglected, has at last been perfected," he reported.

> It is an organization which all honorable men must approve and which heaven itself must bless. I call upon you [veterans], therefore, to organize in every State . . . and rally to the support of the high and peaceful objects of the United Confederate Veterans.[25]

Cunningham mixed business with pleasure while covering the sessions in New Orleans. He distributed his well-traveled tract on the battle of Franklin to interested delegates—a shrewd move because the document served as his credentials to formalize relations with the fledgling society.[26] He also visited Jefferson and Varina Davis at Beauvoir.

By the end of the first plenary session, the deputies had hammered out fourteen articles to a provisional constitution. Jastremski proposed the organization's name, the United Confederate Veterans Association, or UCV. Seen as a guiding force in the amalgamation process, Fred S. Washington secured the election of John B. Gordon of Georgia as its first commander-in-chief. Many powerful positions of the new society would be filled by former officers of the Confederate army.[27]

Cunningham reported the main goals of the new association as laid out in Article II: "The object and purpose of this organization will be strictly social, literary, historical, and benevolent."[28] To him, conformity to these principles became a near-sacred duty; he remained committed to them for the rest of his life.

Cunningham reported in the *American* with great skill and acumen on the formation of ex-Confederate associations at the local, state, and regional levels. He was attuned to their goals of camaraderie, welfare, and vindication, and he appeared with increasing frequency at their gatherings both as a reporter and as a loyal supporter. Former comrades were quick to recognize him as an adept advocate of the Confederate heritage.

Thus, after years of professional struggle, Cunningham achieved modest success through ties with former comrades. Shortly, the *American* would entrust its prize reporter with a project that would forever alter his life. For S. A. Cunningham, the man and the moment had met.

# Chapter 14 General Agent Cunningham

S. A. Cunningham found a comfortable niche in reporting the activities of his former military associates in the United Confederate Veterans Association. In only twelve years the organization swelled to more than sixty thousand members and seventeen hundred "camps." It is estimated that one out of every four living veterans belonged to the fraternity.[1] Why Cunningham delayed so long before joining Cheatham Bivouac remained uncertain. His nomination was aided, albeit indirectly, by the death of Jefferson Davis. When the ex-Confederate organizations learned of Davis's death on 6 December 1889, they rushed representatives to Beauvoir to help the former president's family. John W. Childress and Edward Ward Carmack of the *Nashville American* accompanied fifteen mourners from Cheatham Bivouac.[2] Cunningham kept company with the group and reported on the funeral in the Crescent City. He visited Varina Davis several times and recounted "the melancholy pleasure of being at the quiet home . . . an event that will last with vivid memory." He wrote several features about Davis in retirement during an extended stay at Beauvoir after the funeral.[3]

Following the funeral, Childress invited a number of editors to discuss the historical merits of the Confederate president. Earlier he had suggested that newspapers throughout the South solicit funds to build a monument to the great leader. Childress offered the *American* as the vehicle to spearhead the collection drive, and the consenting newspapermen picked him to preside over a ten-man committee known as the Southern Press Association.[4]

In less than two weeks Childress received over a thousand dollars in donations. While the initial surge overwhelmed the chairman, pledges then dropped sharply. On 6 May 1891 Childress officiated at an urgent session of the Southern Press Association in Nashville, where he reported the alarming decline in public support. The group formed a subcommittee to open dialogue with the UCV to examine other methods of attracting capital. The Southern Press Association simultaneously appealed to the public to set aside 18 June 1891 to stage community fund-raising rallies. Cheatham Bivouac responded with vigor; they canvassed each of Nashville's twenty-five civil wards on the appointed day.[5]

Once again pledges and cash poured in. Childress's work at the *American* suffered from his rigorous travel schedule and collection efforts. When he confided in the Southern Press Association on the enormity of his task at a meeting held in Atlanta they instructed him to appoint a general agent to assume the tedious and time-consuming chores. Without hesitation, he chose his top reporter, S. A. Cunningham. Childress armed the amenable Cunningham with a handwritten letter of introduction "cordially commending him to the people of the South."[6] The editor wisely kept the forty-eight-year-old general agent on the payroll of the *American.*

Childress's selection of Cunningham as general agent was a calculated decision. Indeed, he had laid the groundwork a month earlier in encouraging Cunningham to apply for membership to Cheatham Bivouac. Initially the reporter hesitated.[7] His reluctance could have stemmed from several sources. First, he remained self-conscious about his poor Civil War record. Second, the strict entrance qualifications raised a moral issue. He clearly understood the bylaws of Cheatham Bivouac—especially Article III, section 1, which read:

> None but persons who have served honorably in the Army or Navy of the late Confederate States during the war between the States, serving until the close of the war, unless disability, or honorably released from service, having an unimpeachable war record, and of good standing since, can be members of this organization.[8]

The dilemma was that Cunningham had not served until the end of the war. Like approximately sixty percent of his comrades, he had dropped out early.

Cunningham's failure to remain faithful to the Confederate war effort haunted his memory. Like so many of his comrades, he remained silent as the postwar myth of the Confederate soldier unfolded, knowing full its erroneousness. It must have generated a personal conflict within himself and many of his comrades, and might explain why seventy-five percent of all surviving Confederates opted not to seek membership in the UCV. Although Cunningham failed to meet the minimum membership requirements of the local association, Childress deemed it essential that he "enlist" in order to maximize his status as general agent. Accordingly, he sponsored Cunningham's application.

Cunningham filled out the application form in messy style. The vita was marred by poor penmanship, hurried and incomplete thoughts, frequent cross-outs, and poor punctuation. Such errors on the part of an educated man strongly suggest anxiety.[9] Furthermore, Cunningham described his military service in nebulous terms that purposely mislead the reader: "Was a Fort Donelson prisoner (16 Feb. 1862) Sent to Camp Morton. Exchanged at Vicksburg in Sept 62 Served in Mississippi, Louisiana, in the Georgia Campaigns with Bragg, Johnston and Hood. Was cut off on Hood's retreat but *not* captured."[10] In his statement Cunningham manipulated the truth in such a manner as to imply that his dedication to duty was constant, which in fact it was not. When given an opportunity to explain interruptions in his service record he felt obligated only to explain his absence after December 1864:

> Relying on assurance of Adjt. Gen. J. D. Porter that army would stay at Columbia a certain number of days I was cut off as stated above. While on the way out through intersecution [*sic*] relations a parole was given without any promise from me for two days which I avoided arrest until I voluntarily surrendered May 27, 1865.[11]

In fairness to Cunningham, it should be said that many Confederate veterans from Tennessee explained their final act of service in euphemisms or metaphors.[12] But his narrative, unlike others, is practically indecipherable. His use of evasive language and sketchy detail leads the reader to draw generalizations that are inaccurate. Without question, Cunningham manipulated the evidence to suggest that he was a battle-hardened veteran, but he offered no specific details on combat, as other applicants frequently did. Shifting the blame to an officer for his failure to return to the departed army, it became central to his case that he did not sign the oath of allegiance until after the last Confederate army had surrendered.

The application showed Cunningham at his elusive best. It demonstrated how a person with command of the language could recast the truth. Unfortunately, he resorted to his ability to falsify information whenever it suited him. Years later, one of his closest friends acknowledged that Cunningham had "by his changing a word [in a manuscript] made me say something that I did not do." [13] His habit of recording quasi-truths caused ill will with his acquaintances on several other occasions.

Cheatham Bivouac approved the application and initiated Cunningham on 15 June 1891. Now he possessed the credentials necessary to mount a respectable fund-raising campaign. The *American* congratulated the new general agent "on his deserved promotion." [14] Cheatham Bivouac was extremely proud that one of its own had been selected for such a presitgious assignment.

Cunningham's enrollment in the bivouac increased his involvement with the veterans of Nashville. He frequently filled in as secretary at the monthly meetings because of his literary skills and eventually inherited the role of scribe. At first he drafted letters of invitation, solicitation, and condolence. Later he delivered testimonials for deceased comrades, an important ritual conducted only by fraternal members of high status. Within two years Cunningham represented the Nashville unit as a voting delegate at the state and national UCV conventions. In 1894 he introduced his first resolution at a state convention. He was frequently asked to deliver lectures because of his respectable talent as an orator and involvement in the everyday workings of the bivouac. By the end of the decade, Cunningham was recognized as an undisputed kingpin in the local group. [15]

Immense collection problems faced the general agent for the Davis monument. Childress had turned over lengthy pledge lists, and Cunningham was inundated with correspondence from patrons beyond Tennessee. He traveled endlessly on a limited budget to collect sponsorships. When public interest lagged, his canvasses became less productive. In one jaunt to Marshall County, Tennessee, he pooled only eighty-five dollars. In 1892 he scheduled three six-week tours and traveled from Richmond to El Paso. In these major thrusts the energetic agent acquired many new contracts but he relied on the good intentions of each donor to make payment. [16] On one trip Cunningham chatted with an independent rival in Richmond— probably a UCV-sanctioned agent. But the Tennessean never lost faith in the importance of his mission. "If New Orleans can erect $150,000 worth of Confederate monuments, and Richmond near that amount, should the entire South hesitate in an undertaking to cost only $250,000?" he questioned. [17] From the outset, the general agent considered his position a labor of love.

Locally too Cunningham made substantial progress. For instance, he received more than two thousand dollars from Carmack through the Young Men's Democratic Club. Cash receipts were compiled from a benefit concert held at Nashville's Vendome in March 1890, and the Ladies Auxiliary of the Confederate Soldiers Home donated their gate from a week-long chrysanthemum exhibition. These contributions accounted for almost $4,000 from the Nashville area alone.[18]

Cunningham did not rely exclusively on the graciousness of Nashvillians. He encouraged scholars and well-known ex-Confederates to deliver paid lectures on the character of Jefferson Davis. Throughout 1892 he traveled frequently to other states seeking funds. In these travels he came to realize what Childress already knew—that the position of general agent consumed tremendous time and energy.[19]

The Davis family gave Cunningham much moral support. The general agent maintained an active correspondence with Varina Howell Davis and her two daughters, Winnie and Margaret. These ladies felt at ease discussing sensitive and personal family matters with Cunningham. Mrs. Davis and Cunningham shared each other's grief whenever close friends and family members died.[20] In print, Cunningham unequivocally defended the entire Davis clan. Southern readers respected Cunningham's outspoken loyalty to the former president and first lady. Shortly before her death, Varina Davis thanked Cunningham for his faithfulness. She referred to him as a true "spokesman of the South."[21] Cunningham valued the Davis connection over the years. He watched remorsefully as each family member died: Winnie in 1898, Varina in 1906, and Margaret in 1909.[22] Their deaths contributed to Cunningham's growing melancholia later in life.

Cunningham played a conspicuous role in the reinterment of Jefferson Davis in 1893, joining a host of UCV dignitaries that accompanied the remains by rail from New Orleans to Richmond. Commander Gordon had instructed UCV members to assemble in their local communities and view the passing cortege. During the journey, the entourage was afforded an unexpected measure of public gratitude as it was met by tremendous crowds that often obstructed the tracks and forced the train to stop. Bells tolled and guns saluted the train as it traveled through the South. The citizens of Beauvoir coated the rails with layers of rhododendron and magnolia blossoms. Similar acts of veneration were repeated in countless towns and cities throughout the South. In Richmond an enthusiastic crowd estimated at twenty-five thousand greeted the train. Cunningham stood beside Commander Gordon in reverence before the open grave.[23]

Despite Cunningham's attachment to the Davis memorial project and his relative success in gaining pledges, actual cash contributions lagged, largely because of worsening economic times and the general agent's growing preoccupation with a new journalistic venture. Surely the UCV might pick up the slack for so worthy a cause, he reasoned. Cunningham knew that the body had shown initial interest in cosponsoring the project with the Southern Press Association. In fact, the influential Clement A. Evans succeeded in presenting a resolution to offer the services of the association as the sole collection agency.[24] The resolution might well have been the original source of antagonism between Evans and Cunningham. The two men were on distant and sometimes unfriendly terms throughout the 1890s.

The decision of the UCV to collect contributions unilaterally for the Davis monument caused duplication of Cunningham's efforts. For example, the UCV participated in a community collection drive announced by Childress but did not entrust its receipts to Cunningham. Instead, Commander Gordon issued General Order #58 on 7 May 1892, creating the Davis Monument Committee.[25] He chose W. L. Cabell to chair the select committee which comprised one representative from each Southern state. Each representative in turn appointed a state chairman to coordinate local fund-raising efforts. Cabell nominated W. H. Jackson to represent Tennessee on the standing committee. In a move that would surely confuse any accountant, Jackson selected Cunningham to carry out solicitations in the Volunteer State.[26] The choice of high-ranking ex-Confederates such as Cabell and Jackson illustrated the patriarchal nature of the UCV, a reality that rankled Cunningham. But the UCV's usurpation of his responsibilities as general agent might have been a blessing too. Cunningham obtained easy admittance to all meetings of the Davis Monument Committee. General Jackson's irregular attendance and Cunningham's dependability resulted in the general agent's gradual assumption of more influence within the UCV. As a newspaper reporter and committeeman for Tennessee, Cunningham was able to witness firsthand the inner workings of the UCV hierarchy. He formed a quick opinion of John C. Underwood, the hand-picked finance chairman, whose "dictatorial" style Cunningham found revolting.[27]

Underwood essentially inherited Cunningham's duties as general agent, and the fact did not go without comment from Cunningham, who reported in print on the activities of an "unauthorized" solicitor he called John C. Brain. Apparently "Brain" circulated in Texas and Arkansas, accepting donations for the Davis monument, but never submitted the cash to Cunningham.[28] It is highly likely that Cunningham was jealous of John C. Underwood; could the name John C. Brain have been a pseudonym for Underwood? There is no doubt that Cunningham resented Underwood's appointment, and it planted bitter seeds that blossomed into serious litigation several years later.

Cunningham carefully monitored the actions of the Underwood committee, but the lack of sufficient funding continued to hamper the Davis project. Indeed, by 1896 the UCV had collected less than seventeen thousand dollars—not even a tenth of the anticipated price. Yet the UCV committee voted to lay the cornerstone immediately in Richmond. Thousands of veterans traveled there to take part in the historic ceremony. Many men were "without money, [and] slept in all the parks, on doorsteps, in yards, and even in the streets."[29] The excitement generated by the occasion surpassed that elicited by any memorial activity in recent Southern history.

At the ceremonial laying of the cornerstone, Cunningham sensed that the UCV hierarchy undervalued his role in the project, and he increasingly focused his resentment on the influential Underwood. At first he directed his criticism to the committee's irresponsible decision to lay the cornerstone before sufficient funds had been secured, and then he expressed disapproval of the lengthy work schedule, which would deprive many aging veterans of the pleasure of seeing the finished product. "Let us hope that the action [of the UCV committee] will be reconsidered . . . before funds in hand shall have been expended upon a foundation," he warned.[30] Cunningham even faulted the grandiose design.

Cunningham's foreboding remarks proved to be justified, but at the time he was mocked for lacking vision. Three years later Cabell stunned the UCV by suggesting that the United Daughters of the Confederacy (UDC) assume the duties of solicitation. Cunningham praised the decision; perhaps he even allowed himself a degree of personal vindication. At any rate, construction of the Davis memorial began under the watchful eye of the UDC. The ladies, claimed Cunningham, had demonstrated their superiority in raising money for prior memorial projects.[31]

The unveiling of the Davis monument on 3 June 1903 marked an important occasion in Cunningham's life. As a reporter, general agent, and UCV committeeman, he had turned the project into a personal crusade. On the appointed day, an estimated eighty thousand visitors—twenty percent of them veterans—crammed into Richmond. The assembly was the largest single contingent of ex-Confederates ever to gather. It might even have marked the grandest moment in UCV history. Edward Ward Carmack delivered the keynote address, but Cunningham shared the limelight with no other man when the rank and file greeted the original general agent with a thunderous ovation.[32]

Through his connection with veterans' societies, Cunningham had earned a reputation as an individual dedicated to institutionalizing the Confederate past. He had welcomed the position of general agent as a sacred opportunity, though it required relentless travel, voluminous record-keeping, commitment and boundless energy—the latter two of which Cunningham was characteristically able to give. While his work never met with resounding monetary success, in the process of doing it he contacted many influencial people across the South, and some of them encouraged his dream of establishing a new magazine devoted to perpetuating the Confederate heritage. When S. A. Cunningham founded the *Confederate Veteran* in 1893, at the age of fifty, he finally discovered his life's work.

# Chapter 15 — *The* Confederate Veteran

In 1892 Cunningham interrupted his work as general agent for the Jefferson Davis monument to solve the record-keeping problems that had resulted from the fund-raising for that cause. He proposed to publish a contributors' directory—a list of names of the people who donated money for the monument.[1] Some UCV leaders, like Adjutant General George Moorman, encouraged Cunningham in this project, which would, he said, "enable the Southern people to see from what sections the money is given and also by whom."[2] Cunningham claimed he could handle the heavy commitment that the position of general agent imposed and still find the time to edit the directory. Privately, he knew the latter enterprise would consume a great amount of time. Since he drew no commission as general agent, he felt no obligation to work endless hours on a project for which responsibility was being increasingly usurped by the UCV. In fact, he felt "free from technical restraint" and made a decision to renounce the general agency.[3] Amazingly, some of the factors relevant to founding the *Confederate Veteran* have been secreted for over a century.

It is probable that Cunningham planned from the very beginning to publish more than simply a contributors' list. He was aware of a short-lived journal published in Atlanta in 1890 called the *Confederate Veteran*. T. A. Havron edited the magazine, which contained reminiscences about the Civil War written by ex-Confederates.[4] Cunningham pondered the merits of forming a similar magazine and initiated discussion with many Southerners on its potential value. Unfortunately, he lacked the capital sufficient to implement the scheme. In February 1890 his mother died, leaving him a modest estate.[5] It was not enough to start a new magazine, but his superiors at the *American* gave him significant encouragement and offered the use of their printing facility. This apparently gave Cunningham the impetus he needed to begin publishing.

The first issue of the *Confederate Veteran* rolled off the press in January 1893, and it was a bold venture in light of the editor's limited financial resources. Forty-three subscribers received the first issue, but he optimistically printed five thousand copies. He shipped complimentary copies of the thirty-two-page introductory number to Confederate dignitaries, veterans' societies, friends, and family members. He also sent copies to more than five hundred post offices in Tennessee, hoping to drum up support,[6] then stuffed the remaining unsold volumes into large sacks and tucked them away.

Cunningham announced the goals of the magazine on page one:

> The *Confederate Veteran* is intended as an organ of communication between Confederate soldiers and those who are interested in them and their affairs and its purpose is to furnish a volume of information which will be acceptable to the public, even to those who fought on the other side. It will at once be sent to every Confederate Veteran organization in existence and the patronage of such bodies is earnestly sought.[7]

He believed in his mission statement even though it conflicted somewhat with his earlier announced plan to publish a contributors' directory. "The concept of the *Veteran* was not, after all, an enterprise," he later claimed. "It was rather an evolution, and its beginning was surrounded by no fixed resolve to 'establish a magazine,' but rather to serve a specific purpose."[8] Cunningham's magazine was a bold risk.

Cunningham articulated lofty ideals in the first issue in order to win endorsements and sell subscriptions. He appealed first to Southern nationalism. "The *Veteran* is in the spirit of Southern people who espoused the cause of independence in the sixties," he proclaimed. "Its unparalleled success is attributable to these facts and to their acceptance."[9] Varina Howell Davis and J. William Jones sent reassurances. "Please send your plucky *Veteran* here," requested the former first lady of the Confederacy. "It has my sincere approval and sympathy."[10] Southern newspapers trumpeted the birth of the magazine, but the *Veteran* made its biggest impact on the faceless mass of Southerners. Testimonials from common folks filled its pages. "I am delighted with the *Veteran*," wrote one admirer. "It has the right ring."[11]

Cunningham realized that the *Veteran* desperately needed an official endorsement from the UCV if it was to survive. Throughout 1893 the proprietor appealed to the association's leadership for an approving nod. Despite his requests, Commander Gordon gave no such commendation. In fact, as long as John B. Gordon led the UCV, Cunningham was denied any measure of respect from the association's hierarchy. Although Cunningham showed restraint in what he believed was unfair treatment, after Gordon's death he alluded to "frailties and weaknesses" in the Georgian's character.[12] When the financial panic of 1893 led to the cancellation of the annual UCV reunion—the decision devastated Cunningham; he had laid meticulous plans to file for an official disclosure at that time.[13]

In the first year of the *Veteran*'s existence, Cunningham fought to eliminate several competing publications from the field. He singled out the *Confederate War Journal Illustrated* as the principal rival. The *War Journal*, edited in New York by Marcus J. Wright and Ben LaBree, commenced publication only three months after the birth of the *Veteran*. Both monthlies had the same goal—to highlight the long-neglected field of Confederate history.[14] However, the *War Journal* differed significantly from the *Veteran* in content. The former relied exclusively on contemporary accounts of the Civil War and chose not to publish any postbellum narratives. It also included literary features.[15]

Commander Gordon stung Cunningham when he publicly announced that the *War Journal* was the single most important publication of its kind. Other UCV executives followed suit and deemed the *War Journal* "worthy of full confidence and support." The UCV honored the distinguished Wright at several reunions. Such public acknowledgments shook Cunningham into realizing that the *War Journal* might be given the coveted endorsement at the 1894 reunion.[16]

Cunningham wasted no time in assailing the *War Journal*. At first, he restricted his comments to alleging that it had poor paper quality, brief articles, and too many pictures. When this had little effect, he lost all patience and degenerated into slanderous rhetoric.[17] Cunningham questioned how anything labeled Confederate could possibly be published in New York. "If our people support the New York publication in preference," he lobbied, "it would be a humiliation to the influence that seeks to do all possible for our people at the lowest possible price."[18] Cunningham conveniently forgot about his own New York product, *Our Day*.

LaBree, a Kentuckian, sent a conciliatory note disavowing the Tennessean's vitriolic charges. The *War Journal*, noted its assistant editor, was published and controlled by Southern interests. But Cunningham ignored him and accused his magazine of fraudulence for copying the published subscription list of the *Veteran*. Cunningham distrusted LaBree, whom he referred to as a shrewd and sneaky character. LaBree confronted him several months later at a UCV reception in Washington, D.C. The sheepish Tennessean withdrew from the face-to-face confrontation.[19]

The *War Journal* went out of business in less than two years, but LaBree returned to his native Kentucky to start a monthly called the *Lost Cause*, which was similar in style and format to the *War Journal*. Cunningham found no cause to alter the tone of criticism for this new target, labeling it a "vile, alien instructor in Confederate history." He further slandered LaBree as a hypocrite and concluded that the *Lost Cause* "will sicken any Southerner who will examine it discriminately."[20] Cunningham's attacks did not contribute to the eventual demise of either the *War Journal* or the *Lost Cause*. But his narrow-mindedness and emotional response to rivals were definite character traits forged from earlier journalistic experiences.[21]

Cunningham was dumbfounded by the continued aloofness of the UCV. Not only did he resent Gordon's snub, but he also felt mistreated by George Moorman, whom he erroneously charged with favoritism toward LaBree and J. William Jones.[22] Nevertheless, the editor devised a new strategy aimed at gaining favor with local UCV camps. He mailed a circular to every camp to request an endorsement of the *Veteran* as its official organ.[23] Cunningham printed many letters in the *Veteran* from the rank and file voicing support for an endorsement. In August 1893 Cheatham Bivouac made such a commitment to Cunningham's magazine and instructed its delegates to lobby strenuously for it at the next UCV reunion.[24] The editor stumped energetically around Tennessee and won significant grassroots support.

Still, the UCV hierarchy remained silent as Cunningham continued to make significant progress in winning over its membership. He prepared a souvenir edition of the *Veteran* for distribution at the 1894 reunion in Birmingham, a one-hundred-page special that sold for only twenty-five cents and contained mostly reprinted items. It was an inexpensive attempt to peddle the *Veteran* to a broad range of potential subscribers. The plan worked and the list of patrons grew steadily.[25]

Bolstered by this limited success, Cunningham arrived at the 1894 reunion full of optimism that the association's leaders could no longer ignore the groundswell of support for his magazine. B. H. Teague agreed to introduce a resolution seeking the UCV's acceptance of the *Veteran* as its official mouthpiece. However, the plan went awry when Teague was delayed in reaching the podium. The convention fell rapidly behind schedule, as John C. Underwood monopolized floor time outlining complicated constitutional proposals. An angry Cunningham blamed the "political general," Underwood, for purposely dragging out his presentation. The editor earnestly believed that Underwood had conspired to delay the presentation of Teague's resolution and thus sabotage the organization's endorsement of the *Veteran*. Although the constitutional debate received little attention from Cunningham prior to the convention, it became a pivotal issue afterward. Underwood's plan would have created quasi-military districts with a hierarchical command structure.[26] Cunningham claimed that the association was already "top-heavy with generals" in name only, and that the proposed amendments were unpopular with the UCV membership. Cunningham's audacity offended Commander Gordon because it forced his issuance of General Order # 129, a directive that effectively delayed promulgation of the new constitution until all sides had been heard.[27] This series of events deepened the rift between Gordon and Cunningham.

When Teague finally reached the rostrum, late on the third day, approximately half of the delegates had already gone home. A straw poll taken during the convention had determined that the *Veteran* had the support of eighty-two camps.[28] When Teague called for an official vote, eighty-five camps nodded in approval, but the delegates who remained did not constitute a quorum. The rebuff embittered Cunningham, and he was indiscriminate in his subsequent condemnation of Gordon and Underwood. Some years later, Teague wrote with insight about the incident, "Did you [Cunningham] not make a mistake in your criticism of General Gordon et al., after the Birmingham meeting?"[29] In an intemperate action, Cunningham had alienated the most powerful man in the UCV. Gordon instantly denied Cunningham the right to print the minutes of future reunions in the *Veteran*. By Cunningham's own account, the proceedings were "an ordeal" that resulted in his failure to secure the mandate he had so coveted.[30]

The UCV hierarchy did not ignore Cunningham completely. In fact, the historical committee, chaired by Stephen D. Lee, recommended the *Veteran* to the membership the following year. Cunningham presumptuously interpreted this as evidence of de facto recognition. In 1897, when the reunion was held in Nashville, Lee secured permission for Cunningham to address the convention. The editor inappropriately used the opportunity to scold the crowd: "There should never be a reunion or convention of Confederates . . . without discussing the *Veteran*."[31] Cunningham's singular hard work would insure the survival of the magazine, but this had yet to be proved. Cunningham's journalistic enterprise still teetered on the brink of ruin.

Cunningham had promised that the *Veteran* would remain affordable. Never a shrewd businessman, he added to his dilemma by charging only fifty cents (or half the national average) for a year's subscription.[32] Many readers, however, could not afford even this bargain rate. Foolishly, the editor mailed issues to people who were too poor to pay. In the first year, he printed eighty thousand copies of the *Veteran*, but fewer than two thousand subscribers actually paid for them.[33] To make matters worse, Cunningham notified delinquent subscribers that he would not employ solicitors to collect unpaid bills. "The method of the *Veteran* is on honor," he naively said. "No legal process has ever been used to collect subscriptions, nor will any be. . . . So it is solely upon faith of integrity and good will that this department is conducted."[34] Cunningham chose instead to browbeat his patrons for their failure to pay in a signed cover letter that accompanied the fifth issue.[35] In subsequent issues of the magazine he used a wide range of unimaginative efforts to win support. "The *Veteran* is powerless," he whined, "to accomplish its patriotic and holy purpose as would have been our army commanders to win victories without the co-operation of the soldiers." And further, "the *Veteran* is the most important medium that has ever been printed to represent the principles for which you suffered."[36] He even resorted to military jargon and commanded the rank and file to fall in and sound off for the magazine.[37]

His quest for new endorsements, subscriptions, and advertising kept Cunningham on the road a great deal in the magazine's first year. As it had with *Our Day*, his absence affected content and scheduling of the *Veteran*. The fourth issue, for example, was totally reprinted matter. In habitual bad form, Cunningham missed printing deadlines. Instead of mailing the *Veteran* on the first day of each month as advertised, Cunningham frequently shipped it out between the twelfth and eighteenth days. He confided that the enterprise lost over a thousand dollars in its first year.[38] Only Cunningham could shoulder responsibility for such disorganization. Clearly, his benefactors at the *American* could not carry such a liability indefinitely.

Cunningham also resorted to gimmickry—a common practice among journalists of his time—to attract new patrons. First he purchased twenty lots atop Raccoon Mountain near Chattanooga. He paid five hundred dollars for the property and offered to sell one lot to each drummer who would mail in twenty-five legitimate subscriptions. Later he offered a fourteen-karat watch to any solicitor who would enroll nineteen new patrons, free bicycles to anyone who could collect fifty-eight customers, and a $450 piano to the individual who turned in the most subscriptions in six months. The latter proposal backfired when the winning entry produced only twenty-three names—all from the North.[39]

Though Cunningham relied on advertisements to raise capital, the first issue of the *Veteran* contained none. This dearth of business support, which plagued the magazine throughout its entire history, exemplified one of Cunningham's major flaws. He blamed Northern and Southern firms alike for withholding patronage. "Bear this important fact in mind," he said, "that very few general advertisers have ever patronized the *Veteran*. They do not understand its high, patriotic character or are prejudiced because of its name."[40] What little advertising did appear in the *Veteran* was placed primarily by greater Nashville firms. Advertising was heavy only in the enlarged souvenir editions prepared for the annual reunions.[41]

Cunningham admitted to spending many sleepless nights before making a decision to increase the annual subscription cost of the *Veteran* to a dollar. Some readers protested, but he realized that the move was necessary in order to keep the magazine solvent. He even took out a life insurance policy to keep his creditors satisfied.[42] In his deepest hour of frustration, Cunningham wrote what was perhaps the most poignant appeal ever to appear in the *Veteran:*

> The VETERAN has had faults and made mistakes all the while, but its motives and loyalty to the highest principles of life have never varied. It has been courteous and heroic in vindication of truth, softened and strengthened by memories of the hundreds of thousands who went down to death with approving consciences. By these sacred memories, which are as hopes for the future, let us all press onward . . . until even our enemies will be convinced that our motives were, and are exactly such as make the Christian tread through fire, in the faith that across the river we all may indeed "rest under the shade of the tree."[43]

Cunningham's sincere plea did not fall upon deaf ears.

The financial crisis that threatened the *Veteran* eased noticeably in late 1894 when the Southwestern Publishing House of Nashville, owned by the Methodist-Episcopal Church, South, agreed to print the magazine. S. W. Meek, the manager of the firm, undertook the mechanical end of publishing, and Cunningham retained exclusive control over content and editorial policy. The new arrangement brought more church advertising. The change satisfied Cunningham, and he moved into a new office in the Wilcox Building on the town square. Sharper type, improved paper quality, more ads, and the introduction of photographs all contributed to making the *Veteran* a more appealing product. An enthusiastic Cunningham boldly proclaimed that fifteen thousand introductory copies would be printed, though the subscription list did not warrant such a large issue.[44]

Beginning in 1895 the *Veteran* recorded steady growth. Business stationery and the magazine's masthead proudly publicized the most up-to-date circulation figures. Initial strength of the magazine had been predominantly local—the Nashville post office received eighty percent of all deliveries. By the mid-1890s the *Veteran* had made impressive inroads into the South. At the turn of the century it earned the distinction of being the largest Southern-based periodical. It peaked with a reported twenty-two thousand patrons in 1902. Cunningham estimated that one out of every sixteen living Confederate veterans purchased the monthly.[45] As a matter of fact, the *Veteran* sustained itself above the twenty-thousand mark for many years. These figures suggest that Cunningham succeeded in attracting a new generation of readers to replace those who were dying off. In time the editor enlarged the magazine to forty-eight pages; on special occasions it was expanded to sixty-four. A steady flow of manuscript material helped to increase its quality and variety.[46]

When Cunningham introduced the *Veteran*, it immediately became an important disseminator of the Confederate heritage. Ostensibly he had started the magazine to publicize the names of contributors to the Jefferson Davis monument fund. However, Cunningham disguised another motive in leaving his job as general agent for the monument—a reason never before made public. The executive committee of the Southern Press Association had decided to terminate his appointment in mid-1892. Some facts remain unclear, but it appears that the overzealous Cunningham accepted a retainer from a group seeking to locate the Davis monument in the Virginia capital, and he planned to lobby for the Richmond site at the upcoming UCV reunion. In accepting this money, he placed himself in a compromising position. He naively reasoned that the Southern Press Association would approve of his purpose. In fact, he had grievously overstepped his authority. When the reunion was canceled, Cunningham called for an open meeting to discuss the proposal. He received heated reactions from angry veteran leaders. Not only did he alienate such powerful dignitaries as W. E. Cabell, Clement A. Evans, John B. Gordon, and John C.

Table 2

*Subscriptions to the* Confederate Veteran, *1893–1902 (In Thousands)*

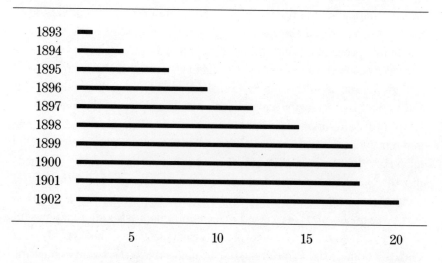

Underwood. "About that time," Cunningham recounted sadly, "there was a coldness manifested towards me by members of the [Southern Press] Association." The displeased body recalled Cunningham in New Orleans and unceremoniously revoked his appointment.[47]

Unfortunately, the episode did not end there for Cunningham. Upon his dismissal, he donated his $200 expense allowance to the coffers of the monument drive. His generosity was viewed suspiciously by the executive board, who did not understand why Cunningham, recently fired, would return monies owed to him. The association ordered an immediate investigation into Cunningham's ledgers and uncovered a mess. The confused executive board summoned Cunningham to a special hearing "to explain certain [accounting] discrepencies."[48] He cast a darker cloud over the case when he replied that financial hardship might interfere with his attendance at the hearing. Cunningham's fears were reinforced when the board charged him with malfeasance.

Prior to Cunningham's defense hearing, he published the first issue of the *Veteran* entirely at his own expense. It was his attempt to explain, in a public forum, all monies on hand. As a sign of good will, Cunningham supplied the executive board with complimentary copies. Oddly, the magazine contained scant evidence of financial accountability.

The unpleasant episode surrounding Cunningham's dismissal as general agent illuminates the true purpose of his founding the *Veteran:* to

Table 3

*Relative Distribution of Circulation of the* Confederate Veteran

| | |
|---|---|
| Ala. | ━━━━━━━ |
| Ark. | ━━━━━ |
| Fla. | ━ |
| Ga. | ━━ |
| Ok. | ▪ |
| Ky. | ━━━━━━━━━ |
| La. | ━━━━━ |
| Md. | ▪ |
| Miss. | ━━━━━━━━━━━━ |
| Mo. | ━━━━━━━ |
| N.C. | ━━━ |
| S.C. | ━━ |
| Tn. | ━━━━━━━━━━━━━━━━━━━ |
| Tx. | ━━━━━━━━━━━━━━━━━━━━━ |
| Va. | ━━━━━━━━━ |

extricate himself from a potential legal suit. Although cooler heads prevailed and Cunningham avoided prosecution, he could not help but believe that his honor had been seriously questioned. It is little wonder that the UCV officially looked upon Cunningham and his magazine with misgiving. His personal conflict with the Southern Press Association and UCV hierarchy delayed an official endorsement indefinitely. But there were other problems. His unimaginative editorials, laborious style, and frequent reliance on overworked themes never appealed to intellectuals. Rarely did he examine controversial issues with fresh perspective. It is no insult to Cunningham that his magazine appealed to popular tastes; the *Veteran* was always intended to be a repository for the reminiscences of common foot soldiers.

Cunningham's relationship with the UCV leadership was unfortunate, especially in light of their shared interest in Confederate vindication. His personality clashes with the upper echelon caused long-lasting distrust. Cunningham enjoyed deeply the camaraderie with rank and file veterans, but he was jealous of Gordon, Underwood, and Wright. His undisguised public criticism of the latter men and private invectives directed at the former did not ingratiate the editor to the decision makers of the UCV, and his periodic complaint about reunion management earned him a reputation as an association gadfly.

Cunningham won a degree of personal vindication once the *Veteran* became solvent. Local UCV camps were generally appreciative of the magazine, and he returned their kudos by attending as many state reunions as possible. In time, Gordon relented and extended tacit approval of the *Veteran*. He recognized Cunningham's genuine service to ex-Confederate causes and appointed him to the general staff in 1902 with the honorary rank of colonel. Two years later the editor was chosen to be a pallbearer at Gordon's funeral. When Stephen D. Lee assumed the commandership of the UCV, Cunningham received greater overt respect at official functions.[49] Now he had free reign to comment on issues of vital importance to Confederate veterans.

# Chapter 16    *Patron and Critic*

As an editor, Cunningham did not endear himself to power elites of the UCV, but that did not inhibit his attendance at their local, state, and regional activities. Never at a loss for words, he felt no restraint in criticizing the organization. He expanded upon his associational interest with the veterans to participate in other groups in the civic, historical, religious, and fraternal realm. Cunningham's membership in these bodies contributed to shaping and enriching his character. They also offer a slightly different window through which to explore his personality.

Cunningham relished his encounters with the rank and file at the annual UCV reunions. He represented Cheatham Bivouac at national functions and testified to his devotion and prominence within the local and regional association.[1]

The business portion of the UCV meetings bored most conventioneers, including Cunningham. They eagerly awaited the moment when the keynote speaker would present a systematic defense of the Confederacy. "The greatest good to be obtained by these reunions is our vindication," stated one UCV official."[2] Cunningham commented that reunions were "largely social and that feature should never lose its charm."[3] When official recognition of the *Veteran* was delayed, a frustrated Cunningham resorted to criticizing reunion management, and his terse opinions irritated and offended UCV leadership.

Cunningham's criticism of reunion management surfaced only after his rebuff at the hands of the Gordon clique in 1894. His biting comments reached full strength the next year when he charged the leadership with mismanaging the Houston reunion. Many veterans, he asserted, were bewildered in the immensely crowded hall. According to the disgruntled editor, there were farcical scenes in which "men undeserving of recognition received the limelight."[4] Confiding in a friend, Cunningham said,

> I presume, however, that you have seen enough of the management of the UCV to know that no opportunity is ever missed to have eulogies paid to the head officials. I sincerely hope that different methods will prevail and that there will be more time given for deliberation upon matters of great moment and importance in connection with our organization.[5]

Perhaps the Houston situation agitated Cunningham more when he discovered the tent office assigned to the *Veteran* completely surrounded by mud and water. Furthermore, the remote location was so difficult to find that it greatly inhibited his chances of luring new subscribers. Most important, he blasted reunion organizers for failing to commend the *Veteran* to the membership.[6]

The following year a comical situation developed when Cunningham arrived at the convention center packing a bundle of *Veteran*s. He halted at the entrance, where a throng of people awaited admission. An individual handing out official admission badges blocked the doorway. In order to expedite the process, Cunningham offered to help distribute the colorful ribbons. The official graciously accepted, and the crowd was quickly handled. When Cunningham attempted to enter the hall, however, the very same worker detained him because he did not possess the necessary admission badge. On another occasion, Cunningham's tent was erroneously leased to a merry-go-round operation. The editor learned a valuable lesson from these snubs. In subsequent years he publicized the precise location of reunion headquarters beforehand.[7]

Over time Cunningham criticized the organization for a wide range of reunion mishaps. But he had one primary ongoing complaint: that annual gatherings tended to honor former officers at the expense of the common soldier. Cunningham typified many veterans who viewed the Civil War as a great (social) leveling experience. In the postwar realm of veteranhood, rank offended Cunningham; he viewed all comrades as equals.[8] "Amid it all [reunions], many of the rank and file of the old rebs could feel somehow they were forgotten or neglected," wrote an aggravated Cunningham. "Most of us are too old to dance, too lazy to tramp in the procession, or participate in other things that have been made dominant features of these so-called reunions. So there seemed to be no place for us."[9] Cunningham offered an unsolicited plan to restructure the UCV. He proposed that all members be reassigned to their original Confederate rank and military detachment.[10] The practices of having female sponsors and maids of honor and granting ficticious military titles irritated him. The UCV hierarchy rejected his scheme.

Some of Cunningham's criticism of reunion management was unjustified. Between 1889 and 1907, an average of twelve thousand veterans and other visitors crammed into host cities to participate in the festivities.[11] These guests placed a great strain on lodgings, food supplies, health care facilities, and meeting hall accommodations. Besides the urban congestion they created, they imposed added economic pressures on host cities.[12] Early on, Southern cities engaged in fierce rivalry to attract the annual reunion, but by 1903 many of them were reluctant to accept the heavy responsibility entailed in holding the expensive social gathering.

This development worked in Cunningham's favor because it allowed him an opportunity to plan a reunion to his own liking. In 1897, when Nashville hosted its first reunion, he worked countless hours to make the Tennessee convention the smoothest in UCV history. He personally handled many of the mundane details.[13] Six years later, when no Southern city bid on holding the upcoming 1904 reunion and cancellation appeared imminent, Bennett H. Young, a rising figure within the UCV, wrote a desperate appeal to Cunningham to solicit Nashville's sponsorship. The editor sampled local opinion and everyone encouraged Cunningham to invite the UCV. The newly-elected commander of the UCV, Stephen D. Lee, credited Cunningham with preserving the reunion.[14]

Cunningham had long aspired "to attend a reunion solely of old comrades. Give this class of noble men a week together undisturbed by others," he requested.[15] The 1904 reunion became his instrument to hold an egalitarian meeting comprised only of former enlisted men. It took place on a pleasant afternoon in an enclosed courtyard at Vanderbilt University, but Cunningham was personally disappointed by the low turnout.[16]

As fiercely as the editor censored UCV leaders, he went out of his way to patronize the ladies' auxiliary, the United Daughters of the Confederacy (UDC). The *Veteran* extolled the virtue of the women's organization and its goal to advance the Confederate heritage. Under the direction of Caroline M. C. Goodlett of Tennessee, the UDC gained in membership and influence. In its early days the UDC made little impact outside the South, but within sixteen years it registered nearly fifty thousand members and became the largest women's association in the country.[17] Outside the South, the UDC was an unknown commodity. "Why I never heard of the Daughters of the Confederacy," confided a Minnesotan. "What are you—a lot of organized anarchists?"[18] Cunningham must have snickered at such a comment.

From its inception, Cunningham provided liberal space in his magazine for coverage of UDC activities. "The *Veteran* nursed the organization in its infancy," he claimed.[19] Cunningham thoroughly enjoyed the company of the ladies and became a familiar fixture at their functions. He considered it an obligation to participate with the local chapter in promoting Decoration Day in Nashville. Cheatham Bivouac recognized Cunningham's ability to get along with UDC members and chose him to represent it at all UDC conferences. He worked vigorously to secure lodgings for visiting UDC dignitaries, sponsors, and maids of honor at both reunions in Nashville.[20] Extensive coverage of every UDC convention earned Cunningham the organization's gratitude. Indeed, the auxiliary became the first ex-Confederate group to openly endorse the *Veteran* as its official organ, and the ladies often invited Cunningham to say a few words at their national meeting. Undeniably a special bond developed between Cunningham and the UDC.

Cunningham's fondness for women was not limited to members of the United Daughters of the Confederacy. One insightful comrade in Cheatham Bivouac described the editor as a man "always with an eye to the ladies."[21] A colleague at the *American* acknowledged that Cunningham "was a typical Southern gentleman of the old school, his deference to and consideration for ladies being one of his marked characteristics." It was frequently said by acquaintances that Cunningham "knew more ladies than any man in the Southern Confederacy."[22] He carried on an active correspondence with leading Southern women including Varina Howell Davis, Winnie Davis, Emilie Todd Helm, Mildred Lewis Rutherford, Caroline M. C. Goodlett, Susie Walker, Katie Behan, and Janet Randolph.

Cunningham presented a pleasing disposition to the ladies, a trait that he groomed over a lifetime and that may have been related to his close bond with his mother and his wife. After they died, he transferred some of his filial and marital feelings to the women's auxiliary. The adoration of a female audience reassured Cunningham and like-minded men of their loyalty to the Lost Cause.

Cunningham felt a masculine sense of duty to shield the UDC from its critics. His defense of its membership and their mission filled the *Veteran*.

He routinely scolded the Southern press for inadequately reporting UDC gatherings. He also played referee in several internal squabbles.[23]

The UDC appreciated Cunningham's intense loyalty to them and the Confederate heritage and presented him with a special service medal in 1905. The editor was deeply touched; he proudly wore the medallion to every public occasion thereafter. The award conspicuously adorned his lapel in several later photographs.[24] This honor should not be confused with the Cross of Honor, a badge that the UDC distributed to some fifty thousand ex-Confederates. In another gesture of appreciation, the Nashville chapter named an auxiliary boy's club they chartered in 1906 the S. A. Cunningham Junior Sons of Confederate Veterans.[25]

Cunningham's wide association with former Confederates also brought him into more direct contact with Union veterans. In 1897 handicapped Ohio veteran William H. Knauss publicized the decoration of Confederate graves at Camp Chase Cemetery near Columbus by mailing invitations to many figures in the GAR and UCV.[26] Cunningham attended the historic occasion and received a warm welcome. After the ceremony, the local GAR camp held a banquet in his honor. In his salute to the group, he undiplomatically demanded "some immediate improvement" in the stone wall that surrounded the cemetery.[27] When Knauss announced that the Camp Chase service would become an annual event, he earned Cunningham's lasting friendship. The editor was encouraged by this early expression of sectional reconciliation, but he remained skeptical about formal ties of brotherhood, or fraternization, between the UCV and GAR.[28]

Cunningham reminded his readers in the *Veteran* that there were approximately thirty thousand unmarked Confederate graves in the North and ten thousand additional plots in national cemeteries.[29] The editor was convinced that only the federal government could adequately maintain so many sites. At the height of the Spanish-American War, President William McKinley announced to the Georgia legislature that "the time has now come in the evolution of sentiment and feeling . . . when in the spirit of fraternity, we should share with you [the South] in the care of the graves of the Confederate soldier."[30] Though McKinley's celebrated Peace Jubilee Speech excited Cunningham, he tempered his appreciation: "O, how sad that it has required a third of a century . . . for the dominant party to realize that we are and have been all the while honorable and true to our oaths of allegiance." He concluded with a challenge to all future presidents to "labor not only to do justice to the memory of the Confederate dead . . .

but let them recognize in the living the tribute that is due them."[31] Influential comrades such as J. William Jones, J. A. Chalaron, and Janet Randolph urged Cunningham to continue his cautious editorial approach to "fraternization." Still, Cunningham recognized McKinley's offer as a major victory for Southern vindication.[32]

Cunningham was dismayed by the growing favor being shown to the idea of "fraternization." He was overwhelmed by the thought of formal associational contacts with men from the other side. "The *Veteran* took the position long ago," he noted, "that the Confederate soldier was more patriotic than the average soldier for the Union."[33] When veterans from both armies met at dedication ceremonies in several national military parks, he voiced alarm. "There is a namby pamby sentiment," he chided, "for conglomerate mixture of the 'blue and gray' putting the blue first, which has been carried to excess."[34] Cunningham feared that such contact with Northern veterans would result in a second class status for the Confederate heritage.

Another big stumbling block to fraternization between the veterans concerned the issue of captured regimental battle flags. This matter first surfaced in 1887 when President Grover Cleveland announced his intention to restore Confederate colors to the Southern states. A flood of objections, including assassination threats, forced the president to rescind the offer.[35] When Cunningham spoke to the Columbus GAR nine years later, he revived the flag issue and commented on its importance to Southerners. He argued that the battle flags were trophies of a forgotten war and charged that the War Department held them illegally. He pleaded for the return of the "sacred cloth" as a gesture of goodwill. The government returned some four hundred flags in 1905, only after Congress passed a joint resolution. A euphoric Cunningham declared that restoration of the battle flags had obliterated sectionalism forever. The ex-Confederate associations wasted no time in displaying the treasured emblems at local, state, and regional reunions.[36]

Despite Cunningham's objection, the notion of holding annual Blue-Gray reunions was gradually becoming more popular among veterans.[37] Cunningham reported on meetings in Evansville (1899), Atlanta (1900), St. Louis (1904), Washington, D.C. (1905), and Memphis (1911).[38] The editor was concerned that it might be demeaning to invite the GAR to the annual UCV convention, and when such an overture was turned down, it ignited his passion. He resented the display of blue uniforms at GAR meetings. Curiously, the gray suits worn by the UCV did not elicit the same level of indignation from Cunningham. In the beginning UCV members were urged to wear conservative dress—black suits trimmed with a red belt. Although Confederate gray was the subliminal favorite among the rank and file, the darker garment remained the unofficial uniform for years.[39]

Cunningham had internalized some deep prejudices about his former foe. The information he disseminated in the *Veteran* convinced him that the traditions of the South contained more value than the common national heritage. In his own mind, the South was the unique entity in American civilization, but its values were in danger of being diluted. Cunningham, for one, would not stand by silently and allow that to occur.

Cunningham overcame his hatred of his former adversaries only with great reluctance. Although the Spanish-American War tempered some of his antagonism, he remained guarded. "The North owes the South much recognition," he asserted,[40] and he printed a sharp warning before the highly publicized joint reunion in 1900:

> There is a mistaken idea by younger people of the fraternal spirit between the veterans. . . . They chime in with a class who were either pig or puppy when *men* were in demand on both sides, and they think the patriotic thing is to amalgamate as speedily as possible. They mistake the spirit of the heroes of both sides.[41]

At the UCV reunion held a month later, disgruntled veterans opposed a resolution to convey fraternal feelings to the GAR. The ensuing demonstration interrupted business for more than ten minutes.[42]

Emotions reached a peak in a nasty incident at the joint reunion in 1900. From the dais, Commander Albert D. Shaw of the GAR charged that the current trend in Southern historical writing was fanning the flames of sectionalism. Commander Gordon, representing the UCV, stepped to the podium and declared angrily that the South would never disavow its righteous motives in fighting the Civil War. The Southern portion of the audience greeted Gordon's retort with wild enthusiasm. But, as Cunningham reported in his account of the incident, Shaw's remarks initiated a Southern backlash that deterred the fraternization movement. To the Tennessean's relief, joint reunions fell into temporary disfavor.[43]

The idea of holding a national Blue-Gray reunion was revived in 1909 when some veterans desired to commemorate the outbreak of war in 1861. A "National Peace Jubilee" did take place at Manassas, and President William Howard Taft delivered the keynote address. The harmonious mood at this gathering contrasted sharply with the earlier exchange in 1900 and fostered the belief that cooperation between the veterans was possible. The Manassas event laid the groundwork for the grandest joint meeting ever held, the Gettysburg reunion of 1913, in which Cunningham played a significant role.[44]

In 1908 a historian named John P. Nicholson had convinced Gettysburg merchants that a Blue-Gray meeting would bring immense economic advantage to their city. Several months later, the Pennsylvania legislature established a reunion commission and asked every state to send a representative to a plenary meeting. Tennessee selected Cunningham, and over the next three years he traveled extensively on behalf of the Gettysburg reunion. He also attended legislative meetings in Pennsylvania and congressional hearings in Washington, D.C.[45] Despite his participation in planning the reunion, however, he was concerned about a possible misinterpretation of fraternization and warned Southerners, "Be on guard comrades! . . . There has never been a more important period for watchfulness than now."[46] More than anything else, Cunningham worried that the gala event might dilute Southern loyalty to Confederate ideals.

On 1 July 1913 more than fifty-three thousand veterans and visitors invaded Gettysburg for the second time in fifty years. Feeble veterans presented special problems for the planners. The age of the participants ranged from 61 to 113. The Red Cross set up a field hospital and treated patients for many ailments, including sunstroke, exhaustion, digestive problems, alcoholism, and diarrhea. Four hundred Boy Scouts were on hand to assist the aging veterans. In all, nine people died during the four-day "love feast."[47]

Perhaps the most memorable event in the three-day reunion was the reenactment of Pickett's charge, on which Cunningham reported:

> One hundred and fifty veterans of the Virginia regiments of the Immortal Division made their slow parade. Under the brow of the ridge, in the Bloody Angle, where the Philadelphia Brigade stood that day, was a handful in blue, scarcely larger, waiting to meet the onslaught of peace. There were no flashing sabres, no belching guns—only eyes that dimmed fast and kindly faces behind the stone wall that marks the angle. At the end in place of wounds or prison or death, were greetings and handshakes.[48]

Cunningham had the honor of delivering the opening greeting on the final day. President Woodrow Wilson closed the reunion in the Great Tent. But neither Cunningham nor Wilson evoked as much enthusiasm as did the reenactment of Pickett's charge.

Feelings of brotherhood initially warmed the seventy-year-old Cunningham at Gettysburg. "It was the most wonderful occasion of the kind that ever took place," he rejoiced. "History has never recorded such a remarkable event, such colossal, munificent and hearty greeting of former foes."[49] But Cunningham questioned whether sectional bitterness had been dealt a lethal blow. He pondered the long-range implications of such meetings, wondering "just what the duty of Confederates is in connection with joint reunions and general movement toward amalgamation."[50] Later, once the euphoria wore off, he warned Southerners not to be deceived by the exchange of goodwill. "That not a word of discord was heard seems incredible [but] don't let anybody imagine that the marvelous experience at Gettysburg have [sic] gotten it [UCV] off its base," he admonished.[51] He also revealed a personal observation: "That suppressed disturbance of spirit exists in regard to fraternity between veterans of the two great armies of the sixties is well known."[52] Cunningham would carry this apprehension to the grave.

By no means did Cunningham limit either his associational ties or his commentaries to veterans' functions. He participated in a wide range of civic and religious organizations in Nashville as well. He remained a devout Christian, guided by this simple creed: "The Christian possesses the inherent hope that makes compliance with the golden rule his guide, and he feels safely protected by the invisible Power against any storms that may come."[53] He attended the Addison Avenue Church in Nashville, where he earned a well-deserved reputation as a humble and faithful parishioner and eventually became an elder and trustee. His favorite hymns included "Lead, Kindly Light," "Nearer My God to Thee," and "How Firm a Foundation." When the Cumberland Presbyterian Church elected to affiliate with the Presbyterian Church, USA (commonly called the Northern Presbyterian Church), the Addison Avenue Church refused to make the change.[54] Shortly thereafter, Cunningham's church declined in attendance, and he played a key role in selling the property several years later. Meanwhile, he transferred his membership to First Church, the largest Southern Presbyterian church in Nashville.[55] Cunningham rarely wrote religious statements of a personal nature in the *Veteran*, but he made this exception in 1908:

HE sees now that all who are human are destined to death ere long, and he realizes more vividly than before that the human race is on trial every hour. A Judge who cannot be deceived is in constant charge of his case, and he may be required to confess any day or hour. Let us have faith and hope, giving good cheer; but let us place charity before all other virtues after integrity—charity that is kind and that endures. Let us be active to help and elevate our fellow-man; then we shall have done what we could.[56]

Cunningham went to the grave with his religious belief intact.

The editor also enjoyed working on historical projects unrelated to the Confederacy. He joined the Tennessee Historical Society in 1880 and read research papers before the group on the battle of Franklin and the story of Samuel Davis. Governor Albert S. Marks chose Cunningham to represent Tennessee at the 1880 King's Mountain Centennial celebration, where he wore a large red sash and was entrusted with a sword owned by the British commander Patrick Ferguson. He also attended the Oregon Exposition (1905) and the Jamestown Exposition (1907) in an official capacity. In 1908 the executive committee of the Nashville Battlefield Association asked Cunningham to assist in placing historic markers around the city.[57] Later in life Cunningham lobbied strenuously to establish a national military park at Franklin. He called an open forum to discuss the proposal, and a modest contingent of veterans attended. In the keynote speech, Cunningham outlined his plan to turn the Carter House, cotton gin, and nearby locust grove into a national shrine.[58]

Perhaps the greatest associational honor ever bestowed upon Cunningham occurred at the 1912 state UCV reunion. In his hometown of Shelbyville, the delegates selected Cunningham as president of the Association of Confederate Veterans, Tennessee. The audience, estimated at about one thousand people, also witnessed the installation of John P. Hickman as major general of the Tennessee division. Cunningham and Hickman were perhaps the two most active members of Cheatham Bivouac. Cunningham presided over the parade and barbecue in the same town square where he had marched off to war half a century earlier. The newly elected president was gratified by the honor his association bestowed on him.[59]

Cunningham's presidential duties were largely ceremonial: he visited camps throughout the state, attended important meetings, and presided over the 1913 reunion. His selection met with universal approval in the

Tennessee press. A representative comment from the *Nashville Banner* said:

> The Tennessee Association of Confederate Bivouacs is to be congratulated upon the wisdom of its action in the selection of S. A. Cunningham as President. Mr. Cunningham is a fine type of gentleman and an unsurpassed type of veteran. His war record contains incidents of real heroism. And in the years since the war few men—we are inclined to believe, no man—has done more for the attainment of those things toward which Confederate veterans, as an organization, strive than Major Cunningham.[60]

A new photograph of Cunningham that appeared in the local press on this occasion was used later as a model for the depiction carved on his tombstone.

Cunningham's religious and historical interests contributed greatly to refining his character, but his involvement in other civic organizations showed his growing urbanity. One such association was the Hermitage Club, an exclusive men's club in downtown Nashville. Housed in an antebellum mansion on High Street, it was well known for its fine decor, meals, and receptions.[61] Cunningham's famous uncle, George Washington Cunningham, belonged to the fraternity and probably sponsored his application. An atmosphere of gentility permeated the club, where members read and discussed papers on a wide range of topics.

Cunningham also participated in less formal civic programs. Always a patriot with a strong sense of community, he often sat on Nashville's Fourth of July committee, and he served on a city committee to discuss the open petition written by Tsar Nicholas II of Russia for a worldwide peace conference.[62] Because he favored a strong local economy, Cunningham became involved in several enterprises to promote growth in Nashville: he belonged to the Nashville Board of Trade, a commission of businessmen dedicated to improving the commercial base of the city, and he often attended sessions of the Chamber of Commerce and Nashville Retail Merchants Association.[63]

As a patron and critic of various associations, Cunningham possessed the confidence to speak out on major issues involving Confederate veterans, the church, historical organizations, and the city he lived in. Sometimes his opinions were inflammatory, as in the debate over "proper histories."

# Chapter 17 "Proper Histories"

For the most part, Cunningham limited his personal thoughts to the editorial page, where he rarely shared original ideas. He seldom wrote feature-length articles. However, he repetitiously discussed commonly held opinions concerning the causes and effects of the Civil War. These brief summations normally ran no more than four paragraphs in length. Contemporaries never considered Cunningham to be intellectually stimulating, but they lauded his dogged determination in capturing the essence and philosophy of popular Southern culture.

Cunningham emphatically rejected the use of certain terms he considered objectionable. From the beginning, he informed patrons that such phrases as New South and Lost Cause were deplorable. He never offered a concise reason; his belief seemed rooted in emotionalism rather than logic. Cunningham refuted the notion that the South had somehow changed after 1865.

> The Old South is sometimes used in contra-distinction. . . . Let all who join in the spirit of progress (?) be careful of this phrase, remembering that the word "New" in such connection was conceived and its adoption urged by a class who came among us for spoils, and sought to put the "bottom rail on top." We have changed conditions, but the dear old South is good enough.[1]

Cunningham repeatedly warned contributors to remove offensive terminology from articles or run the risk of receiving rejection slips. He even scolded patrons who employed the words in private correspondence.[2] So that no one should misunderstand his intent, Cunningham drafted the following masthead in 1906: "The terms 'New South' and 'lost cause' are objectionable to the *Veteran*."[3] The admonition remained a fixture on page one for years.

On a more complicated subject, Cunningham defended the South's right to secede in 1861—not to preserve slavery but to protect constitutional principles. In this the editor reflected mainstream belief that the South had had a legitimate right to secede because the federal government was infringing upon specified constitutional powers reserved for the states. Cunningham posed an important query to his readers. "The Confederacy was lost of course, and the contention is as to whether the principles were maintained."[4] He provided his own rhetorical answer; "The principles of the government for which we fought are being maintained, save as to States rights and slavery," he said. "Constitutional government is the underlying principle for which all good men pray, and will fight."[5] Cunningham's interpretation was that the cause could not have been lost because the ideals for which Southern men had fought continued to live. "No! No! Our cause was not lost because it was wrong," he argued. "Our cause is a living contitutional principle inherent in the nature of our wonderful system of free government. . . . No! No! Our cause was not lost for the reason that it was not wrong!"[6] Cunningham's editorials on the subject of secession reflected the views of his patrons.

Cunningham also mirrored a less persuasive view that the South had always been and still remained unalterably loyal to the principles of the Union. "The men and women of the South of the sixties were as patriotic as those of the North" and "by the laws of the land and by inherent rights they were justified in their revolution, also that by their sacrafices . . . they deserve to be recognized . . . by the civilized world to be as worthy of all honor."[7] Cunningham treated the subject of Southern loyalty as more than simply an academic debate. In the late 1890s, the outbreak of war with Spain gave Southerners the opportunity to prove their commitment to the federal government. "Let us now be honest with ourselves," asserted Cunningham. "For the third of a century we have in vain sought recognition for patriotism by the northern section of the Union." "The duty of Confederate veterans is clear. They should, as they will, be as helpful to the government as practicable."[8] He repudiated the notion that the South had somehow been dishonored in 1865 and maintained his contention that the South had remained a loyal partner in the Union ever since.[9]

As proprietor of the *Veteran* and a white man concerned about maintaining the racial status quo, he uttered statements intended to keep "the bottom rail" in its place. He also preserved a strain of antebellum paternalism in his thoughts. He once commented that white "Southerners are as loyal to the old slaves as they are to each other."[10] Once, he spearheaded a farcical drive to erect war monuments to the black race. Cunningham's actions in this cause were no more than tokenism; he had no real intention of improving the condition of blacks. The closest he came to taking a charitable position was to suggest that the veterans of slavery receive ten acres of land in restitution. The paternalistic Cunningham sympathized with what he called the "old-time darkies" born to slavery but feared that the younger generation of blacks sought social equality.[11]

Cunningham conditionally supported the opinion that blacks should defer to whites and accept what Southerners thought was their proper place in Southern society. At the same time, he lobbied for a "Solid South" on the race issue. Like many whites, he was shocked when Booker T. Washington dined with President Theodore Roosevelt at the White House in 1901. He feared that a violent backlash might result.[12] In the most blatant racist statement Cunningham ever recorded, he said that "until leopards become spotless, and until black becomes white, in fact, the effort of no man for social equality will succeed."[13] Later he sent President Roosevelt a warning on the danger of social equality:

> These expressions are not of sectional consideration, but from a principle as old and as deep as the creation of white and black—and the distinctive color odor. Let his [Roosevelt's] friends in the South be diligent to communicate with him upon the disastrous and grievous results that will come of playing with unquenchable fire.[14]

Cunningham reflected mainstream white Southern sentiment in regard to the race question. From the whites' perspective, "the only solution of this matter is for negroes to accept the situation," explained Cunningham. "Treat the whites with deference, and they will soon realize the best they need ever hope to exist between the races."[15] Cunningham understood and accepted racial segregation as a matter of fact and committed every fiber of his being to maintaining it. Late in his life, he even reversed an earlier opinion favoring the education of blacks; he came to see it as a major social disruption. He even recommended repeal of the 15th Amendment.[16]

Although Cunningham professed to operate the *Veteran* on a nonpolitical basis, he did not shy away totally from the political arena. As his reputation grew, so did his contacts with politicians. When crucial political campaigns on the local and state levels were under way, Cunningham occasionally ran a Democratic fact sheet in the magazine. He wrote about and corresponded with every Tennessee governor beginning with Albert S. Marks in 1879.[17] During a particularly bitter senatorial campaign in 1905, Cunningham found himself in an awkward position when two of his old friends, Robert Love Taylor and Edward Ward Carmack, squared off. Although he attempted to remain neutral, he found it difficult to do so. He accepted a two-page spread in the *Veteran* describing both candidates but apologized to his patrons that it was "unavoidable under the circumstances."[18] Cunningham publicly endorsed neither candidate, although he shared closer bonds with Carmack. During national political campaigns, Cunningham was usually silent.[19]

The issues of race and politics were inextricable in Cunningham's mind. He believed that maintaining the racial status quo depended upon continuation of the "Solid South." At the turn of the century, Cunningham worried that the South was losing its political distinctiveness.

> Four decades have bound men together in sympathy that only makes the condition good faith precedent to unstinted sacrifice for each other. . . . The shame of reconstruction days, while dishonoring the "top rail" was such a blessing to those at the bottom that it is not well to overlook, and the steadfastness of Confederates to principle sealed their devotion to each other. Let us pray that these relations may continue for they have maintained the exaltation of ancestral patriotism.[20]

Much as Cunningham had fretted over race issues during the presidency of Theodore Roosevelt, he distrusted his successor, William Howard Taft, even more. Cunningham was particularly incensed by the Republican's use of the patronage system in appointing blacks to prominent positions in the South.[21] Vigilance became a watchword for the bigoted editor, who proclaimed that

> the bedrock of patriotism in the South is exacting in matters of justice and integrity. Our plea to the South is therefore to remain solid. . . . Every Southerner should be proud of the loyalty and devotion of his fellows throughout Dixie Land. Devotion to our common interest is a guarantee of dignity and the respect with which our people will be possessed as long as we remain united.[22]

Through such appeals to the common man Cunningham gained widespread popular support.

As a journalist, Cunningham was ever watchful of the reputation of the Confederacy and obstinately advocated only the use of history texts containing what he believed to be correct interpretations in Southern schools. This belief in what he considered proper interpretations of Confederate history was one means of maintaining the social standards he espoused. Cunningham was certain that Northern textbook publishers conspired to slander the historic Confederacy. His dedication to preserving the Confederate heritage brought him into closer contact with the influential UCV history committee, which evaluated textbooks and made recommendations on original works. In the *Veteran*, Cunningham reported on the committee's findings. Together, the committee's decisions and Cunningham's advertising influenced the curriculum of several Southern school systems.

The editor worried that "blue-penciled" interpretations of the Civil War were being studied and accepted by Southern children. He disagreed vehemently with the treatment certain history texts gave the war as a rebellion and with their labeling Southerners as traitors. He also discounted what he called the "exaggerated influence of the slavocracy." Cunningham and like-minded comrades on the history committee preferred to believe that the South had fought the war to protect against a violation of constitutional principles.[23]

Cunningham was unwilling to compromise on the issue of history texts. He lobbied vigorously for the removal of Northern interpretations from Southern classrooms. One Confederate veteran, General S. G. French, sent this analysis: "A conquered people seldom have the heart to write the history of their humiliation and defeat, and it is generally left to the victors."[24] Cunningham agreed with French that there was a pressing need to rewrite American history from the Southern perspective.

In his quest to encourage the writing of "proper histories," Cunningham found an ally in the UCV history committee. Three distinguished men chaired the committee over its first twenty years: Clement A. Evans, Stephen D. Lee, and Bennett H. Young.[25] Each shared Cunningham's conviction that Southerners must write their own version of the causes and results of the Civil War. In 1894 the UCV resolved to promote "action by this organization in taking steps for a complete 'renaissance' of history throughout the South" and stated firmly that "the vindication of the South must come from the pens of Southern writers."[26] Armed with this resolution, the history committee set forth to revise the interpretive flow of American history textbooks.

First the committee recommended a list of primary sources they believed would be useful in writing *correct* accounts. "The time is near," proclaimed Stephen D. Lee, "when the painstaking, broadminded, catholic historian can write a history free from prejudice and permeated with the true spirit of liberty-loving Americanism."[27] Cunningham agreed with Lee's appraisal in the *Veteran* and offered to sell, at cost, acceptable reminiscences by notable ex-Confederates. "A leading business feature [in the magazine] is to supply Southern histories and especially that class of war stories which treat the valor of Southern men who served the Confederacy," announced Cunningham.[28] He stockpiled volumes of Jefferson Davis's *Rise and Fall of the Confederate Government and History of the Confederate States of America* and offered them to budding historians at reduced rates. He also promoted recent publications like the biography of President Davis by J. William Jones, which he described as a "Southern Book on a Southern Man by a Southern Author for the Southern People." Clement A. Evans recognized the value of advertising in the *Veteran* and sent Cunningham a complimentary twelve-volume set of his *Confederate Military History.*[29]

In 1892 the Association of Confederate Soldiers, Tennessee, followed the example of the UCV and created a history committee to search for and encourage public school use of histories written by Southerners. Cheatham Bivouac also set up a standing committee, to which Cunningham belonged, to review history books.[30]

Not only did Cunningham support the history committee in its demand for historical revisionism, but he also acknowledged the need for structural reform in the Southern educational system. In 1895 the committee proposed two significant changes to establish prestigious chairs in American history at major Southern universities and to require a year of study of American history in public schools. Cunningham reported these guidelines in the *Veteran* and expanded them to include the preparation of state histories, preservation of local historical data, publication of Southern scholarship, and empowerment of local school boards to censor undesirable historical materials.[31]

At the local level Cunningham urged veterans to publish accounts similar to his own *Reminiscences.* "The importance of regimental histories is such that it behooves every veteran soldier to contribute thereto," he asserted. "Commanders of regiments, if living, should be diligent to prepare a record."[32] Cunningham also called for "proper state histories." In Tennessee he promoted the work of W. R. Garrett and A. V. Goodpasture. Cunningham, like other Tennesseans, addressed the need to create a state archive. Southern colleges—especially those that trained young women for teaching—advertised in the *Veteran.* The editor proudly announced that Peabody College in Nashville led the way in establishing an endowed chair in American history. Finally, Cunningham printed literary reviews of fiction that presented a favorable Southern viewpoint, such as Thomas Nelson Page's *Red Rock: A Chronicle of Reconstruction* and Thomas Dixon's *The Clansman.* [33]

Cunningham and his cronies on the history committee exerted tremendous influence on curricula in public schools and small colleges in the South. Many school boards adhered to the UCV guidelines and enforced strict censorship. The Confederate association succeeded so well that several widely used textbooks were carefully rewritten to include the desired interpretations. The campaign for historical revisionism paid impressive dividends. Northern publishers reacted with alarm at the potential loss of the Southern market, and at what they considered historical "misinterpretation." [34]

The degree to which ex-Confederate lobbyists influenced the educational system of the South is illustrated by a serious quarrel that flared up in 1911. Indeed, the suppressive nature of the "proper histories" contingent was laid bare during the so-called Elson controversy, which started when Cunningham reprinted an article criticizing a Roanoke College history instructor for using an "uncomplimentary" text. [35] The book in question was H. W. Elson's *History of the United States*—a text used in approximately sixty institutions of higher learning. The Maryland UDC had expressed its indignation at the author's treatment of the Confederate experience. J. D. Rodeffer, a faculty member at Roanoke, wrote to Cunningham to defend the choice of Elson's text on the principle of academic freedom. In the *Veteran*, Cunningham criticized Elson's material as being more inflammatory than *Uncle Tom's Cabin.* [36] In a subsequent issue, he claimed, in an unscientific straw poll, that public opinion ran against the history by a three-to-one margin. At this point, Elson wrote to Cunningham appealing for fairness: "I feel that I have been wronged by the recent agitation against my history. The pain of it lies in the fact that I like the Southern people and never meant to offend them." [37] The president of the college interceded in behalf of Elson, but his argument fell upon deaf ears. "There can be no compromise with it," Cunningham told his readers. [38]

Cunningham then criticized the teacher who used the Elson text. In an editorial, he called for a financial boycott of the institution. "Venerable comrades whose sons are students cannot endorse the use of such slander upon what they hold most sacred in life," said Cunningham. "There is not enough money in Virginia to induce patience for a moment with men who would inculcate such doctrine among the people of the South."[39] Cunningham also attacked the president of the college for taking prolonged "begging tours" in the North to secure financial aid for the institution.[40]

In the long run, Cunningham's campaign against the Elson text backfired. While many state UDC and UCV associations condemned the book at reunions throughout 1911 and some schools ceased to use the volume, book sales actually increased dramatically, and Elson's publisher printed a new edition six months ahead of schedule. Cunningham soon lost interest in the "Elson controversy," and it disappeared from the columns of the *Veteran.*[41]

Considering his usual lack of originality, it is significant that Cunningham was able to formulate a spontaneous response in the debate over "proper histories." Through his literary organ, he waged an effective campaign to encourage Southern authorship of texts and the use of texts by Southern writers. It is regrettable that the overzealous editor advocated and applied censorship in this cause, even to the extent of discrediting any volume that he personally considered not to reflect the Southern view.

In his position as editor of the *Veteran*, Cunningham felt a strong moral obligation to support specific needs that had grown out of the Civil War. Among those were soldiers' homes, service pensions, and maintenance of grave sites. Beyond these immediate concerns, he was part of a growing popular movement to memorialize the Confederate heritage for future generations through the erection of granite memorials. A monument-building craze was sweeping the South, and through his involvement in it, several impressive commemorative projects were undertaken.

Cunningham charged national and state governments with conspicuous neglect in the care and treatment of Confederate veterans. He informed his patrons that Federal veterans received thorough care and that he was gratified to see such liberal provisions for them. But he deplored the lack of comparable provision for destitute Southerners. "What mysteries in this world!" he concluded in amazement.[1] Many Southerners shared Cunningham's sense of outrage and objected to what they considered to be a double standard established by the U.S. Congress.[2] The South's recent demonstration of loyalty to the United States in the war against Spain contributed greatly to Cunningham's demand for fair play and equality before the dole.

Cunningham was equally impatient toward Southern state and local governments that handed out meager pensions. Compensation from the six largest Southern states totaled less than a million dollars, and Tennessee paid out only a shameful sixty thousand dollars annually.[3] Each Southern state operated under different qualification requirements, and the resulting lack of uniformity, concluded Cunningham, hurt truly deserving individuals.[4] He reported on the condition of soldiers' homes in the *Veteran* at regular intervals. Destitute ex-Confederates wrote touching messages describing their plight.

The inadequate pension system in Tennessee raised Cunningham's ire, and he conducted a one-man lobby for Confederate pensions throughout his life. He appealed to a special UCV committee on charities to examine and act upon the most desperate cases that crossed his desk. In later years he served on the dole committee for Cheatham Bivouac. He attempted several times to bring the pension issue before the state association.[5] It remained a matter of grave concern to him that Tennessee ranked lowest among the Southern states in its per capita support for veterans.[6]

One of the first items of business conducted by the Association of Confederate Soldiers, Tennessee, in 1889 was to select nine trustees to take charge of the Hermitage property and turn it into a home for Confederate soldiers.[7] Cunningham assumed a personal interest in the home and worked closely with the ladies' auxiliary to improve living conditions there. W. E. Cunningham, a relative with whom he had fought at Franklin, died at the home in 1894.[8] Later, the executive board of the home selected Cunningham to serve as librarian and historian.

Cunningham commended Secretary of War Elihu Root in 1903 for suggesting the compilation of an accurate list of Southerners who had fought in the Civil War. The editor misinterpreted Root's announcement as a first step toward providing a pension for Confederate veterans. The project languished until Cunningham urged every Confederate veteran to write directly to General Marcus J. Wright in the War Department to verify their Confederate service. At the time, Wright was busy preparing documents for the *Official Record of the War of the Rebellion*—a twenty-year assignment. In response to Cunningham's appeal, letters addressed to Wright poured in. Wright asked Cunningham to tone down his petition drive, but the editor was suspicious of Wright because of their earlier competition. He responded sarcastically: "The foregoing is most significant as showing the influence of the *Veteran*. Think of two issues overtaxing the capacity of the United States government to supply information about the records of Confederate soldiers!"[9] Delighting in the jab, Cunningham also realized that Southerners were no closer to receiving a pension in 1908 than they were in 1865.

Cunningham was equally resolved to see honor bestowed upon the graves of fallen comrades. In his first editorial he clearly defined one major goal: to record with "undying devotion" the deeds of the "sacred dead."[10]

Over the years Cunningham was conspicuously present at Decoration Day services held at Mount Olivet Cemetery in Nashville. He worked in close harmony with the local UDC chapter to plan the annual event. Partly because of Cunningham's concern, Nashvillians were treated to elaborate memorial programs.[11]

Cunningham memoralized the passing of veterans in a unique way. In 1897 he started a column known as "The Last Roll," a series of vignettes about recently deceased veterans.[12] It won the instant acceptance of readers and became the single most popular feature in the *Veteran*. Today it is valuable to historians and genealogists. In time Cunningham fretted over the increasingly frequent deaths of Confederate veterans. Indeed, the average veteran was over sixty years old in 1900, and the ranks were becoming depleted. Some camps literally died off; more than five hundred disappeared from the UCV registry between 1907 and 1909. Tennessee camps, once numbering eighty-seven, declined to forty-six by 1912. Ten years after creating the column, Cunningham announced that "the term 'Last Roll' . . . has now a national significance."[13]

Some people pointed out similarities between the South's Decoration Day and the North's Memorial Day and suggested a combined celebration, but Cunningham did not like the idea; he felt that the South should hold its own observance. He believed also that it should have a fixed date.[14] Previously each Southern state had celebrated the holiday anywhere between April 3 and June 3. In 1895 the UCV decided to hold its Decoration Day observation on June 3, the birth date of Jefferson Davis. Commander Gordon issued general order #287 putting this into effect so that "we may have a memorial day as distinct as May 30th is used by the other side."[15] Cunningham agreed with Gordon: "We surely want the little children to grow up with the feeling that one certain day in the year will be set apart for the brotherhood of the Confederacy to renew their own fealty through the honoring of their dead heroes," he said.[16] Even though the UCV later rescinded Gordon's order for a June 3 observance, the holiday became a legal one in seven Southern states shortly thereafter.[17]

Cunningham's greatest work as a journalist was promoting construction of commemorative memorials to the valor of the common Southern soldier. "Though men deserve, they may not win success," read the masthead of the *Veteran*. "The brave will honor the brave, vanquished none the less."[18] Cunningham recognized the power of his message during the golden age of Southern monument-building. Indeed, more monuments to the Confederacy sprouted between 1886 and 1899, when Cunningham was supporting this initiative in his magazine, than in the first twenty years since the end of the war.[19] The style usually featured a Confederate soldier standing atop a granite column. The location, previously the local cemetery, was now more likely to be the town square or courthouse lawn. Southerners willingly met the challenge to build these local and regional memorials as a tribute not only to their war dead but also to their impoverished region. The *Veteran* took full pleasure in reporting on these activities.

Cunningham took special interest in projects in Chicago, Nashville, and Shelbyville. In 1891 Cunningham's arch-rival, John C. Underwood, started a collection to build a statue to honor six thousand Confederates buried in Chicago's Oakwood Cemetery. He received official UCV sanction when Adjutant General George Moorman appealed to every camp to make a $10 donation.[20] Underwood, unlike Cunningham, proved to be an adept fund-raiser; he even elicited contributions from Northerners. On the day the monument was unveiled, Memorial Day 1895, floral arrangements including palmettos, moss, and magnolia blossoms arrived in Chicago from Charleston, New Orleans, and Pensacola. Many distinguished Confederate and Federal veterans attended the ceremony in a remarkable outpouring of reciprocal respect.[21]

Cunningham attended the dedication and reported favorably on its bipartisanship. Although he had been stung by Underwood's rebuffs in Birmingham and Houston, he praised Underwood for exercising "diligence and zeal in the success of this movement in Chicago that deserves recognition and expressions of gratitude from every Confederate organization."[22] Cunningham's report was typical of Southern press response, which generally voiced elation over the exhibition of brotherhood. Some reviewers optimistically predicted that sectional hatred had been dealt a lethal blow. Wade Hampton of South Carolina summarized the experience as a "noble emblem of a restored union and reunited people."[23] Underwood's success became a model for Southern communities to follow by building their own Confederate monuments. It also contrasted sharply with Cunningham's inept handling of the Davis memorial drive.

Nashville caught monument fever in 1897, the city's centennial year. Festive celebrations were planned around a six-month-long exposition which attracted thousands of visitors. In the same year Nashville hosted the national UCV reunion for the first time. City planners dedicated Centennial Park in West Nashville along with a replica of the Parthenon. Contemporaries dubbed the building Tennessee's "greatest contribution

*The S.A. Cunningham Camp of the United Son's of Confederate Veterans, Centennial Park, Nashville, 1908. Cunningham is standing at far left. This photograph appeared in the* Confederate Veteran *16 (May 1908).*

to the gilded age." Cunningham marveled at the cultural accomplishments of Nashville during the year-long celebration and did much to advertise the city as the "Athens of the South."[24]

Cunningham collaborated with a group of Nashvillians to erect a monument in Centennial Park to honor the gallantry of the "private soldier." A member of Cheatham Bivouac first conceived the idea. One of Cunningham's old acquaintances, Ben M. Hord, chaired the solicitation drive, which took twelve years to raise four thousand dollars. The finished product—a Confederate soldier resting against a rifle—was dedicated on 19 June 1909. A bronze tablet on one side of the monument contained an alphabetical list of the 540 members of Cheatham Bivouac.[25]

Cunningham's hometown, Shelbyville, followed by hundreds of other Southern towns, built a monument to their local heroes. Although Cunningham had not resided in Bedford County for more than twenty-five years, he had kept in close touch with relatives and friends. Veterans in Frierson Camp wished to co-sponsor a memorial with the local UDC chapter, and the editor joyously publicized the plan. It is a tribute to the middle Tennessee community that it raised the monument in only two years. Senator Thomas B. Turley attended the unveiling in Willow Mount Cemetery, and Bishop Thomas F. Gailor of Nashville delivered the oration.[26] A group photograph shows Cunningham standing next to the granite shaft— a scene oft repeated in many subsequent dedications. Such rituals honoring the valor of the average Southern fighting man were always important to Cunningham, but none was as sacred as the one erected in Shelbyville to commemorate his fallen friends and neighbors.

While Southern communities lifted monuments to glorify the heroism of local Confederate soldiers, a regional scheme with an identical purpose was unfolding. Hopes to build a tabernacle to display war relics and describe the actions of the Southern soldier dated back to 1892, when Senator John W. Daniel of Virginia, addressing the UCV convention, called for a regional campaign to fund a "Battle Abbey." The following year Nannie Nutt contributed an article to the *Veteran* entitled "A Confederate Westminster." The author envisioned a similar national mausoleum to preserve Confederate memories. At first there was some confusion over the concurrent drives to build the Davis monument and the proposed Battle Abbey. Cunningham astutely recognized the difference. Both movements appealed to his desire to memorialize the Confederate heritage.[27]

In November 1894 the Battle Abbey advocates received a tremendous boost when a blind philanthropist, Charles Broadway Rouss, offered to make a substantial donation. Rouss had been a prosperous merchant in prewar Winchester, Virginia, and he served as a private in Company B, 12th Virginia Cavalry, during the war. Later he moved to New York City and amassed a fortune in the retail business. By the mid-1890s he had forty branch outlets that grossed $12 million annually.[28] He not only sympathized with Nutt's suggestion to build a Confederate museum but took the initiative and mailed a circular to several UCV camps, making the following appeal:

What is to become of . . . our records and cherished relics when the last of our veterans who are their custodians shall have passed away. . . . Should they not be collected and provision be made for their preservation as a rich inheritance to our children and a patriotic object lesson for generations to come?[29]

His open letter suggested that thousands of small donations should be collected so that the memorial hall would truly be a people's project rather than a private shrine funded by one wealthy benefactor. "The theory of the movement to establish the Memorial association," he said in a second appeal, is "that every confederate veteran should have a proprietary interest in the institution: that each one of them should feel that he had contributed something toward perpetuating the memories of the great struggle in which he has borne a part."[30] In such a "Temple of the Lost Cause,"

Rouss argued, each Southern state would have space to display its records, relics, mementos, and portraits. The millionaire became consumed by the project and devoted great energy to it for the next three years.[31]

Cunningham grasped Rouss's proposal as a once-in-a-lifetime opportunity to erect a central repository to glorify the Confederate heritage. The editor printed a letter of commendation from Stephen D. Lee, chairman of the UCV history committee. Equally enthusiastic, Commander Gordon issued a circular endorsing the project. Similarly excited, Tennessee veterans set up a state organization to collect contributions.[32]

Cunningham anxiously awaited the upcoming debate on the Battle Abbey scheme at the UCV convention. When the assembly met, Commander Gordon stunned the audience by reading an offer from Rouss to donate up to $100,000 for the Battle Abbey proposal. The veterans cheered wildly as Rouss's personal representative, Colonel Robert C. Wood, approached the podium. There, he clarified one important point: that Rouss would *match* whatever amount the UCV collected.[33]

Gordon accepted Rouss's challenge on behalf of a grateful organization. He immediately called for the formation of a committee representing each Southern state. Cunningham hoped to receive the post, but he was passed over in favor of General W. H. Jackson. Several months later Gordon signed General Order #145 creating the Confederate Memorial Association (CMA), the title coming from Rouss. W. D. Chipley of Florida chaired the committee of trustees, which included Clement A. Evans of Georgia and W. L. Cabell of Texas. Cunningham pictured the fifteen-man committee on the cover of the November issue of the *Veteran*.[34] The first session of the CMA was scheduled to meet in Atlanta in October 1895. Cunningham attended and reported on the proceedings.[35]

From the outset the process of choosing a location for the Battle Abbey was tainted by geographic partisanship. Cunningham and his comrades in Cheatham Bivouac set out to win the coveted museum for Nashville. The Bivouac formed a committee to explore fund-raising possibilities and picked Cunningham to chair it. He advised delegates "to use their influence with the State Convention to ask the Rouse [sic] committee to locate the memorial in Nashville."[36] The editor urged the state convention to prepare an exhibit of Tennessee's war relics for presentation to the CMA. Undoubtedly, Cunningham hoped to demonstrate his state's ability to respond quickly in the collection of memorabilia. He focused on one major goal: it was "very important to have it [Battle Abbey] located in Nashville."[37] W. R. Garrett urged "in a very earnest speech that the Cheatham

Bivouac should without delay take the lead and secure its location in Nashville."[38] Despite later disclaimers, Cunningham's motive to win the Battle Abbey for Nashville was deeply rooted in selfishness, as it was with men from the other competing cities.

Over the next few months Cunningham's committee hatched another scheme to win the Battle Abbey. First, they asked each member of Cheatham Bivouac to contribute one dollar. This suggestion complied with Rouss's wish to solicit small donations. Second, the local committee canvassed Nashville thoroughly and collected $285. Third, the plenary council wisely asked for assistance from the local UDC chapter.[39] Under Cunningham's guidance, Cheatham Bivouac undertook aggressive steps to secure the Battle Abbey for Nashville. Some locals hoped that winning the Battle Abbey would be the crowning prize to the celebration that would take place when the city hosted the Tennessee Centennial Exposition.

Cunningham was present when the first session of the Confederate Memorial Association convened in Atlanta. He, Marcus Toney, and G. H. Baskette were prepared to deliver a strong case for Nashville. To their surprise, other Southern cities were equally well prepared to make presentations. The Nashvillians made their presentation first and were followed in succession by representatives from Washington, D.C., Richmond, New Orleans, and Atlanta. Rouss voiced his preference for the nation's capital, a choice roundly criticized by the UCV and UDC.[40] The stalemated committee decided that the cities in contention for the honor should amass as great an amount of capital for the building as possible before the next UCV reunion, in May 1896, in Richmond. There the committee would announce its final decision.[41] From the beginning, Nashville, New Orleans, and Richmond led the list of potential host cities.

Cheatham Bivouac rebounded from its disappointment and formed a new committee headed by Robert Morris to prepare an advertising strategy for the Richmond reunion. Cunningham and his comrade John P. Hickman orchestrated a three-pronged attack to win unanimous support for the Nashville site. They planned to send prominent Tennessee veterans to Richmond as lobbyists; to encourage important civic leaders from Nashville to visit Richmond; and to transport two uniformed companies of Cheatham Bivouac's renowned marching units, companies A and B, to the Richmond meeting to perform.[42] They also organized a medieval Battle Abbey tournament to raise funds. The event was held in Nashville's Cumberland Park, and General W. H. Jackson served as master of ceremonies. The partisans deemed it a resounding success.[43]

At the Richmond reunion, the CMA shocked the convention when it delayed indefinitely its final decision on the location of the Battle Abbey. Cunningham shared the dismay of Rouss's assistant, Colonel Robert C. Wood, who requested the formation of an administrative panel, or executive board, to intervene in the deadlock and make a final determination.[44] The CMA agreed to Wood's suggestion and created the executive board. Unfortunately, the new watchdog group added to the bureaucratic confusion because its duties overlapped those of the CMA. To Cunningham's utter consternation, the board selected John C. Underwood for the position of superintendent and secretary for the Battle Abbey.[45] Cunningham seethed with envy, but the new superintendent partially mollified his overt displeasure by choosing Nashville as the setting for the committee's first meeting. Underwood expressed a willingness to coordinate the project from an office in the Tennessee city and directed all contributions to be deposited in the Fourth National Bank of Nashville.[46] Through these moves, he hoped to avert the wrath of Nashvillians, who had already collected a substantial amount of money.

Apparent harmony soon gave way to new tensions arising from the way the CMA had managed the Battle Abbey campaign. Cunningham figured prominently in the dissatisfied element. The CMA had held a second meeting in November 1895 and filed a charter for incorporation with the state of Mississippi. Commander Gordon commended the CMA activities to that point, but critics began to question details of the charter shortly after it was filed.[47] J. A. Chalaron, president of the Louisiana Historical Association and a leading New Orleans promoter, was the most outspoken member of the newly created executive board.[48] He argued that the document was illegal because the CMA had yet to deposit any funds. Indeed, the funds collected so far—$20,000—existed only on paper. Chalaron also pointed out Rouss's failure to match the UCV pledges to date and lashed out at the composition of the executive board, which, though it did not represent every state, included Rouss's personal representative, A. G. Dickinson.[49] General Jackson defended Rouss and upbraided Chalaron for attempting to set up what he regarded as petty barriers. The emotional debate brought about one positive change: Rouss agreed immediately to match all UCV and UDC pledges.[50]

Chalaron's scathing rebuke brought to the surface other concerns that men like Cunningham had been keeping to themselves. The most serious challenge to the management of the Battle Abbey centered on the disposition of funds already on hand and the unmet pledges. Remembering earlier criticism leveled at him by many of the same people currently in charge of the Battle Abbey fund, Cunningham enjoined the fray. When Underwood had assumed the superintendency of the executive board, the CMA records accounted for $16,000 in hand. Yet the superintendent receipted only $9,400 to the former administrators. CMA president W. D. Chipley urged that future draft accounts should be signed jointly by Clement A. Evans, representing the CMA, and Underwood, representing the executive board.[51]

Cunningham became irrevocably immersed in the dispute when he charged that Underwood was misappropriating funds. He knew for a fact that Tennessee alone held cash reserves totaling over six thousand dollars. Through an agreement between the Tennessee Centennial Exposition and Cheatham Bivouac, a third of the proceeds from the daily admissions to the exposition had been transferred to the Battle Abbey account.[52] Cheatham Bivouac threatened to freeze its collection until the financial questions and the matter of the memorial's location had been resolved.[53]

Confusion in Nashville over the accounting methods of the executive board reached a crisis point. An official Bivouac task force headed by Cunningham and Hickman confronted Jackson and Garrett, Tennessee's representatives respectively to the CMA and the executive board. Following the interrogation, the dissatisfied investigators drafted a resolution to examine the "appropriation and use of the Rouss Memorial Fund."[54] This action, the most serious challenge to date, clearly illustrated the mounting dissatisfaction of Cunningham and his comrades with the management of the Battle Abbey campaign. Their discontent was destined to spread to the state level and beyond.

The executive board, armed with assurances from Underwood that construction of the Battle Abbey could begin as early as mid-1898, turned to the explosive issue of location. The subject deeply divided committee members. Any decision formulated by the executive board would require approval from the UCV membership. By all indications the upcoming reunion in Atlanta would be tumultuous because of this issue. One of Cunningham's friends from North Carolina, William L. DeRossett, expressed a growing determination among veterans not to contribute any more money until the executive board published its decision about the location of the hall.[55] In a prophetic statement, Cunningham defended his right to print DeRossett's controversial remarks. "The *Veteran* has heretofore withheld all criticisms adverse to the movement," he stated, "but as the questions involved are to be taken up at Atlanta the discord had as well be known."[56] Like many other veterans, Cunningham awaited the showdown in Atlanta.

When Clement A. Evans informed the UCV convention that the executive committee had chosen to place the Confederate Memorial Institute in Richmond, a riot nearly broke out. Emotional protests halted the proceedings, and Chalaron demanded to address the throng. The leaders on the podium attempted to silence him, but to no avail. In point of fact, the executive board was rent by a bitter internal struggle before it ever reached a final decision on the site of the Battle Abbey.

On the stage, an angry Chalaron charged the executive board with bad faith for violating the understanding that the Battle Abbey would be built in the state with the largest net contribution. He understood that Virginia lagged behind several other Southern states. Chalaron indicted the UCV leaders, especially Underwood, for dishonoring the dead heroes of the South by accepting Northern donations. He wrote to forewarn Cunningham that the final decision of the executive board "confirmed my fears of unfairness, of deception and of out-and-dried methods in the whole affair."[57] Only with great difficulty did Commander Gordon restore order, and the assembly stamped its reluctant approval on the executive board's recommendation. The Louisiana division immediately severed its financial tie with the Battle Abbey project.[58] Sharing in their disenchantment, Cunningham and Chalaron began an intensive correspondence that continued for several years.

Cunningham agreed completely with Chalaron's assessment. The Tennessee delegation, too, deeply resented the final choice of Richmond. After it returned from Atlanta, Cheatham Bivouac carried out its earlier threat to freeze all of its contributions. It also succeeded in bringing an injunction to withhold all assets collected by the Association of Confederate Veterans, Tennessee.[59] The state association in Mississippi followed a similar course. Cunningham printed the feelings of many resentful Southerners in the *Veteran*.

To this point, Cunningham's view of the Battle Abbey fiasco was primarily that of a highly opinionated partisan of Nashville. His interjection of his personal biases against Underwood into the controversy marked a major turning point in the history of the Confederate Memorial Institute. Indeed, his vociferousness unknowingly planted the seeds of his own potential ruin. In the ensuing battle over the Battle Abbey, Cunningham nearly destroyed the object he cherished more than life itself—his magazine.

# Chapter 19 Battle over the Battle Abbey

To say that Cunningham was extremely disappointed with the selection of Richmond as the site for the Battle Abbey is a great understatement. His resentment focused squarely upon one person, John C. Underwood. Cunningham's animosity against the superintendent had simmered for years. The sensitive editor interpreted Nashville's loss of the Battle Abbey as a personal insult—the most recent in a long and painful series of snubs by Underwood. Cunningham believed that Underwood's successes had always come at his expense. His quest for personal satisfaction marked the beginning of a long, costly, and desperate battle over the Battle Abbey.

On 26 January 1899 Cunningham wrote to one of the CMA's trustees expressing his lack of confidence in Underwood's leadership of the Battle Abbey project. He questioned the superintendent's business methods and was disgusted by his dictatorial and egotistical personality.[1] The editor despised Underwood's pomposity and complained that he never listened to the UCV membership. In March Cunningham's select committee in Cheatham Bivouac audited Underwood's local ledgers. The evidence they uncovered led them to conclude that Chalaron's allegation of mismanagement was accurate. Moreover, they discovered that most of the contributions dating to Underwood's superintendency came from wealthy Northerners. Cunningham interpreted this revelation as a "radical and fundamental departure from Rouss's original offer."[2]

Friends warned Cunningham to temper his public criticism of Underwood, but to no avail. In April the editor launched a series of scathing attacks against his rival. He rationalized his frustrations to readers of the *Veteran:* "In his last personal appeal the writer asked if *seven years* was not long enough to wait for a share of the courtesies extended to a multitude." Clearly, he still held Underwood accountable for his earlier failure to win an official endorsement from the UCV. Cunningham fully understood the consequences of printing his true feelings. He prophesied that the eventual battle with Underwood "threatens to be the bitterest and most prolonged that the writer has ever engaged in. It will involve a multitude of friends and patrons but it may result in a blessing to millions of people." Cunningham expressed confidence should his opinions be tested in court, saying that he had *"never been defeated in a public controversy."*[3] Only time would verify the accuracy of his optimism.

After the Charleston reunion in 1899, Cunningham lost all patience with Underwood, the executive board, and the CMA. In a ten-page editorial published in June, he ripped vengefully into Underwood's financial report. He explained that the ledgers were misleading: $42,000 in pledges, $100,000 in the Rouss fund, and $6,000 on deposit in the Fourth National Bank of Nashville.[4] Cunningham challenged the accuracy of these figures, claiming they were "bold" and "nauseating," and contended that very little hard cash existed. He became indignant with Clement A. Evans's poorly timed announcement that Underwood was due a $7,700 commission. Cunningham challenged a plan to purchase oil paintings valued at $60,000 for the hall. He argued it was not only financially reckless, but also went beyond the prescribed powers of the superintendent.[5]

Cunningham held nothing back when he rebuked Underwood in formal proceedings before the UCV historical committee. In his comments, the editor singled out Clement A. Evans for censure, claiming that he "insolently disregarded warning and appeal from as worthy veterans as live."[6] Publicly, Cunningham exonerated Commander Gordon from blame, supporting the claim that he had been too busy with official business to monitor Underwood. Privately, however, Cunningham agreed with Chalaron that Gordon had lowered the dignity of the UCV by his unwavering support of Underwood.[7]

Cunningham's solution to the accounting quagmire was to freeze all UCV funds and force the executive board to make a proper accounting to the association membership. He reminded all sympathizers that he remained a staunch advocate of the Battle Abbey concept "regardless of what may have been considered 'unfair methods' to fix the location" at Richmond.[8]

Three months after writing his first damning editorial, Cunningham alluded to a related problem—poor record keeping. The editor complained that the superintendent used a "smearing indelible pencil" and neglected to enter pledges promptly. Cunningham blamed the CMA for failing to monitor the business practices of the executive board. "For some years now the Board has given out so meager reports that the public is kept in absolute ignorance of the facts," he scolded.[9] Straying from the point, Cunningham also slandered Underwood's war record on the grounds that he had never carried a gun. (Underwood had served as a recruiter.) Addressed to a veteran audience that readily conceded that combat soldiers had made the truest sacrifices during the war, this was no insignificant charge.

Cunningham did not have long to wait for Underwood's response. While an impressive array of veterans listened intently to Cunningham's challenge to the executive board, its superintendent took exception to the remarks. On 28 July 1899 Underwood demanded that Cunningham "fully retract the insinuations . . . which are derogatory of the Executive Committee and of myself."[10] The superintendent also threatened legal action if Cunningham failed to comply with his demands.

In the meantime, Underwood reportedly wrote a sixteen-page defense of his actions in the *Lost Cause.* In the treatise, he expanded the demands to include fifty thousand dollars in damages.[11] The editor lost his composure and replied that Underwood's lengthy defense was "well-paid for." John P. Hickman sent a rejoinder to the Lexington-based magazine defending Cunningham, but it was not promptly printed.[12]

S. A. Champion, Cunningham's legal counsel, had unpleasant news for Cunningham: he declared the second editorial flagrant and wrong.[13] Worse, he counseled, the executive board possessed the financial and legal resources to destroy the *Veteran.* Although distraught, Cunningham stubbornly refused to issue a retraction. He and the Southwest Methodist-Episcopal Publishing House were issued a warrant on 2 August 1899.[14] The editor was defiant. He wrote in the *Veteran,*

> When the testimony is all in I feel that a just public must see that I am censurable only in waiting so long before making known the unfortunate methods of Underwood as Superintendent and agent of the Confederate Memorial Institute.[15]

Cunningham felt that he must endure any possible legal proceeding as a part of his personal duty to expose Underwood as a fraud. "Not a stone is to be procurred," said Cunningham, "that would cause humiliation and dishonor."[16]

In a letter discussing the impending trial, Chalaron suggested that Underwood's lawsuit was only "a method of advertising himself and of attracting attention to the Confederate Memorial Association." Chalaron encouraged Cunningham to proceed with his attack. "Do not feel ashamed of yourself for the great wrong you have inflicted on so disinterested and deserving a Confederate patriot," he stated, referring with sarcasm to Underwood.[17]

Privately, the prospect of the upcoming trial disturbed Cunningham. Publicly, his opinions fluctuated in the *Veteran*. One editorial remark sounded especially patronizing: "I am not going to be mad at him [Underwood] however much I may regret what he has done."[18] In a more conciliatory mood, he offered Underwood space in the *Veteran* to explain his position. Then, in a moment of self-doubt, he requested a "general expression of sentiment" from sympathetic patrons prior to the hearing. Cunningham published excerpts from ninety-two letters that praised him and admonished the superintendent.[19] One cheered Cunningham's famous editorial as "dignified but incisive, well written and strongly put." The writer concluded, "I believe you are right and ought to be, and will be sustained by the veterans throughout the South." He predicted that Underwood would "pale away into utter insignificance under the influence of the scathing rebuke."[20] Bolstered by the response he received, the editor published a satirical story in which he demeaned Underwood.[21] However, as the court date approached, the gravity of the legal battle overwhelmed Cunningham. It clearly disrupted the continuity of his editorials.

Cunningham's Nashville friends rallied to his defense. Comrades in Cheatham Bivouac passed a comforting resolution of support only two days after the court summons was delivered. At the Bivouac's request, several UCV camps sent Cunningham letters of encouragement.[22] Meanwhile, Underwood claimed, in an interview in the *Dallas News*, that he could account for every penny contributed to the Battle Abbey project.[23]

Cunningham received a particularly unexpected reaction from one member of the executive board, B. H. Teague, the friend who first introduced the *Veteran* to the UCV reunion in 1894. Teague staunchly defended the board's actions and soundly criticized Cunningham for printing injudicious remarks. Teague perceived the lawsuit between Cunningham and Underwood as detrimental to the UCV in general and the CMA in particular. He hoped to appease the temper of both men: "I write to you," he told Cunningham, "as I have written to him that I hope some means may be adopted by which this lamentable affair may be adjusted with peace and satisfaction to all parties."[24]

Teague was especially affronted that Cunningham had attacked the "honor and integrity" of the entire executive board. He said in his letter,

Though it may be an individual assault of words by you in your editorials, yet the CMA and the Confederate veterans believe it to be one by "the people of Nashville," i.e. those interested members of Cheatham Bivouac and other veterans. I do not believe the Executive Committee would withhold *anything* from the veteran body.[25]

Teague regretted that Cunningham had found it necessary to espouse Nashville's cause at the expense of all ex-Confederates. "Its editor should not have let his personal feelings from a 'conviction of public duty' . . . embroil himself and personal friends into a lamentable controversy," scolded Teague.[26] Unquestionably, Cunningham's editorials had alienated the leaders of the UCV. Teague also intimated that Cunningham's tirade stemmed from Underwood's coolness toward the *Veteran* at the Birmingham reunion in 1894, where Underwood had been expected to offer a resolution making the magazine the official organ of the UCV. "Am I mistaken in thinking perhaps his failure to do so," Teague asked, "is to some extent a cause of dislike on your part?"[27]

The South Carolinian argued that Underwood had not compromised the wishes of the executive board in locating the Battle Abbey in Richmond. Rather, the board had reached that decision through open and democratic means. The public discussions, asserted Teague, had always been attended by Tennessee's representative. "Individually," said Teague, "we believed it appeared, that Richmond had not only offered more as an endorsement, but that each believed from opinions expressed by veterans in conversation that the majority favored Richmond." Finally, Teague censured Cunningham for soliciting acclamations of support from individual UCV camps. "I do not espouse the 'cause of the man,'" he chided; "I espouse my own cause as an integral part of the CMA and it is very *grievious* [*sic*] to me that my comrade should expect me to be more loyal to him than to myself, my board, and my state. It is your mistake to expect loyalty under your attack."[28] Teague's correspondence illustrates the depth of animosity that Cunningham's editorial had generated.

On 3 October 1899 the libel case opened in Nashville's sixth circuit court before Judge Charles D. Clark. The plaintiff demanded that Cunningham admit to libel, print a retraction, eulogize Underwood in the *Veteran*, and pay $4,700 in court costs. Cunningham's lawyer reviewed the grievances that led the editor to draft his editorial about Underwood. They included improper acceptance of Northern contributions for the Battle Abbey, offensive and improper financial demands on Rouss, misappropriation of funds to purchase paintings, display of rude and selfish manners toward Nashvillians during the 1897 reunion, and behavior as a false friend of the South.[29] Champion portrayed Cunningham's relationship with Underwood as a cooperative one and argued that it was Cunningham's duty as editor of the official organ of the UCV to report any improprieties. When Cunningham testified, he revealed provocative new information. Though he first acknowledged that Underwood's selection as superintendent of the Battle Abbey was based on his successful work on the Oakwood Cemetery monument in Chicago, he charged that most of the monies he collected came from a lecture given by Commander Gordon. Second, Cunningham had taken literally the statement of W. D. Chipley that the final location of the Battle Abbey would not be discussed until full funding had been achieved. When the executive board selected Richmond in 1898, many veterans, including Cunningham, considered it a breach of faith. Third, Cunningham offered what he claimed to be evidence of Underwood's lack of moral integrity: Cunningham had warned a Charleston woman not to allow Underwood to reside at a family member's home during the 1899 reunion. He based this advice on Underwood's "questionable morality."[30]

During his instructions to the jury, Judge Clark concluded that Cunningham's editorials were libelous. However, he explained that the malicious comments might have been based on an understanding of "conditional privilege"—that is, that Cunningham's opinion as editor of the *Veteran* might have been offered in good faith. The judge ordered the jury to determine whether this was the case.[31]

The jury requested clarification on several legal points before it began deliberation. Judge Clark explained that the jury could fine one defendant and release the other from responsibility. As a result, the verdict found the publisher without fault and reached a split decision on Cunningham. The jury foreman stated after the trial that "at no time was it agreed to fine Mr. Cunningham over one cent."[32] A new trial date was set.

In the meantime, Cunningham traveled to New York City to discuss the lawsuit with CMA benefactor Charles Rouss. The philanthropist offered to intercede in Cunningham's behalf and speak with Underwood. Cunningham accepted this offer, but Underwood set conditions for the talk that were so offensive Cunningham refused to consider them. "I don't blame you," said Rouss later.[33]

The Underwood-Cunningham lawsuit received considerable attention in Cheatham Bivouac. Prior to the hearing, the Bivouac discovered that its bank account, which was supposed to have been frozen, had been mysteriously withdrawn, along with the state fund. The Bivouac immediately elected to "wash its hands of the whole matter."[34] It urged the state association to follow suit, with Cunningham playing an active role. The Bivouac also determined to recover the missing money. It first threatened to bring suit against the CMA but then withdrew the resolution for fear that it might further embarrass the Battle Abbey movement. In a calmer moment, the Bivouac requested that the executive board return Tennessee's portion of the fund, which it had decided it would prefer to invest in a state memorial building. To everyone's surprise, Evans could not trace Tennessee's deposit. Nashville veterans remained bitter for years.[35]

Before the UCV reunions in 1900 and 1901, Cunningham took extraordinary steps to bring the libel case before the membership for discussion. Against legal advice from Champion, he hoped to gain an audience with the body "regardless of the legal tribunals outside."[36] Cheatham Bivouac supported Cunningham in his bid for vindication. It also pushed for creation of a special UCV committee to investigate the cause of the libel suit.[37]

Cunningham passed an important hurdle when the committee on resolutions agreed to hear his plea. But when William P. Tolley introduced a resolution favorable to Cunningham, the committee sat in stony silence. The cautious members were "immovable against any inference" that could possibly be used in court against the CMA.[38] Cunningham was frustrated by the lack of support, and he labeled the meeting a "whitewashing." His accusation hurt the feelings of another potential ally. "I am sorry that you are so wrought up over this matter," explained Tolley, "as that you would do your best friends the great injustice you have done me."[39]

The rank and file veterans turned a deaf ear to Cunningham's desperate appeal for help, and with good reason. The executive board issued a financial statement that showed more than $65,000 in cash deposits and an additional $59,000 pledged. More important, Rouss released the remainder of his matching donation.[40] Underwood's position never appeared stronger, and Cunningham, conversely, was viewed with contempt. The editor sheepishly acknowledged defeat when he printed the financial report on the last page of the *Veteran* without comment.[41]

Cunningham's morale plunged as the retrial approached. The lack of public support sapped the Tennessean's normal vitality. In August he traveled secretly to New York City for some unknown purpose only to be hospitalized.[42] An official hospital release stated that he was being treated for an old ailment, but it is more likely that he suffered an illness brought on by the stress of the libel suit. A friend of forty years, Lewis Tillman, sent a timely note to remind Cunningham that goodness always followed evil and that God would make things right.[43] The message of goodwill improved Cunningham's spirits.

Before the retrial began, Cunningham's lawyer embarked upon a new course. He besought the editor to enlist as many character witnesses as possible either to sign a deposition or to appear in person at the trial.[44] Cunningham sought a second opinion of the new strategy from Malcolm McNeil, a Chicago attorney. McNeil offered to interview witnesses favorably disposed to the Tennessean.[45]

Cunningham felt confident that he could rely upon many Southern friends. For instance, he knew that J. A. Chalaron would collaborate in an effort to remove Underwood from the superintendency. Chalaron had worked as assiduously to secure the institute for New Orleans as Cunningham had for Nashville, and both men felt swindled by the final decision favoring Richmond. Furthermore, Chalaron had resigned in protest from the executive board. "I battled strenuously with the Board against what I thought was a nefarious tendency," he told Cunningham.[46] Thus it came as a great surprise when Chalaron notified Cunningham that he would be unable to testify at the hearing. He did, however, inform Cunningham that Rouss's assistant, Colonel Robert C. Wood, would mail pertinent documents to John P. Hickman.[47] In an even more startling revelation, the publisher of the *Veteran*, S. W. Meek, declined an invitation to testify. Meek insisted that he knew nothing of substance or value about the case. While his attorney professed to be "in good spirits," Cunningham fell victim to despair.[48] His closest associates seemed to be washing their hands of the entire affair.

When the retrial convened on 25 February 1901, Cunningham was burdened with additional bad news. The Southwest Methodist-Episcopal Publishing House asked the court for a severance with the editor. Their lawyer argued that the *Veteran* was the sole property of Cunningham and that the publishing house was merely responsible for printing and mailing the magazine. In an unusual decision, Judge Walter Evans overruled the motion. The trial took a strange twist when Evans denied to hear the testimony of Cunningham's character witnesses, invalidated McNeil's depositions, and refused the publisher's proofreader an opportunity to testify.[49]

When the trial ended six days later, Judge Evans instructed the jury in the same manner as Judge Clark had done in the first trial. "I am satisfied that certain parts of the publication are in themselves libelous," he stated. Then, in an error, he told the jury that they could demand compensation damages against both Cunningham and the publishers but punitive damages only against the editor. The jury followed Evans's instructions and fined the defendants collectively $15,000, and assessed Cunningham an additional $10,000.[50]

The editor was crushed. He was in no financial position to pay the exorbitant settlement. The publishers generously paid $12,000 toward the collective fine, but Cunningham claimed insolvency. The stunning effect of the settlement illustrates that the editor of the *Veteran* operated on a very thin margin. Judge Evans sympathized with Cunningham's plight and suggested the victorious plaintiff accept a reduced amount. He hinted that such a benevolent act might persuade Cunningham not to file an appeal. But Underwood, bent on a course to ruin Cunningham and the *Veteran*, refused. Although Cunningham was mentally and physically exhausted, he had no alternative but to file an appeal.[51]

At this point in his life-and-death struggle for the *Veteran*, Cunningham suffered a staggering personal loss—the untimely death of his only son, Paul Davis Cunningham. Although they had often lived apart from each other, especially in Paul's adolescence, father and son were very close. Cunningham had printed several sketches of Paul in the *Veteran*. He was doubly affectionate toward his son because the young man resembled his mother in physical appearance. Certainly Laura Davis Cunningham's religious training had been instrumental in shaping the boy's character.[52] Paul had studied civil engineering at Emory College, and with the assistance of his father he was hired as an apprentice by the Louisville and Nashville Railroad. When he contracted pneumonia in 1890, he convalesced at Beauvoir under the personal care of Varina Howell Davis. For the rest of the decade, father and son shared quarters at the Maxwell House. When the Spanish-American War began, Paul joined the United States Engineer Service assigned to the command of Colonel William Black. It was Black's assignment to disinfect the streets of Havana and thereby reduce the threat of yellow fever. The highly successful program, in which Paul

Cunningham played an important role, resulted in Paul's promotion to the rank of chief engineer.

In 1901 the service reassigned Paul to work with Black as a consulting engineer for the International Boundary Commission. He accompanied a joint American-Mexican surveying team responsible for mapping the thirteen-hundred-mile course of the Rio Grande. The expedition experienced an inordinate number of delays. At one point Paul was bitten by a rattlesnake and returned to El Paso for treatment. After he rejoined the survey team in July 1901, he drowned under suspicious circumstances while floating a treacherous rapid. An old friend at the *Nashville American*, William H. Bumpus, personally delivered the tragic notice to Cunningham at the Maxwell House.[53] Initially the editor appeared to react with little emotion and displayed outward courage. But the trauma induced by the tragic news remained with him for the rest of his life. Mrs. W. R. Lyman, a friend and hostess to Cunningham on his frequent visits to New Orleans, later recalled that Paul's unfortunate death was a devastating loss to Cunningham. It is uncertain what happened to Paul's body.[54]

Immediately following Paul's death, Cunningham received condolences from many sources.[55] The grieving father assumed the unpleasant task of notifying his eighty-four-year-old father-in-law about the death. William B. Davis had been particularly fond of his grandson. Already in declining health, he passed away within a month. "A truer, better nobler man did not live in his time," eulogized Cunningham.[56] Within the short span of five weeks, Cunningham had lost two close family members.

After these tragedies, the court decision appeared less important to Cunningham. As the appeal process dragged on, he seemed detached and melancholy. "The Lord be praised that there is no other motive than which is designed to establish eternal truth," he lamented. At this time of personal loss and professional controversy, Cunningham leaned heavily upon his religious faith. "The grievous experiences of the last year or so have removed all other ambitions from the management than to establish [an] enduring record of the merits of the Southern people," he confessed.[57]

In the throes of despondency, Cunningham no longer possessed the physical strength to pursue his own vindication. As in an earlier struggle for survival against what he perceived to be insurmountable odds, he relinquished the will to fight.

# Chapter 20 Desperate Times

Many of Cunningham's comrades and readers were jolted by the outcome of the lawsuit. The UCV leaders turned a cold shoulder to him. Clement A. Evans wrote a typical note to Cunningham that was totally devoid of compassion:

> *Individually* and *personally* I have wished to intervene and adjust the matter without touching it *officially*, but you have never given me the authority nor opportunity to do so. Personally, I would be glad to have the matter settled.[1]

Evans's remarks expressed the general feeling among the veterans that the ongoing litigation had had a detrimental effect on the Battle Abbey project.[2] In the face of impending defeat, Cunningham obtained one satisfying endorsement from Rouss. "You have won my friendship and esteem by your energy and enterprise and I am very much in sympathy with you."[3] But kind words alone would save neither Cunningham nor his magazine. These were desperate times, and he needed irrefutable evidence to revitalize his sagging case.

In the months following the retrial, Cunningham returned to court six times to justify an appeal. His lawyer in Chicago observed that the two trials were remarkably similar in the way the judges instructed the juries. Perhaps, queried McNeil, Judge Clark had discussed the case with Evans prior to the retrial. Such an action would invalidate the results. Cunningham's courtroom counsel also planned to present new evidence that Underwood had surreptitiously renegotiated a commission clause in his contract with the CMA. Champion prepared to argue another legal flaw—that neither judge had permitted a severance of the defendants as warranted by Tennessee law.[4] Finally, the defense attorney implied that both magistrates had erred in refusing to allow testimony concerning Cunningham's reputation. Champion finally succeeded in securing an appeal in the U.S. Circuit Court of Appeals, Cincinnati.

Cunningham frantically sought to gather fresh evidence to prove that Underwood involved himself in the Battle Abbey project purely for personal gain. Cunningham corresponded with one remaining ally on the executive board, George Reese, who revealed to the beleaguered editor that Underwood had *never* been elected to the superintendency and sensed "unrest and dissatisfaction" on that point.[5] Reese believed that the committee erred a second time in not publicizing a contract revision issued to Underwood. The new terms allowed for twenty-five percent commission to replace the flat fee of $4,500 a year. Reese agreed with Cunningham that Underwood should be removed from office. "A defeat would be worse than silence," Reese said.[6]

The editor hurriedly published the startling news in the *Veteran*.[7] The confidential data proved invaluable to the appeal, though its importance was not fully realized until Underwood's lawyers filed an injunction against the CMA to obtain the commission. The ensuing uproar effectively froze the unpaid portion of the Rouss contribution and delayed construction of the Battle Abbey for a decade. It also saved the *Veteran* magazine.

Cunningham contacted J. A. Chalaron and requested financial documents pertinent to the case that might be on file in Louisiana. "Underwood is pressing his suit in a desperate way and would spend much money to crush me," confided the frantic editor.[8] Curiously, he drafted the appeal on Maxwell House stationery rather than using the familiar *Veteran* letterhead; this gave his request a more personal touch.

After Cunningham's disclosure of Underwood's secret commission, public favor shifted gradually to the editor. Recent revelations clearly embarrassed the UCV leaders. Clement A. Evans handled the delicate matter of informing the UCV conventioneers about the secret contract. After confirming its existence, he explained that it was necessary because Rouss refused to pay Underwood's retainer beyond 1899. In order to avert an ugly scene at the reunion, Evans proposed to lay the Battle Abbey cornerstone immediately. One debater questioned the wisdom of beginning construction when so much of the monies were still in unpaid pledges. Another speaker reasoned that Underwood's commission would drain the existing cash reserve by a third. Matters worsened when the executive board disclosed that Underwood had made an unauthorized withdrawal of $24,000 from the Battle Abbey treasury earlier that year. These actions cast the superintendent in a questionable light for the first time.[9]

Then, in a historic development, the convention adjourned a day ahead of schedule so that the executive board could hold an emergency session. In a vote of confidence, the board extended Underwood's contract for two years. Cunningham accused them of paying the superintendent under the table. Clearly the Underwood-Cunningham feud was splitting the veterans' association apart.[10]

In April 1902 the federal appellate court decided that Cunningham had been denied his constitutional rights when both trial judges drew improper conclusions and gave faulty advice to the juries.[11] The humiliating litigation had ended. The front cover of the *Veteran* proclaimed vindication for its editor in bold red letters. In a brazen twist, Cunningham filed a countersuit to collect court costs. Wisely, he later dropped the issue.[12]

Less than a week after the appellate court exonerated Cunningham, the UCV held its annual reunion. Naturally, much of the talk centered on the surprising turn the court case had taken. Unfortunately, the controversy surrounding the Battle Abbey was not over. In fact, disharmony within the UCV was at an all-time high. Such vocal veterans as Chalaron supported Cheatham Bivouac's resolution for the return of all funds so that each Southern state could construct its own memorial hall. He pointed with pride to a significant contribution from Varina Howell Davis to the Louisiana Historical Association. "Every state can erect its own building for such a purpose," agreed Cunningham, "and should do it without aliens [Northerners]."[13] The proposition received considerable attention, and some zealous veterans even advocated dividing the Rouss donation among the state associations.[14]

Tempers exploded at a critical meeting of the executive board held three weeks before Cunningham's ultimate court victory ostensibly to discuss the recent death of C. B. Rouss and its implication for the Battle Abbey. Certainly Rouss's passing shrouded the future of the memorial hall. Speculation arose that the project might never be completed, and this had some basis in fact: Rouss's assets were frozen; the Underwood-Cunningham appeal was forthcoming; and Underwood's litigation against the CMA for failure to pay his commission created confusion. The executive board wisely elected to debate these divisive issues behind closed doors. While George Reese planned to force Underwood's resignation, other stalwart members sought a contract extension. Reese invited Cunningham to travel to Atlanta and "talk plainly" with Evans. Cunningham went, but neither he nor Reese succeeded in speaking to Evans. The editor was barred from the meeting room, inside which Evans proceeded to "read [Reese] quite a lecture." Reese had no desire to "precipitate unpleasantness in the Board," so he sat in silence for the duration of the session.[15]

Cunningham did not remain so composed. "To refuse admission of the editor of the official organ, also the daily press, and to enjoin secrecy by the members is inconsistent with the spirit of the movement," fumed the irate editor.[16] He suspected that the board would not disclose full details of the closed-door gathering. He distrusted Evans's motives and inferred that mischief had taken place. Evans was aware of Cunningham's uncomplimentary opinions. In his own defense, he wrote that "reporters interviewed me and all their questions were fully answered. You [Cunningham] had all opportunity to report our proceedings and I do not know why you did not."[17] Evans's statement did not satisfy the editor of the *Veteran*.

Cunningham vented his frustration in another inflammatory editorial. Stung, Evans responded, "I am not encouraged by your illiberal and unfair editorial comments on my account of the Atlanta meeting."[18] This incident typified how rarely Evans and Cunningham ever saw eye-to-eye on UCV policy-making.

The tide of public opinion swung solidly behind Cunningham shortly after news broke of his vindication in the courts. Evans sensed the shift and was conspicuously absent from the 1902 reunion. In his place, Robert White read the complete financial report of the board. A Dallas newspaper interviewed Evans, who refuted Cunningham's earlier charges of secrecy. He lamented that "any intimation of that character is as ungenerous, as it is unfair and unjust."[19] John P. Hickman recounted to Cheatham Bivouac that Evans's statement was "not very flattering."[20]

Cunningham and Evans did agree on one point—that Underwood's pursuit of damages against the CMA posed a real threat to the Battle Abbey. In executive session Evans now turned on Underwood, disclosing that the superintendent had failed to attend a single meeting in 1902. Reversing his earlier position, he chastised the superintendent for negligent bookkeeping, and recommended that the CMA hire legal counsel and remove Underwood from the superintendency. Accepting the suggestion, the executive board installed J. William Jones as Underwood's replacement.[21]

The Battle Abbey project remained in peril as long as Underwood pursued his case against the CMA. In 1905 the former superintendent won a startling $16,000 settlement, but an appeal overruled the deci-

sion. Underwood threatened to bring the case before the United State.
Supreme Court, but then he lost interest and dropped the matter.[22]

After an eight-year legal hassle that nearly crushed the Battle Abbey,
gravely endangered the *Veteran*, and tarnished the reputation of its editor,
Cunningham could put the regrettable episode behind him. The Confederate Memorial Institute opened its doors in 1921, but Cunningham and
many of his cronies did not live long enough to attend its dedication.[23]

The Battle Abbey imbroglio was probably unavoidable, especially considering the personalities involved. Cunningham's irritating nature, neu-
roticism, self-righteous and condescending tone, and defensiveness delayed any quick resolution of the issues involved. Neither were his enemies
without fault. Finally, in any case, the editor was exonerated and allowed
the freedom to explore topics that would carry his magazine into the
twentieth century. For Cunningham, two separate monument drives—for
memorials to Samuel Davis and Richard Owen—would cap his long and
illustrious career in journalism.

# Chapter 21  Crowning Glories

Early in the history of the *Veteran,* Cunningham learned about Samuel Davis, a Tennessee cavalryman who was captured, tried, and executed by the Federal army for spying. Fascinated by Davis's tragic story, Cunningham volunteered to spearhead a drive to build a monument to the heroic youth. He also resolved to see a memorial erected to the prison commandant at Camp Morton, Richard Owen. Cunningham believed that the monuments that were eventually built were the "crowning glories" of his life. His motives in working for them were personal: there was a distinct connection between Sergeant-Major Cunningham's inglorious military service and editor Cunningham's indefatigable zeal to glorify the "Boy Hero of Tennessee" and the "Good Samaritan of Camp Morton." Getting the monuments erected was a form of self-exoneration, a way of making amends for his poor war record.

Cunningham first became aware of Samuel Davis at a public lecture sponsored by the Literary Society of Nashville in 1895.[1] The pathetic story about Davis's capture and execution had gone practically unnoticed by Tennesseans, and it touched the editor deeply.[2] He published two eyewitness accounts of the execution and almost immediately was swamped by correspondence from interested readers.[3]

It is an understatement to suggest that Cunningham was intrigued by the character of Sam Davis and contributed greatly to its perpetuation in Tennessee history and folklore. Davis was born in 1842 on a cotton plantation near Smyrna in middle Tennessee. When the Civil War broke out, he enlisted as a scout in the 1st Tennessee Cavalry. In November 1863 a Federal detachment captured Davis in possession of military intelligence for General Bragg. Interrogated by General Grenville M. Dodge, the young prisoner steadfastly refused to identify his source of information. The Federal officer had no recourse but to find Davis guilty of espionage. The twenty-one-year-old cavalryman was hanged in Pulaski on 21 November 1863.[4]

Davis's sad fate gripped Cunningham, and he promised a thorough account of his deeds in the *Veteran*. The editor appealed to knowledgeable Tennesseans for reminiscences about Davis, but he could not have anticipated the cascade of personal accounts that poured in from eyewitnesses, neighbors, quasi-historians, and folklorists. As soon as any story of the "boy hero of Tennessee" appeared on his desk, regardless of its veracity, Cunningham printed it.[5] The Davis story touched on several themes that were important to Cunningham's Victorian readership: demonstrated manliness based on self-denial, devotion to a principle or cause, and sacrifice in the name of a higher law.[6] "The model character of Sam Davis has kindled anew the courage and firmness of the Confederate soldier element," he wrote, "and it points afresh to principles that are more than life."[7] The Davis mystique totally absorbed Cunningham, whose interest bordered on obsession.

The tremendous affection displayed by Tennesseans for Sam Davis led Cunningham to reevaluate plans to memorialize Otho F. Strahl, his commander who had died at Franklin. In the summer of 1895 the editor suggested the construction of a memorial to Davis on the state capitol grounds. "Such a monument embodying a history of that character," explained Cunningham, "would ever convey exaltation of mind and an influence that would strengthen manhood."[8] The editor anticipated a positive response and volunteered to collect donations for the project. With dramatic flair, he appealed for pledges to be postmarked on 27 November, the thirty-second anniversary of Davis's execution.[9] Coincidentally, it also marked Cunningham's wedding anniversary and the birth date of his son.

Cunningham's plan for the memorial won immediate endorsement and financial assistance from distinguished ex-Confederates such as Varina Howell Davis, John B. Gordon, and J. William Jones. In letters to the *Veteran*, many ex-Federals, led by Grenville M. Dodge, testified to the bravery of young Davis. One eloquent booster declared that Sam Davis would attain the national fame of Nathan Hale. However, the Sam Davis memorial drive remained largely a Tennessee enterprise.[10]

Despite initial public enthusiasm for the Davis monument, Cunningham had collected only $400 after months of advertising. He therefore devised new approaches. First he suggested that each veteran collect as many dimes as possible and forward them to Nashville on 21 July, another unpublicized but significant date: Cunningham's birthday.[11] He proposed to invest what he referred to as the common man's contribution in interest-bearing government bonds. Cunningham then organized a graveside memorial service at the Davis homestead. He took complete charge of program and transportation arrangements, and fancied the excursion to be an afternoon of "appropriate songs and music." A modest number of people attended the emotional gathering.[12]

In an important editorial entitled "How Shall Sam Davis Be Honored?" Cunningham contributed personally to what became a plethora of Davis articles. Shortly thereafter he presented a biographical lecture on Davis to the Tennessee Historical Society. The *American Historical Magazine* published this sketch, and Cunningham reprinted it several times in his journal.[13] In the final year of his life, Cunningham drafted a pamphlet that illustrated Cunningham's close identification with Davis.[14]

In 1897 Cunningham received a letter from the Reverend James Young, the Federal chaplain who had befriended Davis before the boy's execution. The letter disclosed that Young had been in possession of Davis's Confederate overcoat since the execution day. He was becoming increasingly infirm, and he wished to return the jacket to the South before he died.[15] Cunningham jubilantly accepted the gift. When the treasured garment arrived at his office, he locked it safely in a cedar chest beside his desk. He displayed it during a highly publicized UDC meeting in Nashville. "When it was shown," he later recalled, "every heart was melted to tears and there we sat in that sacred silence. Not a sound was heard save the sobs that came from aching hearts. It was a time too sacred for words."[16] Later that year Cunningham exhibited the coat at the national UCV reunion.

Shortly after these exhibitions, Cunningham concocted a bizarre scheme to attract more contributions to the sagging monument drive: he offered to furnish a photograph of himself wearing the cherished overcoat.[17] An engraving was struck for the prints, but Cunningham "shrank from having them printed." "The truth is," he revealed, "that while the plate is ready now, and in a few minutes a number of prints could be made, I have not the courage to have it done."[18] A collector of historic memorabilia brashly requested a clipping from the famous overcoat. Cunningham tersely rebuked him for being "out of place."[19]

Cunningham turned his attention to finding a qualified sculptor for Davis's monument. Varina Howell Davis assisted in this endeavor by introducing him to George Julian Zolnay.[20] On the recommendation of the former first lady of the Confederacy, the editor hired the Hungarian artist. Zolnay's task would be difficult because no portrait of Davis existed from which to model a bust. The sculptor prepared a composite from physical descriptions recollected by Davis's relatives. His first effort evoked complaint because it resembled the artist himself. Other critics chimed in; some disapproved of the subdued facial expression, while others objected to what they called the alien background of Zolnay.[21] These detractors were silenced after a time, and Zolnay completed his work, much to Cunningham's satisfaction.

The general assembly generously apportioned $5,000 and granted its permission to erect the Davis monument on capitol hill. The lawmakers formed a committee headed by Cunningham to choose an appropriate site.[22] The group wasted little time in selecting the southwest capitol entrance at Vine and Cedar. A gleeful Cunningham observed that the monument "will give increased sympathy and admiration for the patriotic hero—awakening emotions akin to worship."[23] The Sam Davis project now entered its final phase.

In 1902 Cunningham neared nervous exhaustion brought on by the stressful litigation with Underwood, so he transferred responsibility of finishing the collection to the Tennessee UDC. The ladies made little progress other than securing one significant pledge from their national association. After a six-year lapse, Cunningham announced that sufficient private contributions were on hand to begin construction. His eager comrades in Cheatham Bivouac also pushed to see the statue unveiled. In a typical melodramatic touch, Cunningham called for a referendum on the subject—twenty thousand letters postmarked on November 27—for "sentimental reasons." Some followers complied, and contractors broke ground almost immediately.[24] The Sam Davis monument was unveiled on 29 April 1909. By his own assessment, Cunningham considered the ceremony a "crowning glory" of his life.[25]

The second jewel in Cunningham's crown was the result of his desire to pay homage to Richard Owen. Inexplicably, prisoners' reminiscences were popular at the turn of the century, and Cunningham devoted an entire issue of the *Veteran* to this theme.[26] The first mention of a memorial to Richard Owen followed Cunningham's attendance at the 1906 GAR convention. At the Minneapolis gathering he listened attentively to a raging debate over a UDC proposal to build a monument to Henry Wirz, the notorious commandant of Andersonville prison.[27] The Tennessean identified with the graphic descriptions of suffering by Federal prisoners, which rekindled memories of his own incarceration. Cunningham mentally contrasted Wirz's record with that of the humanitarian commandant of Camp Morton. As the Sam Davis monument entered its final stage, he explored the possibility of sponsoring a bronze tablet to Owen. He received encouragement from many Tennesseans.[28]

Cunningham realized that he would have to bear much of the financial responsibility for the Owen project. "So nearly all of the Camp Morton prisoners are dead," he explained, "that I had an ambition personally to pay tribute to Colonel Owen."[29] He discussed the proposed Owen memorial in every editorial throughout 1911, but reluctant Southerners had contributed only $161 after a year. This poor response did not slow the editor from drafting a letter to the Indiana legislature to request permission to place a memorial tablet on capitol hill. He even traveled to Indianapolis to discuss the plan with Governor Thomas R. Marshall. Cunningham won Marshall's endorsement and secured a joint legislative resolution empowering Representative William W. Spencer to assist Cunningham with the arrangements.[30] Cunningham devoted full attention to the Owen project in 1911. He hosted several fund-raising dinner parties in Indianapolis but the collection never exceeded $700. His thirteen-page ledger shows that contributions rarely topped a dollar each.[31] When Cunningham accepted a tablet design that would cost more than the budget allowed, he cheerfully paid the difference. "The editor . . . would live on bread and water that this most worthy undertaking be worthily executed," he insisted.[32] Cunningham prepared a pamphlet on Owen for distribution during the 1913 Christmas season to help defray the added expense. He admitted that the Owen drive was motivated by patriotism and personal gratitude.

When the monument was finished and in place, Governor Samuel Ralston accepted the tablet at the unveiling. "We should never look upon it without recalling the noble qualities of heart and soul of S. A. Cunningham," the Hoosier proclaimed in his opening remarks.[33] In the keynote address, Cunningham informed the audience in a lighthearted manner that many ex-Confederates considered Owen to be a "renegade Kentuckian." On a more serious note, he recounted the kind treatment that Owen had bestowed upon Confederate prisoners at Camp Morton. At the conclusion of the ceremony, he placed a copper box in the base of the pedestal, the contents of which remain unknown to this day. Then the tablet was sealed.[34]

At the conclusion of the ceremony, Cunningham summed up his feelings about his work on the Owen memorial:

I have done it through the aid of fellow prisoners, other comrades, and our friends. My conviction is that, in so far as undying souls take cognizance of what is done after their careers have been ended, more than four thousand are glad with me, and that in the greatest reunion ever to occur there will be greetings to me for this deed.[35]

After spending a lifetime in commemorative exercises for the Confederate heritage, Cunningham had paid the ultimate tribute to a former foe.

There is little doubt that Cunningham assumed a religious fervor in his work on the Sam Davis and Richard Owen monument drives. But were his motives as unselfish as the editor wanted others to believe, or was he driven by painful memories of his own Civil War experience and a need to identify himself with a hero to suppress the memory of his own questionable service to the Confederacy? Surely assuming some of Davis's perfection by such identification would have soothed Cunningham's tarnished self-image. And the two men had similarities that Cunningham could base such a bond on. Davis's boyhood closely resembled Cunningham's own. Like Cunningham, Davis had grown up in middle Tennessee on a rural farm with strict but religious parents. They "were old-fashioned people, God-fearing, simple-mannered, neither rich nor poor, and Sam grew up in the quiet ways of the Southern country boy," explained Cunningham.[36] Cunningham and Davis both turned eighteen in 1861, and when hostilities broke out, they both left school to join the Army of Tennessee. Cunningham frequently superimposed the familiar language of his own wartime diary on his accounts of Davis's experience, as when he wrote, "The peace and beauty of the [Smyrna] farm gave place to the wearisome tramp, the pangs of hunger, the cries of the wounded, and the pale faces of the dead."[37] It was clear that after a lapse of fifty years, vivid memories of the Civil War continued to haunt Cunningham.

Cunningham and Davis shared other important similarities, including a strong Christian faith, likeable personalities, and, above all, a commitment to the principles of honor and duty. "Next to God, above even his tender love for his mother and home, Sam cherished that old-time sense of 'honor,'" explained Cunningham. "The honor which gives my hero place among the immortals was of the kind that . . . gave one's life in devotion of duty."[38] In this Victorian language Cunningham penned not only Davis's biography but also his own fantasy autobiography, taking a new sense of self-worth from his association with Sam Davis.

Beyond identifying himself with Davis, Cunningham expounded un-

abashedly upon Davis's likeness to Jesus Christ. "In [his] faith to principles [it] is almost divine," recounted Cunningham, "and it recalls even
the sacrifice of the Galilean whose hands and feet were nailed to a cross."
Indeed, he wrote, "There has been no greater test of character since the
crucifixion. Eternity of bliss to such a man! Glory to his name!" he concluded loftily. Cunningham preached to Southerners from the front cover
of the *Veteran* that Sam Davis, like Jesus, "did not die in vain."[39]

Cunningham portrayed the events leading to Davis's execution as analogous to Christ's Passion. It will be recalled that Davis was captured in
1863 while scouting for the 1st Tennessee. The arresting Federal officer demanded that Davis reveal his source of information, just as earlier
judges had enjoined Christ to disclose the source of his knowledge. Davis
showed great composure in his resolve not to cooperate with his accusers.
Here in his analogy Cunningham cast General Dodge in the role of Pontius
Pilate: the reluctant warrior forced by his authoritative position to choose
between duty and conscience. Dodge convened a military tribunal to hear
Davis's case just as Pilate had compiled evidence from the council of chief
priests. Like Christ, Davis chose to remain silent throughout the interrogation. Davis's superior, Captain H. B. Shaw, had also been captured, but
he did not acknowledge Davis, and he remained silent on the source of his
intelligence. Shaw's uncooperative attitude sealed Davis's fate. His role
was drawn by Cunningham as parallel with that of Simon Peter, who denied Christ. Found guilty, both Davis and Christ were sentenced to die on
a Friday morning. Shortly before his execution, Davis entrusted to Chaplain James Young his Confederate overcoat, an action analogous to that in
which a Roman soldier received Christ's seamless robe at the crucifixion.

Cunningham loved and respected Sam Davis for many of the reasons he
revered Christ. Both Davis and Christ faced death stoicly, with courage,
reverence, and grace. And in the end, it was Cunningham's identification
with Davis's life and death that would cleanse him of wartime unfaithful-
ness to the Confederacy, just as he believed his worship of Christ would
cleanse him of all other sins.

Finally, Davis offered a short statement at the execution site, just as
Christ had done. The exact wording went unrecorded by contemporaries,
so Cunningham determined to produce the definitive version. After extensive research, he issued the following: "I would rather die a thousand
deaths than betray a friend or be false to duty."[40] Perhaps the editor was
unaware that an identical passage is purported to have been uttered by
another stoic hero of the South, Robert E. Lee.[41] Although the authen-

*Photograph taken at the dedication of the Sam Davis monument in Nashville.*
*Davis, a Confederate cavalryman, was captured by Union forces and executed*
*as a spy in 1863. Cunningham spearheaded the drive to raise funds for the*
*memorial. The Nashville chapter of the United Daughters of the Confederacy is*
*in the foreground; Nashville's Cheatham Bivouac color guard is in the*
*background. (Courtesy of the Tennessee State Library and Archive)*

ticity of the source is arguable, Cunningham's rendition has endured. It
appears in many prominent places: on the Davis monument in Nashville,
at the Sam Davis Museum in Smyrna, on the famous stained-glass window in the Tennessee Room at Richmond's Confederate Museum, and in
many reputable books on Tennessee history. As recently as 1986 a national
magazine for schoolchildren printed a drama of the Davis tragedy in which
it quoted Cunningham verbatim.[42] Whether or not Cunningham's statement was historically accurate is insignificant. What is important is that
it is accepted by and incorporated into the Southern folk fabric.

While Cunningham's motives in perpetuating Davis's memory were
largely personal, it must be emphasized that Samuel Davis is a hero for
Tennessee and the nation. In laying down his life for his country, the
cavalryman exemplified all that is noble and unselfish in soldiery. Cunningham's subconscious motives for glorifying Davis should neither tarnish nor
discredit his work in recording Davis's heroism for future generations.
The monument that stands silently on capitol hill speaks loudly to the
proud Confederate heritage of Tennessee.[43]

In his own judgment, Cunningham's two greatest accomplishments were the Sam Davis memorial and the Richard Owen tablet. The former released Cunningham from the psychological burden of a dismal war record through his identification with a hero. The latter enabled the editor to accept with finality the verdict of 1865. Thanks to his work on these memorials, the bitterness, hostility and shame associated with his past abated. As all men must do, he made peace with himself. For S. A. Cunningham, the Civil War had finally ended.

# Chapter 22 *"Having Done What He Could"*

By the end of 1912 Cunningham had reached the summit of a long and satisfying career in journalism. Accolades had been slow in coming at first but had increased steadily over the years. In great measure, his willingness to operate on a thin margin and other sacrificial choices brought about the success of the *Veteran*. Cunningham's fiery loyalty to the Confederate heritage embroiled him in controversies, but he survived each one. Eventually he won respect and support from every ex-Confederate body. By the end of his forty-two-year career, he had published a rich tapestry of Confederate military history for a younger generation of Southerners. When he went to the grave, he did so as a leading exemplar of the Confederate heritage.

In the twilight of his career, Cunningham was noted for publishing well-edited articles. He treasured one particular commendation from his old regimental commander. "As I get older," claimed James D. Tillman, "the *Veteran* seems to get better." Nashvillians came to recognize Cunningham as a prominent civic figure and its foremost authority on the Confederate heritage. The *Nashville City Directory* reserved its entire 1912 back cover to advertise the *Veteran*. The following year, the magazine adorned the front cover.[1]

Cunningham's health first showed signs of deterioration in 1901, at the height of the Underwood libel suit, when the trauma of his son's sudden death irritated a nervous condition. Thereafter, many observers believed, the editor slipped in and out of depression. Certainly a morose tone filtered onto the editorial page. Cunningham noted with sadness the increased number of deaths among his comrades and close friends with each passing year. He frequently ordered his favorite flower, the American Beauty rose, for the funeral coffins of deceased ex-Confederates.[2] Having out-lived most of his immediate family and friends, Cunningham had become a lonely man. He included rare photographs of his son and wife in several "Last Roll" columns.[3] At another sentimental time, he asked patrons to mail twenty thousand letters of congratulations on his birthday.[4] A full-page picture of Cunningham embellished the cover of the *Veteran* in 1910; this was an unusual occurrence.

The editor showed signs of advanced physical degeneration in 1909. Shortly after the dedication of the Sam Davis memorial he succumbed to "violent attacks" caused by an abscess after the removal of wisdom teeth. He convalesced for several weeks but admitted to a "deep depression."[5] The frightening episode reminded Cunningham of his own mortality. He also reflected on his work with the *Veteran*. Initially, the editor expressed self-doubts about the worthiness of his career in journalism. He eventually snapped out of this nostalgia phase to conclude that the *Veteran* provided a record to instruct the younger generation on the merits of the Confed-erate experience. Cunningham's increasing feebleness troubled him, and he pushed a resolution through Cheatham Bivouac calling on the UCV to charter the *Veteran* at the 1913 reunion.[6]

Cunningham's premonition of death led him to write a will. While he was convalescing in Arkansas with Virgil Y. Cook,[7] Cunningham drafted the document himself—a personal touch in keeping with his intimate owner-ship of the *Veteran*. "This is written by myself and may not be strictly legal in every sense," he explained, "but it is believed that my motives of integrity and duty would prevent anyone taking advantage of any such error."[8] His assets included two life insurance policies totaling $5,000 in value, a personal library, and the *Veteran*. "For what I possess I am so deeply indebted to the generous patriotic people of the South that I feel it due them to contribute what I have as herein briefly set forth to the perpetuation of such history as is so far recorded in the *Veteran*."[9] He bequeathed $1,000 to Mrs. Thomas (Addie) Wakefield, his sister; estab-lished a board of trustees headed by Cook to manage the *Veteran;* and des-ignated Edith Pope, his long-time secretary, to operate the magazine.[10] It was paramount in Cunningham's mind to address the issue of perpetuating the message of the *Veteran*.

Cunningham's physical deterioration was chronicled by several North Carolinians in 1911. In a highly critical account to Professor J. G. deRoul-hac Hamilton, Rebecca Cameron stated that Cunningham was "not to be judged by the social standards of a gentleman." In the same correspondence, she made reference to a comment made by William DeRossett that Cunningham was the "very roughest specimen that ever sat at his table."[11] This gossip, if reliable, is testimony to Cunningham's declining health because it contrasted sharply with his widely-held reputation of gentility.

Though Cunningham seldom discussed his own journalistic accomplishments in print, in his sixty-ninth year he described his productive career with sincere humility. "No, no. The founder of the *Veteran* asks no honor," he said. "He is simply doing his best in a cause so sacred that he asks nothing of himself. He doesn't expect any other reward than that of the consciousness of having done what he could."[12] Four months later, during the Christmas season, he penned the most personal article ever to appear in the *Veteran*.

> The rounding out of twenty years' service has long been the wish of a contrite heart. . . . Twenty years in directing a periodical—a monthly magazine—from its founding by one of ownership and management has rarely occurred in the history of journalism. And then to be the authorized representative of all the great Confederate organizations . . . should satisfy the ambitions of any human being. The character of work has ever been an inspiration, while the responsibility has been constantly exacting. Throughout this fifth of a century the one purpose has been to give expression to eternity. Faults in the work have been many. . . . But at all times the best has been done that could be under the circumstances.[13]

Throughout 1913 the editor battled several debilitating ailments but refused to give in to them. He took a rare vacation to the Panama Canal and laid out plans to build a monument to Daniel Decatur Emmett, the composer of "Dixie."[14] He also worked on the Sam Davis and Richard Owen pamphlets for distribution at Christmastime, but these combined narratives were published posthumously, for, on 20 December 1913, S. A. Cunningham went to the ultimate Confederate reunion he had long anticipated.[15]

Cunningham had announced two years before his death that he desired to be buried in his hometown. He had also requested that his grave be marked with a simple granite block and inscribed to read "Founder of the Confederate Veteran." But on the day of his interment, Susie Gentry, great-niece of Meredith P. Gentry, suggested in the *Nashville Banner* that Tennesseans erect a monument to honor the deceased editor. Commander Young liked the plan and convened a meeting of interested veterans fol-

*Cunningham's casket, draped in the Stars and Bars and guarded by his Cheatham Bivouac comrades. From* Confederate Veteran *22 (January 1914).*

lowing the interment in Shelbyville to discuss it. They agreed to sponsor a people's monument for which donations were not to exceed five dollars a person. Young asked Edith Pope to act as treasurer of the fund. The committee originally chose to locate the monument in Nashville's Centennial Park.[16]

The Cunningham memorial project dragged on for seven years. Despite their original enthusiasm, Confederate organizations collected less than $4,000. Consequently, the committee decided to modify its original plan. In 1921 the UCV and UDC unveiled on the grave site an eight-foot obelisk with a chiseled visage of Cunningham.[17]

Pope made a valiant effort to keep the *Veteran* solvent. Lawyers estimated that the editor's estate would sustain the magazine for several years. Moreover, Cunningham had compiled an ample reserve of articles for publication. But the distinctive Cunningham flair was missing.[18]

The board of trustees, announcing its commitment to maintain the *Veteran*, established a set of bylaws and agreed to meet annually. Future sessions were filled with business concerns ranging from salaries and hiring new staff to discussing a proposed Cunningham Memorial Museum in Nashville.[19]

Edith Pope faced insurmountable problems as editor. The decrease in the number of remaining veterans combined with declining public interest in the magazine, and many subscribers neglected to pay the $1.50 rate even though it remained fixed for the next two decades. As a result, the subscription list dwindled. By 1914 the social and cultural importance of the Confederate tradition had subsided.[20]

To continue on a smaller budget, Pope reduced the length of the journal and published shorter articles. In a more drastic cut, she began publishing the *Veteran* on a bimonthly basis. The UDC graciously subsidized the magazine in its last years, but the financial burden became excessive. Pope issued two special notices in 1932 pleading with customers to pay their bills. She even reduced the cover price by twenty percent. But none of these measures helped. The Great Depression finished off the magazine, which had teetered on the brink of foreclosure for several years. It is a tribute to Cunningham's farsighted planning and Pope's diligence in carrying out his vision that the magazine lasted for nineteen years after Cunningham's death.

The last issue of the *Veteran*, in December 1932, did not go unnoticed. "Wholly aside from sentimental considerations," said the *Arkansas Gazette*, "this magazine has been a great repository of history, and a valuable supplement to formal works. . . . The South, where traditions are still so deeply rooted, must profoundly regret the passing of this magazine."[21]

Edith Pope was a faithful employee for the thirty-nine-year existence of the *Veteran*. It is appalling that Cunningham mentioned her only once, in an 1894 editorial that recognized her tireless service to the goals of the magazine. He wrote,

> Like many other Southern women to whom the war is as a dream, she is an ardent believer in the sacred principles her father and friends fought for and is a worshiper of the memories of the 'lost cause' and is devoted to the story of its victories and defeats, and the valor of its brave soldiers and heroic leaders.[22]

Pope reciprocated later with kind remarks of her own. "We are feeling the loss of our Editor very keenly," she confided to a friend several days after Cunningham's death.[23] But she bravely carried out his instructions and policies until the magazine folded. Two years after the demise of the *Veteran*, she was asked by two dealers in historic letters to write a biographical sketch of Cunningham and agreed to do so, but the project was never finished. Ten years later, she commissioned the same agents to sell Cunningham's personal set of the *Veteran*.[24] In her retirement, she continued to serve the Tennessee UDC, once as an honorary president and chair of the powerful history committee. Edith Pope died on 24 January 1947.[25]

# *Epilogue*

"T he South was his passion," Dr. James I. Vance said
of Cunningham, "and he loved it passionately with every fiber of his
being."[1] The indomitable spirit of the editor to present the Confederate
heritage in unmistakable terms led him to recognize the historical mission
of his life's work, the *Confederate Veteran.*[2] While he was a man of no
more than average intellect, the magazine he so zealously produced for
twenty years is an irreplaceable document in Southern historiography.

Cunningham's influence is still apparent. Distant relatives are accepted
into organizations of Confederate descendants because of his participation
in the Civil War.[3] Beginning in 1921, the UDC sponsored the Cunningham Memorial Scholarship at Peabody College in Nashville. In the following decade, a syndicated radio broadcast, lauding the former editor, was
heard throughout the South. In more recent times, the *Encyclopedia of
the Civil War* (1986) includes an entry describing the *Veteran* along with a
photograph of its founder. A complete bound set of the magazine is an expensive commodity among used and rare book dealers today. But, perhaps
the greatest testimonial to the enduring power of Cunningham's message
was the rebirth of the *Confederate Veteran* in Murfreesboro in 1985, and
shortly thereafter the creation of the *Journal of Confederate History* at
Middle Tennessee State University, also in Murfreesboro.[4]

S. A. Cunningham spoke loudly to thousands of common Southern men
and women who survived and adapted to the most cataclysmic event of
nineteenth-century America. William Faulkner wrote with considerable
feeling about Cunningham's generation in describing the lesson that all
Southern men must come to grips with concerning their Confederate
heritage.

It's all *now* you see. . . . For every southern boy fourteen years old, not
once but whenever he wants it, there is the instant when it's still not yet
two o'clock on that July afternoon in 1863, the brigades are in position
behind the rail fence, the guns are laid and ready in the woods and the
furled flags are already loosened to break out and Pickett himself . . .
looking up the hill waiting for Longstreet to give the word and it's all
in the balance, it hasn't happened yet, it hasn't even begun yet, it not
only hasn't begun yet but there is still time for it not to begin against
that position and . . . yet it's going to begin, we all know that, we have
come too far with too much at stake and that moment doesn't need even
a fourteen-year-old boy to think *This time. Maybe this time.*[5]

The Civil War made an indelible imprint on the character of S. A. Cunningham, and through his meticulous preservation of the Confederate
heritage, Cunningham affected the way that war was remembered. The
man and the heritage were inextricably bound together.

# Notes

## Prologue

1. *Nashville American*, 30 April 1909.
2. James I. Vance Collection, Scrapbook no. 1, 1899–1917, Manuscript Division, Tennessee State Library and Archives (hereafter cited as TSLA). The description of the dedication by Dr. H. M. Hamill, chaplain-general of the United Confederate Veterans (UCV), is in the introduction to Sumner Archibald Cunningham, *Sam Davis: The Story of an Old-Fashioned Boy* (Nashville: Confederate Veteran, 1914); *Nashville Tennessean*, 27 December 1913; *Confederate Veteran* 21 (July 1913): 323 (hereafter cited as *CV*).
3. Whenever Fields's troupe visited Nashville they always performed "Dixie" in front of the *Veteran* office. The practice continued even after the deaths of Cunningham and Fields. See S. A. Cunningham File, Methodist Publishing House Archive, Nashville, Tenn.
4. See *Nashville Tennessean*, 21 December 1913; *Nashville Banner*, 22 December 1913; *Shelbyville Gazette*, 25 December 1913; *CV* 22 (January 1914): 6–10.
5. *CV* 22 (January 1914): 12; *Nashville Banner*, 22 December 1913.
6. James I. Vance Collection, Scrapbook no. 1, TSLA.
7. James I. Vance Collection, Scrapbook no. 1, TSLA; S. A. Cunningham File, United Daughters of the Confederacy Library, Richmond, Va; Jerry W. Cook, *Obituaries of Our Ancestors as Transcribed from the Shelbyville Gazette, Bedford County, Tennessee* (Wartrace, Tenn., 1990): 56.
8. The 1962 recollection of Sarah Buchanan Robinson is in the possession of Sally Moulder of Shelbyville, Tenn. Also see V. Y. Cook to William E. Mickle, 23 December 1913, Adjutant General's Correspondence, United Confederate Veteran's Association Collection, Louisiana State University.

# Chapter 1: Family Ties

1. Humphrey Cunningham (13 April 1777–15 August 1836) lived with his wife, Margaret Patton Cunningham (12 June 1780–3 February 1847), and their nine children in the militia district of Captain Benjamin Hewitt. See the Frederick Brown Bible in Helen Crawford Marsh and Timothy Richard Marsh, *Bedford County, Tennessee, County Clerk's Office, Tax Lists, 1812; Who's Who in Tennessee: A Bibliographical Reference Book of Notable Tennesseans of Today* (Memphis: Paul and Douglas Co., 1911): 411.

2. Frederick Brown Bible, 135.

3. "Bedford County Tax List, 1836," *Bedford County Historical Quarterly* 3 (1979): 36. Also see *Bedford County, Register's Office, Deed Book FF; Tennessee Records of Bedford County, General Index to Deeds, 1808–1840*, 3 vols. (Nashville: Historical Records Survey, Works Progress Administration, 1940): 73; *Map of Bedford County, Tennessee* (Philadelphia: D.G. Beers, 1878).

4. Richmond was a thriving community in the mid-1830s. It boasted a store, church, chartered academy, and one of twelve county post offices. See R. L. Patterson, "Richmond," *Bedford County Historical Quarterly* 3 (Spring 1979): 10; Amie Caldwell McGrew, "Bedford County Communities," *Bedford County Historical Quarterly* 1 (Spring 1977): 4.

5. In 1840 J. W. C. Cunningham owned no slaves and paid only five dollars in property taxes. In fact, only fifty-eight slaves lived in the entire nineteenth civil district. See *Bedford County, Tennessee, County Clerk's Office, Tax Lists 1839; U.S. Department of Commerce, Bureau of the Census, Sixth Census of the United States, 1840; White Population.* (Hereafter, all census reports will be cited in short form.)

Sarah Cunningham died on 17 August 1837 and was buried in the Couch family section of Zion Hill Church Cemetery near Wartrace. See Marsh and Marsh, 69; private records of Sally Moulder, assistant to the county clerk, Bedford County, Tenn.

6. *Marriage Records, Tennessee*, Microfiche Collection, Church Library, Church of Jesus Christ of Latter-Day Saints, Eugene, Oreg.; *Nashville Daily American*, 4 March 1890; *Shelbyville Gazette*, 6 March 1890. Catherine Clinton argues that Southern women were the guardians of the culture, and "modeling" religious virtue was an important component. See Catherine Clinton, *The Plantation Mistress: Women's World in the Old South* (New York: Pantheon Books, 1982): 90–95.

7. Cunningham's sister and niece also attended school through 1860. See *8th Census, 1860, White Population.* For more on the local education system, see Rose Tate Stewart, "Pioneer Schools of Bedford County and their Masters," History Room, Bedford County Library, Shelbyville, Tenn.; *Who's Who in Tennessee:* 411; *Centennial Celebration, 4th of July, 1876. At Shelbyville, Bedford County, Tennessee* (Chattanooga: Crandall, 1877): 17; A. V. Goodpasture, *A History of Tennessee* (Nashville: Goodspeed, 1886): 882; Stanley J. Folmsbee, Robert E. Corlew, and Enoch L. Mitchell, *Tennessee: A Short History* (Knoxville: University of Tennes-

see Press, 1969): 273; J. K. P. Thompson file, *Civil War Questionnaires*, 22 vols. (Nashville: Tennessee Historical Commission, 1922): 8: 124; Thomas D. Clark, *Pills, Petticoats and Plows: The Southern Country Store* (New York: Bobbs-Merrill, 1944): 174–75.

8. Three-fourths of all children enrolled in private academies came from the slaveholding and yeoman classes. See Fred Arthur Bailey, *Class and Tennessee's Confederate Generation* (Chapel Hill: University of North Carolina Press, 1987): 46–50, 151–52.

9. S. A. Cunningham remained a faithful Cumberland Presbyterian all of his life. See *Who's Who in Tennessee*, 411; *Minutes of the Twenty-seventh General Assembly of the Cumberland Presbyterian Church in the United States* (St. Louis: Republican, 1857): 67. The rural churches in Bedford County were important social centers too. Preaching often mingled with singing and fellowship. See Gilley Stephens, "Early Church History of Bedford County," History Room, Bedford County Library, Shelbyville, Tenn.

10. Thomas L. Connelly, *Civil War Tennessee: Battles and Leaders* (Knoxville: University of Tennessee Press, 1979): 13. The richness of Bedford County is further documented by its large production of oats, rye, horses, mules, cattle, sheep, and hogs. See Goodpasture, *History of Tennessee*, 861–65; *Centennial Celebration*, 13–16; *Shelbyville Times-Gazette*, 7 October 1969, p. 17; Roger L. Hart, *Redeemers, Bourbons and Populists: Tennessee, 1870–1896* (Baton Rouge: Louisiana State University Press, 1975): 140.

11. Stephen V. Ash, *Middle Tennessee Society Transformed, 1860–1870: War and Peace in the Upper South* (Baton Rouge: Louisiana State University Press, 1988): 21.

12. See *CV* 14 (June 1906): 256. For more on the upward mobility of the yeoman class, see Blanche Henry Clark, *The Tennessee Yeoman, 1840–1860* (Nashville: Vanderbilt University Press, 1942).

13. *8th Census, 1860, Slave Abstracts; 8th Census, 1860, White Population;* Donald B. Dodd and Wynette S. Dodd, eds., *Historical Statistics of the South, 1790–1970* (University: University of Alabama Press, 1973); Folmsbee, Corlew, and Mitchell, *Tennessee*, 217.

14. *6th Census, 1840, Slave Abstracts; 7th Census, 1850, Slave Abstracts; 8th Census, 1860, Slave Abstracts.* Of the five slaves owned in 1850, three were females aged 23, 9, and 4. The males were aged 6 and 3. The additional slaves in 1860 were all females aged 9, 7 and 5. It is not known how Cunningham acquired the new slaves. See *8th Census, 1860, Slave Abstracts; Shelbyville Gazette*, 7 October 1969, p. 24.

15. Historian Gavin Wright argued that many middle-class farmers supported the Confederacy only because they hoped to own more slaves in the future. For more on the psychological implications connected with loyalty to the Confederacy, see Gavin Wright, *The Political Economy of the Cotton South: Households, Markets, and Wealth in the Nineteenth Century* (New York: Norton, 1978): 144–57; Reid Mitchell, *Civil War Soldiers: Their Expectations and Their Experiences* (New York: Touchstone Books, 1988): 7–8; Rollin G. Osterweis, *The Myth of the*

*Lost Cause, 1865–1900* (Hamden, Conn.: Archon Books, 1973): 4; Ash, *Middle Tennessee Society,* 10, 15, 44.

16. See Chase C. Mooney, *Slavery in Tennessee* (Bloomington: Indiana University Press, 1957): 122; *7th Census, 1850, Slave Abstracts; 8th Census, 1860, Slave Abstracts.*

17. *7th Census, 1850, Agricultural Schedule; 8th Census, 1860, Agricultural Schedule.* Also see *Bedford County, Register's Office, Deed Book DDD.*

18. Helen Crawford Marsh and Timothy Richard Marsh, *Cemetery Records of Bedford County, Tennessee* (Shelbyville, Tenn.: Marsh, 1976): 69.

19. Catherine Clinton argues persuasively that uncles were highly valued during emergencies for family and financial assistance. Lacking clearly defined legal rights widows were usually at the financial mercy of men. See Clinton, *The Plantation Mistress,* 5–8.

20. *CV* 5 (July 1897): 339.

21. See "Sumner A. Cunningham and the Confederate Veteran Magazine," *Southern Magazine* 34 (1934): 26, 49. For more on the role of women modeling the lessons of culture to their kin, see Clinton, *The Plantation Mistress,* 95.

22. C. Vann Woodward, *Thinking Back: The Perils of Writing History* (Baton Rouge: Louisiana State University Press, 1987): 35.

## Chapter 2: The Civil War Approaches

1. Ten of Bedford County's twenty voting districts voted traditionally for the Whig party. Cunningham's nineteenth civil district was Democratic, thus his family's political leanings were in the minority. See *Shelbyville Expositor,* 11 October 1861; *Centennial Celebration,* p. 24; W. Dean Burnham, *Presidential Ballots, 1832–1896* (Baltimore: Johns Hopkins University Press, 1955): 215, 742.

2. Thelma Jennings, *The Nashville Convention: Southern Movement for Unity, 1848–1851* (Memphis: Memphis State University Press, 1980): 95, 236. G. W. Cunningham was an established planter in 1850. His real estate and agricultural productivity tripled that of J. W. C. Cunningham. See *7th Census, Agricultural Schedule, Bedford County, Tennessee; U.S. Census, Agricultural Schedule, Bedford County, Tennessee, 1860.*

3. Judge H. L. Davidson made this comment eleven years after the war ended. See *Centennial Celebration,* 24. For statewide returns, see *History of Tennessee,* 519, 534; Marcus Wright, *Tennessee in the War, 1861–1865: Lists of Military Organizations and Officers from Tennessee in both the Confederate and Union Armies* (New York: Williamsbridge Press, 1908): 9. Bedford County not only disfavored secession. The county seat at Shelbyville remained a hotbed of Unionism throughout the war. In fact, the town earned the wartime nickname "Little Boston." See *Shelbyville Times-Gazette,* 7 October 1969, p. 69; Goodpasture, *History of Tennessee,* 872; Ash, *Middle Tennessee Society,* 69–73.

4. See Oliver P. Temple, *Notable Men of Tennessee: From 1833 to 1875* (New York: Cosmopolitan Press, 1912): 234. Meredeth P. Gentry was a successful farmer,

lawyer, and politician with a national reputation. He served in the Tennessee state legislature in the 1830s and in the House of Representatives from 1839 to 1853. Gentry, a lifelong Whig, ran unsuccessfully for governor in 1855 on the Know-Nothing ticket. He retired from politics to manage his Bedford County plantation, Hillside.

5. *Nashville Daily American*, 18 January 1889. Also see *CV* 21 (January 1913): 5.

6. Gentry sold his farm in 1861 and invested all of the proceeds from the sale (reportedly over $100,000) in Confederate war bonds. Gentry also won a seat and served with distinction in the Confederate Congress. See *Shelbyville Times-Gazette*, 7 October 1969, p. 55; Folmsbee, *Tennessee*, 235; Temple, *Notable Men of Tennessee*, 234–42; *CV* 19 (September 1911): 424. Some men converted to secession only after the conflict became sectional in nature. See Reid Mitchell, *Civil War Soldiers: Their Expectations and Their Experiences* (New York: Touchstone, 1988): 9.

7. *Our Day* 1 (May 1883): 110.

8. "Thomas Rawlings Myers' Memoirs, March 28, 1916," *Bedford County Historical Quarterly* 5 (Spring 1981): 59.

9. *Shelbyville Expositor*, 11 October 1861. The extreme northern and southern districts of Bedford County contributed the most volunteers to the Confederate army. See *Shelbyville Times-Gazette*, 7 October 1969, 69.

10. Although some were reluctant to volunteer, they enlisted largely because of their loyalty to family and home. See Mitchell, *Civil War Soldiers*, 10–16; Larry J. Daniel, *Soldiering in the Army of Tennessee: A Portrait of Life in a Confederate Army* (Chapel Hill: University of North Carolina Press, 1991): 14.

11. Thomas L. Connelly, *The Army of the Heartland: The Army of Tennessee, 1861–1862* (Baton Rouge: Louisiana State University Press, 1967): 25, 33–38; Wright, *Tennessee in the War*, 9. By December the state had furnished seventy-one regiments.

12. *Bedford County, Register's Office, Deed Book DDD*. Also see *CV* 21 (January 1913): 5.

13. S. A. Cunningham, *Reminiscences of the 41st Tennessee Regiment* (Shelbyville: Commercial Press, 1872): 3; Confederate War Records Division. Record Group 241, in *Compiled Service Records of Confederate Soldiers Who Served in Organizations From the State of Tennessee, 41st Infantry, A–C*, roll 281 (Washington D.C.: Archives, 1959). Hereafter cited as *Confederate Archives*, roll 281. Also see *CV* 21 (January 1913): 5; Richard M. McMurray, *Two Great Rebel Armies* (Chapel Hill: University of North Carolina Press, 1989): 91. Reid Mitchell suggests that such community send-offs became institutionalized with speeches, flag presentations, and a barbeque held in the town square. See Mitchell, *Civil War Soldiers*, 11. For an original picture of Cunningham in his homespun attire see *CV* 3 (December 1895): 379.

14. Cunningham, *Reminiscences*, 3; *Confederate Archives*, roll 281.

15. See Bailey, *Tennessee's Confederate Generation*, 77–78. In *Embattled Courage: The Experience of Combat in the American Civil War* (New York: Free Press, 1987); 7–15, Gerald Linderman suggests that the enlistees were testing them-

selves against feminine influences in their lives. Similarly, Reid Mitchell (p. 17) suggests that family honor was a powerful incentive for enlistment. Indeed, the recruits not only represented their families. It was part of the masculine role to defend the homeland.

16. Peter Maslowski analyzed fifty wartime diaries and concluded that Civil War soldiers fought for one of three reasons: love of country, belief in a better future, or belief in certain basic issues. See Maslowski, "A Study of Morale in Civil War Soldiers," *Military Affairs*, 34 (1970): 123. For a similar view, see Wright, *The Political Economy of the Cotton South*, 144–57.


## Chapter 3: The Experience Begins

1. J. M. Lindsley, ed., *The Military Annals of Tennessee: A Review of Military Operations with Regimental Histories and Memorial Rolls* (Nashville: Lindsley Publishers, 1886): 510.

2. Robert Farquaharson was born in Banff, Scotland. He emigrated to Tennessee in the 1830s. During the Mexican War he rose to the rank of major with the 1st Tennessee Volunteers. See Robert Farquaharson Biographical Sketch, Manuscript Division, Tennessee State Library and Archive; Cunningham, *Reminiscences*, 3; Lindsley, *Military Annals*, 510–11; W. J. Davidson, "Diary of Private W. J. Davidson, Company C, Forty-First Tennessee Regiment," in Edwin L. Drake, ed., *The Annals of the Army of Tennessee* (Nashville: A. D. Haynes, 1878): 16; William F. Amann, *Personnel of the Civil War*, 2 vols. (New York: Yoseloff, 1961): 1:128.

3. Lindsley, *Military Annals*, 510; Confederate War Records Division, Record Group 241; in *Consolidated Index to Compiled Service Records of Confederate Soldiers, M253 Cumm-Curles*, roll 111 (Washington, D.C.: National Archives, 1959). Also see Bailey, *Tennessee's Confederate Generation*, 79; Daniel, *Soldiering in Army of Tennessee*, 15, 106.

4. The weapons shortage in the Army of Tennessee was a sad story. Some soldiers did not receive proper weapons until April 1862. For more information on Confederate weapons, see Claud E. Fuller and Richard D. Steuart, *Firearms of the Confederacy* (Huntington, W. Va.: Standard Publications, 1944): 224; Fairfax Downey, *Storming the Gateway: Chattanooga, 1863* (New York: McKay, 1960): 35–36; Bell I. Wiley, *The Life of Johnny Reb: The Common Soldier of the Confederacy* (Baton Rouge: Louisiana State University Press, 1978 reprint): 287–90; Stanley Horn, *The Army of Tennessee: A Military History* (New York: Bobbs-Merrill, 1991): 58; Connelly, *Army of the Heartland*, 29.

5. Cunningham, *Reminiscences*, 1–43; *CV* 18 (October 1910): 456; Linderman, *Embattled Courage*, 37; Daniel, *Soldiering in Army of Tennessee*, 23. David Donald described this early crisis in training camp: "The distinctive thing about the Confederate army is that Southern soldiers never truly accepted the idea that discipline is necessary to the effective functioning of a fighting force." See Donald, "The Confederate As a Fighting Man," *Journal of Southern History* 30 (1959): 180.

6. Thomas Connelly referred to the productive cordon between Nashville and Macon as the Confederate heartland because of its tremendous wealth in raw materials, manufacturing, and urban centers. See Connelly, *Army of the Heartland*, 3–8; Peter Franklin Walker, "Building a Tennessee Army: Autumn, 1861," *Tennessee Historical Quarterly* 16 (June 1957): 99–116.

7. Some men received flintlock rifles on 4 January 1862. See Cunningham, *Reminiscences*, 4.

8. See Cunningham's reflection in *Nashville Daily American*, 24 October 1889.

9. The half-life of a Southern regiment was fixed at one year. A full regiment, ideally a thousand men, would be reduced to fewer than two hundred effectives within three years. The average Southern soldier was ill and/or wounded six times during the war. The odds of not surviving were one to four. Three times as many soldiers died from disease as from battle-related injuries. Medical problems were so acute that one volume of the *Official Record* was devoted to diarrhea. The usual pattern for illness among new regiments started with an outbreak of childhood diseases like measles. See Paul E. Steiner, *Disease in the Civil War: Natural Biological Warfare in 1861–1865* (Springfield, Ill.: Charles C. Thomas, 1968): 8–12; Stewart Brooks, *Civil War Medicine* (Springfield, Ill.: Charles C. Thomas, 1966): 6–11, 108; Wiley, *Life of Johnny Reb*, 244–46; Connelly, *Army of the Heartland*, 70.

10. Cunningham, *Reminiscences*, 4. The provisional Confederate government of Kentucky resided in Russellville. See Thomas Connelly and Archer Jones, *The Politics of Command: Factions and Ideas in Confederate Strategy* (Baton Rouge: Louisiana State University Press, 1973): 74; James J. Hamilton, *The Battle of Fort Donelson* (South Brunswick, N.J.: Yoseloff, 1968): 12; Arndt M. Stickles, *Simon B. Buckner, Borderland Knight* (Chapel Hill: University of North Carolina Press, 1940): 118–19; Charles P. Roland, *Albert Sidney Johnston: Soldier of Three Republics* (Austin: University of Texas Press, 1964): 290; Connelly, *Army of the Heartland*, 109.

11. Cunningham, *Reminiscences*, 4; Hamilton, *Battle of Fort Donelson*, 62; Stickles, *Buckner*, 132. B. F. Cooling maintains that Gen. Albert Sidney Johnston's defense was marred by "muddled indecision." Not once did Johnston inspect Fort Henry or Fort Donelson. Furthermore, he spread the command too thin over six separate areas. See Benjamin Franklin Cooling, *Forts Henry and Donelson: The Key to the Confederate Heartland* (Knoxville: University of Tennessee Press, 1987): 57, 126–28.

12. See Connelly, *Army of the Heartland*, 115–16; Stickles, *Buckner*, 132.

13. *War of the Rebellion: A Compilation of the Official Records of the Union and Confederate Armies*, 128 vols. (Washington, D.C.: Government Printing Office, 1880–1901), Series 1, 7: 341–42. Hereafter cited in notes to this chapter as *O.R.* 7.

14. Hamilton, *Battle of Fort Donelson*, 83–93; I, *O.R.* 7: 329, 337, 346–47; Horn, *Army of Tennessee*, 84; Stickles, *Buckner*, 128–30. The late arrival of the 41st illustrates Johnson's desire to withdraw the Confederate forces to Nashville. See Cooling, *Forts Henry and Donelson*, 138.

15. Cunningham, *Reminiscences*, 4. Also see Wiley, *Life of Johnny Reb*, 24.

16. The *Carondelet* peppered the town and fort with 158 shells in two hours but retreated when a shot from a Confederate shore battery tore into its hull. See Connelly, *Army of the Heartland*, 118; Cooling, *Forts Henry and Donelson*, 142–45; Horn, *Army of Tennessee*, 88; *Nashville Daily American*, 10 March 1890.

17. Cunningham, *Reminiscences*, 4–5; *Nashville Daily American*, 10 March 1890. For general comments on this type of experience, see Wiley, *Life of Johnny Reb*, 29; Linderman, *Embattled Courage*, 124; Mitchell, *Civil War Soldiering*, 63.

18. Cunningham, *Reminiscences*, 5; Horn, *Army of Tennessee*, 89; Connelly, *Army of the Heartland*, 114; Cooling, *Forts Henry and Donelson*, 147, 272.

19. Cunningham, *Reminiscences*, 6. The coming of nightfall often brought disorganization as soldiers often separated from their regiments. See Wiley, *Life of Johnny Reb*, 74.

20. A historian commented on the battle of Fort Donelson, "The more individualistic soldiers would pause with an organized unit and add to its fire power no matter what his regimental badge said. The more insecure would wander around through the fields, up and down the firing lines telling everyone he was searching for his regiment." See Hamilton, *Battle of Fort Donelson*, 208. Wiley (p. 31) similarly described the first fight as an informal affair. In fact, it was exceptional when a soldier finished a fight with his original unit. See Wiley, *Life of Johnny Reb*, 31.

21. Cunningham, *Reminiscences*, 6; I, *O.R.* 7: 344; Hamilton, *Battle of Fort Donelson*, 166–86; Stickles, *Buckner*, 141; Cooling, *Forts Henry and Donelson*, 171–74.

22. Hamilton, *Battle of Fort Donelson*, 240–41; Connelly, *Army of the Heartland*, 122; I, *O.R.* 7: 332. Cooling points out that political haggling between Pillow and Buckner in 1857 may have been at the core of their miscommunication at Fort Donelson. See Cooling, *Forts Henry and Donelson*, 132, 181–87.

23. See *Nashville Daily American*, 10 March 1890.

24. Ibid.; Cunningham, *Reminiscences*, 6.

25. Hamilton, *Battle of Fort Donelson*, 319; Cooling, *Forts Henry and Donelson*, 205, 213. Some members of the 41st Tennessee escaped and were reassigned to the 35th and 44th Tennessee. See *Confederate Archives*, roll 281.

26. For more on the lack of will to fight, see Richard E. Beringer, Herman Hattaway, Archer Jones, and William N. Still, Jr., *Why the South Lost the Civil War* (Athens: University of Georgia Press, 1986): 336–67. For specific references to this problem at Fort Donelson, see Cooling, *Forts Henry and Donelson*, xiii.

27. See *Nashville Banner*, 22 December 1913. Mitchell argues that the dehumanizing aspects of the Civil War—disease, filth, and sudden death—changed men forever. The war became a major psychological transformation in their lives. See Mitchell, *Civil War Soldiers*, 56; Cooling, *Forts Henry and Donelson*, 269–71.

## Chapter 4: Camp Morton

1. See *Nashville Daily American*, 10 March 1890. For complete surrender figures, see Cooling, *Forts Henry and Donelson*, 216–23.

2. The Federals sent the Southern enlisted men captured at Fort Donelson to Camp Douglas (Chicago), Camp Chase (Columbus, Ohio), Camp Butler (Springfield, Illinois), or Camp Morton (Indianapolis). See Hattie L. Winslow and Joseph R. H. Moore, *Camp Morton, 1861–1865* (Indianapolis: Indiana Historical Society, 1940): 253.

3. See *CV* 1 (September 1893): 273.

4. Cunningham, *Reminiscences*, 7; Cooling, *Forts Henry and Donelson*, 219.

5. Cunningham, *Reminiscences*, 7; *CV* 5 (January 1897): 33; *Indianapolis Daily Journal*, 24 February 1862; Winslow and Moore, *Camp Morton*, 256.

6. Cunningham, *Reminiscences*, 8. Within three weeks the prison population grew to 3,233, including 395 members of the 41st Tennessee. See *Indianapolis Daily Journal*, 17 March 1862; Winslow and Moore, *Camp Morton*, 258; *Confederate Archives*, roll 281; *Selected Records of the War Department Relating to Confederate Prisoners of War, 1861–1865*, roll 102 (Washington, D.C.: U.S. National Archives, 1959). Hereafter cited as *War Department*, roll 102.

7. Cunningham, *Reminiscences*, 8; "Thomas Rawlings Myers' Memoirs, March 28, 1916," *Bedford County Historical Quarterly* 5 (Fall 1981): 60; *Indianapolis Daily Journal*, 24 February 1862.

8. For more on the preparation of Camp Morton, see Winslow and Moore, *Camp Morton*, 256–76; Cunningham, *Reminiscences*, 8; James Carnahan, "Treatment of Prisoners at Camp Morton," *Century Magazine* 42 (1891): 757–75.

9. *CV* 5 (January 1897): 33.

10. Cunningham, *Reminiscences*, 11. Richard Owen was the son of Robert Owen, the Scotsman who founded the utopian settlement at New Harmony, Indiana. See Charles M. Cummings, "Richard Owen, Teacher in Tennessee," *Tennessee Historical Quarterly* 28 (1969): 273–96.

11. Cunningham, *Reminiscences*, 9; Winslow and Moore, *Camp Morton*, 262–70.

12. *Indianapolis Daily Journal*, 24 February 1862; Winslow and Moore, *Camp Morton*, 252–60, 305; From February to August 1862, 265 prisoners died at Camp Morton. See Ibid., 312.

13. Cunningham, *Reminiscences*, 8.

14. *Confederate Archives*, roll 281.

15. The easiest hospital to escape from was located on Meridian Street. The Federals closed it in April. See *Indianapolis Daily Journal*, 4 April 1862.

16. *CV* 10 (September 1912): 405.

17. This incident concerned the community and probably influenced Owen's removal as commandant two months later. Two weeks after the incident, Owen ordered a crackdown on knives and small pistols in the prisoners' possession. See *Indianapolis Daily Journal*, 16 April 1862; Winslow and Moore, *Camp Morton*, 274–75.

18. For Cunningham's version of the Fourth of July episode, see Cunningham, *Reminiscences*, 9–10. Also see Winslow and Moore, *Camp Morton*, 288.

19. Evander Shapard of Shelbyville recalled that evening as a "silent celebra-

tion." As the camp quieted down, Shapard said that the prisoners shared a genuine sense of joy. See *CV* 8 (May 1900): 211.

20. Prior to the mass escape, only thirteen prisoners had successfully fled from Camp Morton. Cunningham's half-brother, Joseph, and a kinsman, William, joined the party that left on July 14. See *Indianapolis Daily Journal*, 17 July 1862; *Confederate Archives*, roll 281; Cunningham, *Reminiscences*, 10; I, *O.R.* 4: 225; Winslow and Moore, *Camp Morton*, 292.

21. Cunningham, *Reminiscences*, 11. If a prisoner signed the Federal loyalty oath, which included a proviso that he should never bear rebellious arms again, he could go home immediately. Many prisoners of war viewed with contempt those men who signed the oath.

22. Ibid. Also see Mitchell, *Civil War Soldiers*, 47. For other accounts of the Camp Morton episode, see the Charles F. Blackwell file, *Civil War Questionnaires* (Nashville: Tennessee Historical Commission, 1922), 1: 224; Winslow and Moore, *Camp Morton*, 295.

23. *CV* 10 (April 1912): 151.

24. Cunningham, *Reminiscences*, 11; *Nashville Daily American*, 14 September 1891. The actual departure of prisoners from Camp Morton occurred as follows: 1,238 on August 23, 773 on August 24, 990 on August 27, and 107 soldiers on September 3. See Winslow and Moore, *Camp Morton*, 297–98.

25. See Mitchell, *Civil War Soldiers*, 44–45.

## Chapter 5: Reluctant Warrior

1. I, *O.R.* 17, pt. 2:699; Cunningham, *Reminiscences*, 12; *CV* 4 (March 1896): 71; *Confederate Archives*, roll 281; Winslow and Moore, *Camp Morton*, 299–300. The regiment reelected Colonel Farquaharson to the command even though he was not present for the reorganization. Some of the officers had already reunited with the 41st. Farquaharson had been released from Camp Warren, in Boston, two weeks earlier. See I, *O.R.* 4: pt. 3: 640; Cunningham, *Reminiscences*, 12; Lindsley, *Military Annals*, 510; *Confederate Archives*, roll 281.

2. Cunningham, *Reminiscences*, 12.

3. Ibid.; *Confederate Archives*, roll 281; *CV* 22 (January 1914): 9.

4. Cunningham, *Reminiscences*, 14; Samuel Carter, *The Final Fortress: The Campaign For Vicksburg, 1862–1863* (New York: St. Martin's Press, 1980): 88.

5. John Gregg of Texas remained the commander of the brigade to which the 41st Tennessee was attached until he was wounded at Chickamauga in September 1863. See Ezra J. Warner, *Generals in Gray; Lives of the Confederate Commanders* (Baton Rouge: Louisiana State University Press, 1959): 118–19.

6. Cunningham, *Reminiscences*, 14–15; I, *O.R.* 17: pt. 2: 781.

7. I, *O.R.* 52: pt. 2: 382.

8. Cunningham, *Reminiscences*, 15. Also see Carter, *Final Fortress*, 90; Gilbert E. Govan and James W. Livingood, *A Different Valor: The Story of General Joseph E. Johnston, C.S.A.* (New York: Bobbs-Merrill, 1956): 171–73; I, *O.R.* 17:

pt. 1: 666; Carter, *Final Fortress*, 99; Robert U. Johnson and Clarence C. Buel, eds., *Battles and Leaders of the Civil War*, three vols. (New York: Century, 1887): 3: 463.

9. Cunningham, *Reminiscences*, 15; Davidson, "Diary," 18; I, *O.R.* 17: pt. 2: 821; I, *O.R.* 10: pt. 2: 926; Edward Cunningham, *The Port Hudson Campaign, 1862–1863* (Baton Rouge: Louisiana State University Press, 1963): 6; *Battles and Leaders* 3: 589; J. William Jones and R. A. Brock, eds., *Southern Historical Society Papers*, 30 vols. (Richmond: Southern Historical Society, 1876–1907): 14, 305. Hereafter cited as *SHSP*.

10. Cunningham, *Reminiscences*, 15; Davidson, "Diary," 19.

11. See *CV* 1 (October 1893): 308.

12. Davidson, "Diary," 19–21. See I, *O.R.* 15: 1033, 1062; Report of Inspector General Charles M. Fauntleroy, I, *O.R.* 15: 943.

13. Cunningham, *Reminiscences*, 15; Davidson, "Diary," 19. At this time Gregg's brigade reported 757 soldiers absent. The quarantined 41st Tennessee represented three-fourths of that total. See I, *O.R.* 15: 965.

14. See *CV* 4 (February 1896): 48; Cunningham, *Reminiscences*, 15; Davidson, "Diary," 22.

15. Cunningham, *Reminiscences*, 16; *SHSP* 14: 308; I, *O.R.* 15: 271; *Battles and Leaders* 3: 590. Eleven Federal vessels comprised the flotilla directed by Admiral David Porter.

16. Lindsley, *Military Annals*, 510.

17. I, *O.R.* 15: 273–74; Edward Cunningham, *Port Hudson Campaign*, 32; *SHSP* 14: 308; Lindsley, *Military Annals*, 510; Cunningham, *Reminiscences*, 16; I, *O.R.* 15: 275, 278–79. The Federals returned on May 21st and carried their siege to a successful conclusion on 8 July 1863. See Edward Cunningham, *Port Hudson Campaign*, 35.

18. Cunningham, *Reminiscences*, 15. Also see Davidson, "Diary," 127; John Lipscomb file, in *Civil War Questionnaires* 5: 34.

19. Connelly, *Autumn of Glory*, 96; Govan and Livingood, *A Different Valor*, 193; I, *O.R.* 15: 1069.

20. Davidson, "Diary," 167. Also see Cunningham, *Reminiscences*, 17. David Donald has noted that Southern soldiers seldom marched in order, even under ideal conditions. Every army in the Confederacy suffered from straggling and from carelessness with its equipment. See David Donald, "The Confederate Soldier as a Fighting Man," *Journal of Southern History* 30 (1959): 181.

21. *CV* 20 (August 1912): 389; Cunningham, *Reminiscences*, 17; I, *O.R.* 24: pt. 3: 840.

22. I, *O.R.* 24: pt. 3: 849, 851–52; Govan and Livingood, *A Different Valor*, 198. See I, *O.R.* 24: pt. 3: 858.

23. Cunningham, *Reminiscences*, 17; Lindsley, *Military Annals*, 512. The citizens of Raymond planned a dinner for the Confederates on 12 May. To their disappointment, the army was routed that afternoon. See Carter, *Final Fortress*, 190.

24. See *CV* 12 (January 1904): 12; 17 (June 1909): 269.

25. Cunningham, *Reminiscences*, 17–18; *CV* 9 (June 1901): 257.

26. See Mitchell, *Civil War Soldiers*, 185–86. Confederate casualties totaled 506, approximately fifteen percent of the entire command. See I, *O.R.* 24: pt. 1: 739. For a description of the heavy skirmish at Raymond, see Cunningham, *Reminiscences*, 18; Davidson, "Diary," 171; Lindsley, *Military Annals*, 512; I, *O.R.* 24: pt. 1: 736–739, 743.

27. A Federal officer, H. K. Nelson, recalled Raymond in *CV* 12 (January 1904): 12.

28. Cunningham, *Reminiscences*, 18. General Johnston was quite ill, but he made the trip to Jackson. See Govan and Livingood, *A Different Valor*, 197, 203–4; *Battles and Leaders* 3: 478; Horn, *Army of Tennessee*, 214–15; Joseph E. Johnston, *Narrative of Military Operations, Directed in the Late War between the States* (Bloomington: Indiana University Press, 1959 reprint): 168; I, *O.R.* 24: pt. 3: 877; Horn, *Army of Tennessee*, 215.

29. Edwin C. Bearss and Warren Grabau, *The Battle of Jackson, May 14, 1863* (Baltimore: Gateway Press, 1981); 13, 44.

30. Cunningham, *Reminiscences*, 19. Also see Johnston, *Narrative*, 177; I, *O.R.* 24: pt. 1: 785; Carter, *Final Fortress*, 192.


## Chapter 6: Year of Decision—1863

1. I, *O.R.* 24: pt. 3: 925.

2. Thomas Connelly estimated that ten thousand deserters and absentees from the western departments were hiding in the mountains of northern Alabama. See Connelly, *Autumn of Glory*, 109.

3. *Confederate Archives*, roll 281; Davidson, "Diary," 216.

4. Cunningham, *Reminiscences*, 20; *CV* 5 (July 1899): 298; Lindsley, *Military Annals*, 510; Wiley, *Life of Johnny Reb*, 39; Davidson, "Diary," 214. One scholar of Civil War diseases commented, "Often, water supplies were shared by drinkers, bathers, launderers, cooks, horses, mules, the commissary's cattle, flies, mosquitoes, and other fauna as well as, unwittingly, some protozoa and bacteria coming from skins, nearby latrines, and other obvious sources. Healthy or chronic carriers of the agents of dysentery, malaria, typhoid fever, tuberculosis, and other diseases were present in every sizeable group of Americans." See Steiner, *Civil War Diseases*, 6–7, 35; Daniel, *Soldiering in Army of Tennessee*, 73.

5. *CV* 14 (August 1906): 344; Cunningham, *Reminiscences*, 20–21; Govan and Livingood, *A Different Valor*, 213–14; Davidson, "Diary," 215.

6. *CV* 6 (July 1899): 298.

7. Cunningham, *Reminiscences*, 21–22; *CV* 1 (April 1893): 113; 4 (March 1896): 71; Govan and Livingood, *A Different Valor*, 216; Horn, *Army of Tennessee*, 220; I, *O.R.* 24: pt. 1: 246; Johnston, *Narrative*, 206–207. In the retreat, Johnston abandoned 60 locomotives and 350 railcars at Grenada. See Jeffrey N. Lash, "Joseph E. Johnston's Grenada Blunder: A Failure in Command," *Civil War History* 23 (1977): 117, 122.

8. Davidson, "Diary," 281. Also see I, *O.R.* 24: pt. 1: 246; Connelly, *Autumn*

*of Glory*, 137; Horn, *Army of Tennessee*, 221; Nathaniel C. Hughes, *General William J. Hardee: Old Reliable* (Baton Rouge: Louisiana State University Press, 1965): 159–160; Govan and Livingood, *A Different Valor*, 218.

9. I, *O.R.* 24: pt. 3: 1031; 26: pt. 2: 164; Lash, "Johnston's Grenada Blunder," 121; Davidson, "Diary," 281.

10. Cunningham, *Reminiscences*, 22. Also see Davidson, "Diary," 281–82.

11. Cunningham, *Reminiscences*, 23. Also see Lindsley, *Military Annals*, 510; Davidson, "Diary," 282.

12. I, *O.R.* 30: pt. 4: 608.

13. Cunningham, *Reminiscences*, 23. For more on hospital train transportation, see Brooks, *Civil War Medicine*, 37.

14. Cunningham, *Reminiscences*, 23; Davidson, "Diary," 325; I, *O.R.* 30: pt. 4: 635; Connelly, *Autumn of Glory*, 183, 187–192; Fairfax Downey, *Storming the Gateway: Chattanooga, 1863* (New York: McKay, 1960): 73; I, *O.R.* 30: pt. 4: 608.

15. The Federals were using the new Spencer repeating rifle. Downey noted that "the startled Confederates heard a new and terrible sound, not familiar volleying of muzzle-loaders, rattling and rolling and dying away, but a steady roar, a torrent of fire and lead" (p. 39). Also see Horn, *Army of Tennessee*, 256; Charles M. Cummings, *Yankee Quaker, Confederate General; The Curious Career of Bushrod Johnson* (Rutherford, N.J.: Fairleigh Dickinson University Press, 1971): 255.

16. Born in Bedford County in 1841, Tillman graduated from Western Military Academy in Nashville in 1860. His family sympathized with the Tennessee Unionists. When the war broke out he enlisted in the 48th Tennessee but transferred to the 41st Tennessee after the regiment reorganized in 1863. He led the 41st during Farquaharson's absence and succeeded to command in 1864. Tillman surrendered the regiment in North Carolina in 1865. See George Newton Tillman, *Tillman Genealogy* (Nashville: McQuiddy Printing, 1905): 5–7; William Henry McRaven Papers, Manuscript Division, TSLA; Jay Guy Cisco, *Tennessee Authors, Short Biographical Sketches of All Authors Past and Present Who Have Made Their Homes in Tennessee* (Nashville: Cisco, 1907): 107; *CV* 4 (February 1896): 49; I, *O.R.* 30: pt. 2: 17; 47: pt. 3: 735.

17. I, *O.R.* 30: pt. 2: 462–68, 496; Connelly, *Army of Glory*, 223–24, 229; Horn, *Army of Tennessee*, 270; Cummings, *Bushrod Johnson*, 260–66.

18. Connelly, *Autumn of Glory*, 226; I, *O.R.* 30: pt. 2: 467, 498; *History of Tennessee*, 586; Davidson, "Diary," 329; Horn, *Army of Tennessee*, 273; Cummings, *Bushrod Johnson*, 268. Hood's division suffered forty percent casualties (Gregg's brigade tallied forty-five percent).

19. Connelly, *Autumn of Glory*, 227; Horn, *Army of Tennessee*, 273.

20. Cunningham, *Reminiscences*, 25.

21. Ibid.

22. Maney was born in Franklin, Tennessee, in 1826. A veteran of the Mexican War, he was instrumental in forming the 11th Tennessee. Maney commanded the brigade that comprised the 41st Tennessee from November 1863 until June 1864. He was promoted to division commander in August 1864. See Warner, *Generals in Gray*, 210; I, *O.R.* 31: pt. 2: 660; pt. 3: 685; Hughes, *Hardee*, 168; Christopher

Losson, *Tennessee's Forgotten Warriors: Frank Cheatham and His Confederate Division* (Knoxville: University of Tennessee Press, 1989). For more on the restructured command, see Connelly, *Autumn of Glory*, 250; Connelly and Jones, *Politics of Command*, 71; James Lee McDonough, *Chattanooga—A Death Grip on the Confederacy* (Knoxville: University of Tennessee Press, 1984): 273–74.

23. Cunningham, *Reminiscences*, 25; McDonough, *Chattanooga*, 136; Downey, *Storming the Gateway*, 137; Horn, *Army of Tennessee*, 296.

24. *Confederate Archives*, roll 281; Cunningham, *Reminiscences*, 26. Bell Wiley noted that fevers recurred often among Confederates partly because of exposure and also because of soldiers' failure to seek treatment. See Wiley, *Life of Johnny Reb*, 244–69.

Forsyth had become a large hospital station. Later, during the Atlanta campaign, approximately twenty thousand sick and wounded Confederates filled the hotels, courthouse, stores, schools, and private homes. See *Forsyth, Monroe County, Georgia; Sesqui-centennial, 1823–1973* (n.p.: n.d.): 38.

25. The Davis family followed a pattern similar to that of Cunningham's family. The family descended from Scottish stock. Two brothers, Archibald and Thomas Davis, moved to central Georgia in 1821 and purchased farms near the Towaliga River four miles southwest of Forsyth. The rich piedmont was ideal for raising cotton. Thomas Davis had seven children. One of the sons, William B. Davis, purchased 202 acres near the town of Brent. In 1837 he married a cousin, Martha T. Davis. The couple had five children, including Laura N. Davis, born in 1848. William B. Davis had become a successful planter by 1860, owning more than eight hundred acres and thirty-eight slaves. The plantation produced over seventy bales of cotton annually, and the family fortune exceeded $43,000. In politics, the Davises supported the Whig party and opposed secession. They supported the Confederacy only after hostilities had commenced. For primary and secondary accounts of Cunningham's future relatives and general information about Monroe County, see *CV* 9 (August 1901): 342; Joseph T. Maddox, *Some Mid-1800 People: Monroe County, Georgia* (n.p.: n.d.): introduction; *Monroe County, Georgia; A History* (Forsyth: Monroe County Historical Society, 1979); *Monroe County Cemeteries*, Miscellaneous file, Atlanta, Georgia Department of Archives and History, n.d.; George Roffalovich, *An Historical Sketch of Monroe County* (n.p., n.d.); Silas Emmett Lucas, Jr., ed., *Some Georgia County Records; Being Some of the Legal Records of Bibbs, Butts, Fayette, Henry, Monroe and Newton Counties, Georgia* (Easley, S.C.: Southern Historical Press, 1977); *Monroe County, Court of the Ordinary, Marriage Records, Book A; 6th Census, 1860, Agricultural Schedule, White Population, Slave Abstracts, Monroe County, Georgia; 8th Census, 1880, White Population; Forsyth Sesqui-centennial.*

26. Cunningham married Laura N. Davis on 27 November 1866. See *CV* 22 (January 1914): 9; Cisco, *Tennessee Authors*, 107.

27. Cunningham, *Reminiscences*, 26. Also see *Confederate Archives*, roll 281.

28. In late September the hospitals in Georgia overflowed with more than thirteen thousand patients. As many as seventeen percent of the army contracted

pneumonia. See Steiner, *Civil War Diseases*, 17. Also see Wiley, *Life of Johnny Reb*, 254, 346; Connelly, *Autumn of Glory*, 230.

29. I, *O.R.* 31: pt. 2: 749; Hughes, *Hardee*, 175; *Confederate Archives*, roll 281; Howell and Elizabeth Purdue, *Pat Cleburne, Confederate General* (Hillsboro, Tex.: Hill Junior College Press, 1973): 248–55. One member of the 41st Tennessee remembered that he "fought all round the missionary ridge." See John T. Gregory file, *Civil War Questionnaires* 4: 176. For more general information concerning the movement and placement of the 41st Tennessee, see Horn, *Army of Tennessee*, 300; Purdue, *Cleburne*, 255; Thomas R. Hay, "The Battle of Chattanooga," *Georgia Historical Quarterly* 8 (1924): 131; *SHSP* 8: 470; Connelly, *Autumn of Glory*, 276.

30. Sam R. Watkins, *"Co. Aytch," Maury Grays, First Tennessee Regiment; or, A Side Show of the Big Show* (Chattanooga: Chattanooga Times Press, 1900): 102–103.

31. For the psychological impact of such experiences, see Linderman, *Embattled Courage*, 64, 125, 128, 161; Bailey, *Tennessee's Confederate Generation*, 86.

32. See Lindsley, *Military Annals*, 513–15. Mitchell claims that the fatality ratio in the Confederate army was 1:3, the highest of any American war per capita. See Mitchell, *Civil War Soldiers*, 180.

33. See Linderman, *Embattled Courage*, 18. Mitchell also argues that Civil War soldiers were highly motivated to protect their family and homeland. Thus, there were many reluctant men who elected to stay in the service rather than desert. See Mitchell, *Civil War Soldiers*, 17, 38–42.

34. Mitchell, 172; Mitchell, "The Perseverance of the Soldiers" in Gabor S. Boritt, ed., *Why the Confederacy Lost* (New York: Oxford University Press, 1992): 121.

35. See Mitchell, *Civil War Soldiers*, 42, 81, 171.

## Chapter 7: Hopelessness

1. Cunningham, *Reminiscences*, 26; *Confederate Archives*, roll 281; Connelly, *Autumn of Glory*, 277; I, *O.R.* 31: pt. 3: 824; Horn, *Army of Tennessee*, 312.

2. Watkins, *"Co. Aytch,"* 106–7.

3. Cunningham, *Reminiscences*, 26; Comments of Dr. John Farris are found in Daniel, *Soldiering in Army of Tennessee*, 103. Also see Wiley, *Life of Johnny Reb*, 37–58, 132; Linderman, *Embattled Courage*, 119.

4. Cunningham, *Reminiscences*, 26–27; Horn, *Army of Tennessee*, 315.

5. I, *O.R.* 32: pt. 2: 571. President Davis sent a letter of appreciation to Otho Strahl's brigade for its patriotic gesture. See I, *O.R.* 32: pt. 2: 667.

6. Cunningham, *Reminiscences*, 27; Hughes, *Hardee*, 190; I, *O.R.* 32: pt. 3: 670.

7. G. Clinton Prim, Jr., "Born Again in the Trenches: Revivals in the Army of Tennessee," *Tennessee Historical Quarterly* 43 (Fall 1984): 250–72; Herman Norton, "Revivalism in the Confederate Armies," *Civil War History* 4 (1960): 417;

Samuel Carter, *The Siege of Atlanta, 1864* (New York: St. Martin's Press, 1973): 93; John P. Dyer, *The Gallant Hood* (Indianapolis: Bobbs-Merrill, 1950): 234. Bell Wiley argued that the American Bible Society, South, was well organized in preparing and distributing huge amounts of religious materials. He believed that revivals appealed to the South after military setbacks or when the prospects of death increased. He noted that the leaders were positive religious role models, that many soldiers came from religious backgrounds, and that the literature was convincing. Some historians estimate that as many as 150,000 soldiers converted to Christianity during the Civil War. See Wiley, *Life of Johnny Reb*, 176–84; Daniel, *Soldiering in Army of Tennessee*, 122; Gardiner H. Shattuck, Jr., *A Shield and Hiding Place: The Religious Life of the Civil War Armies* (Macon: Mercer University Press, 1987): 2–9.

8. *CV* 1 (January 1893): 15.

9. Cunningham, *Reminiscences*, 28; Daniel, *Soldiering in Army of Tennessee*, 123; Prim, "Revivals in the Army of Tennessee," 263. April and May 1864 saw the largest number of conversions in the Confederate army. On 1 May, more than two thousand soldiers, including Cunningham, converted or reconfirmed their faith.

10. Shattuck, *A Shield and Hiding Place*, 109, 135.

11. Cunningham, *Reminiscences*, 28; Wiley, *Life of Johnny Reb*, 134; Hughes, *Hardee*, 182; Linderman, *Embattled Courage*, 262; Daniel, *Soldiering in Army of Tennessee*, 77.

12. *CV* 14 (March 1904): 104.

13. See Carter, *Siege of Atlanta*, 81; Hughes, *Hardee*, 192; Wiley, *Life of Johnny Reb*, 132; Richard M. McMurray, *John Bell Hood and the War for Southern Independence* (Lexington: University of Kentucky Press, 1982): 100.

14. Cunningham, *Reminiscences*, 27.

15. Ibid.; Linderman, *Embattled Courage*, 167, 174.

16. Cunningham, *Reminiscences*, 29; I, *O.R.* 38: pt. 4: 678; Purdue, *Cleburne*, 292; *Battles and Leaders* 4: 263; Govan and Livingood, *A Different Valor*, 248–65; Connelly, *Autumn of Glory*, 323.

17. Cunningham, *Reminiscences*, 30; *CV* 1 (February 1893): 48; *CV* 3 (October 1895): 316.

18. Cunningham, *Reminiscences*, 30. The Confederates were spoiling for a fight at Cassville. See Connelly, *Autumn of Glory*, 345; Govan and Livingood, *A Different Valor*, 271–273.

19. For a copy of the speech, see Johnston, *Narratives*, 579.

20. Govan and Livingood, *A Different Valor*, 275–76; Connelly, *Autumn of Glory*, 346. See Johnston, *Narrative*, 323; John B. Hood, *Advance and Retreat: Personal Experiences in the United States and Confederate Armies* (New Orleans, 1880): 101–08; Connelly, *Autumn of Glory*, 348–50; Richard M. McMurray, "Confederate Morale in the Atlanta Campaign of 1864," *Georgia Historical Quarterly* 54 (1970): 229.

21. Cunningham, *Reminiscences*, 30. Also see Johnston, *Narratives*, 425.

22. Cunningham, *Reminiscences*, 31. Also see the controversial study Grady

McWhiney and Perry D. Jamieson, *Attack and Die: Civil War Military Tactics and the Southern Heritage* (University: University of Alabama Press, 1982); William J. McNeil, "A Survey of Confederate Soldier Morale During Sherman's Campaign through Georgia and the Carolinas," *Georgia Historical Quarterly* 55 (1971): 16; Connelly, *Autumn of Glory*, 354–56; Carter, *Siege of Atlanta*, 134; Govan and Livingood, *A Different Valor*, 280; Archer Jones, *Confederate Strategy from Shiloh to Vicksburg* (Baton Rouge: Louisiana State University Press, 1961): 11; Hughes, *Hardee*, 207. For an outstanding description of breastworks, see Horn, *Army of Tennessee*, 329–31.

23. Cunningham, *Reminiscences*, 31. Also see Connelly, *Autumn of Glory*, 358; Carter, *Siege of Atlanta*, 157.

24. Cunningham, *Reminiscences*, 31. At the beginning of the war, soldiers viewed sniper fire as cowardly. But as the reliance on earthwork defenses increased, sharpshooting intensified. See Linderman, *Embattled Courage*, 72, 147.

25. Cunningham, *Reminiscences*, 32. Sciatica is a rheumatic complaint, a pain along the course of the sciatic nerve. It causes pain in the lower back, the backs of the thighs, and the buttocks and hips.

26. At this point in the campaign, Confederate hospitals filled with sick soldiers. In July the Army of Tennessee was reduced to forty-five percent of its effective strength primarily because of illnesses. See James O. Breeden, "A Medical History of the Later Stages of the Atlanta Campaign," *Journal of Southern History* 35 (1969): 40–49. Wiley adds that rheumatism was the disease most easily feigned by the soldiers. See Wiley, *Life of Johnny Reb:* 255.

27. Cunningham, *Reminiscences*, 32. Atlanta became a clearinghouse for sick and wounded Confederates. Throughout June, boxcars full of soldiers arrived at the train depot and volunteers rushed them to makeshift facilities. See Carter, *Siege of Atlanta*, 169; Connelly, *Autumn of Glory*, 388; Breeden, "Medical History," 37, 55; Daniel, *Soldiering in Army of Tennessee*, 77. In July, nine percent of all hospital patients were furloughed to make room for the increasing number of wounded.

28. Horn, *Army of Tennessee*, 338; McMurray, "Confederate Morale," 230; I, *O.R.* 38: pt. 5: 865.

29. Cunningham, *Reminiscences*, 32; I, *O.R.* 38: pt. 3; 647. A Quaker from Ohio, Strahl moved to Dyersburg, Tennessee, in 1858. At the age of twenty-seven, he practiced law and invested in local farms. The 41st would remain in Strahl's charge until his death at Franklin. See Warner, *Generals in Gray*, 119; Charles M. Cummings, "Otho French Strahl; 'Choicest Spirit to Embrace the South,'" *Tennessee Historical Quarterly* 24 (1965): 341; *Confederate Archives*, roll 281.

30. Cunningham, *Reminiscences*, 32; *CV* 2 (May 1894): 151. Bell Wiley and Larry Daniel claimed that vegetables and sweets were in big demand with the troops in the summer of 1864. See Wiley, *Life of Johnny Reb*, 99; Daniel, *Soldiering in Army of Tennessee*, 60–62.

31. Cummings, "Strahl," 352; Hughes, *Hardee*, 230; Horn, *Army of Tennessee*, 358; Carter, *Siege of Atlanta*, 218; Connelly, *Army of Glory*, 444–51.

32. *CV* 2 (May 1894): 151.

33. Cunningham, *Reminiscences*, 33–34; I, *O.R.* 38: pt. 3: 708. Also see Purdue, *Cleburne*, 373.

34. Cunningham, *Reminiscences*, 33. Also see Brooks, *Civil War Medicine*, 31; Connelly, *Autumn of Glory*, 462–63; Carter, *Siege of Atlanta*, 308.

35. No amount of Southern patriotism could hide the fact that the Confederacy was doomed militarily by mid-1864. See Mitchell, *Civil War Soldiers*, 179.

36. Cunningham, *Reminiscences*, 34. Also see Linderman, *Embattled Courage*, 246–50; Connelly, *Autumn of Glory*, 467–70; Purdue, *Cleburne*, 382. Hood later charged that the Confederate army was unwilling to attack breastworks. See Hood, *Advance and Retreat*, 131–32.

## Chapter 8: Going Home

1. Thomas B. Hay, *Hood's Tennessee Campaign* (Dayton, Ohio: Morningside Press, 1976 reprint): 20. Mitchell argued that "a soldier's lack of enthusiasm for battle made little difference so long as his loyalty remained constant." He concludes that desertion did not mean that Confederates had repudiated their cause; rather, their initial commitment to the Confederacy was weak. See Mitchell, *Civil War Soldiers*, 81, 171.

2. See *Confederate Archives*, roll 281.

3. Horn, *Army of Tennessee*, 372.

4. Cunningham, *Reminiscences*, 35; *CV* 7 (July 1904): 338. Also see Horn, *Army of Tennessee*, 372; Connelly, *Autumn of Glory*, 479.

5. Cunningham, *Reminiscences*, 35.

6. Ibid.; *CV* 6 (July 1899): 296. For the hostile reaction of Southern troops fighting against Negro opponents, see Mitchell, *Civil War Soldiers*, 174–75.

7. Cunningham, *Reminiscences*, 36; Wiley, *Life of Johnny Reb*, 95–103. One veteran noted that many Confederates picked up Federal canteens on the battlefield, blew them apart with powder, poked holes in one end for a grate, and used the other end as a frying pan. See *New Orleans Times-Democrat*, 5 March 1893.

8. See Cunningham, *Reminiscences*, 36.

9. I, *O.R.* 39: pt. 2: 851; 35: pt. 1: 730; Connelly, *Autumn of Glory*, 487; Cummings, "Strahl," 352. Ironically, Cunningham would finish his Confederate service under the same commander with whom he had started.

10. Cunningham, *Reminiscences*, 37. Also see I, *O.R.* 35: pt. 1: 663; Bailey, *Tennessee's Confederate Generation*, 84; Horn, *Army of Tennessee*, 383; Hay, *Hood's Tennessee Campaign*, 82; Horn, *The Decisive Battle of Nashville* (Baton Rouge: Louisiana State University Press, 1956): 2.

11. Cunningham, *Reminiscences*, 37.

12. W. T. Crawford, "The Mystery of Spring Hill," *Civil War History* 1 (1955): 106; *SHSP* 4 (1881): 524, 536. Stewart's corps never did cross the creek that day. Instead, it bivouacked on the south bank. Also see Purdue, *Cleburne*, 400; Hay, *Hood's Tennessee Campaign*, 89–92.

13. Cunningham, *Reminiscences*, 38.

14. *CV* 18 (January 1910): 20; 1 (January 1893): 31. For a recent study that discusses the Southerners' lack of the will to fight either because of an original lack of faith in the Confederacy or because of its subsequent military setbacks, see Richard E. Beringer, Herman Hattaway, Archer Jones, William N. Still, Jr., *Why the South Lost the Civil War* (Athens: University of Georgia Press, 1986).

15. Cunningham, *Reminiscences*, 38–39. Connelly (p. 501) points out that this expression of courage was pointless because the Federals could easily have chosen any of three alternative routes around the sleeping Confederates. Still, from generals to privates, the army was deeply upset by what it believed was the lost opportunity at Spring Hill. See Horn, *Army of Tennessee*, 395; Dyer, *The Gallant Hood*, 289; Mitchell, *Civil War Soldiers*, 195.

16. Connelly, *Autumn of Glory*, 503; Hay, *Hood's Tennessee Campaign*, 117–19.

17. Cunningham, *Reminiscences*, 38. Also see Thomas L. Connelly and James Lee McDonough, *Five Tragic Hours: The Battle of Franklin* (Knoxville: University of Tennessee Press, 1983): 68; Jacob D. Cox, *The Battle of Franklin, November 30, 1864* (New York: Scribner's Sons, 1897): 93; Hay, *Hood's Tennessee Campaign*, 119. For interesting information on command problems and comparisons, see Richard M. McMurray, *Two Great Rebel Armies: An Essay in Confederate Military History* (Chapel Hill: University of North Carolina Press, 1989).

18. Cunningham, *Reminiscences*, 38; Horn, *Army of Tennessee*, 403; Cunningham quote in Bromfield L. Ridley, *Battles and Sketches of the Army of Tennessee* (Mexico, Mo.: Missouri Printing Co., 1906): 422. Also see Connelly and McDonough, *Five Tragic Hours*, 109.

19. Cox, *Battle of Franklin*, 94. Also see Cunningham, *Reminiscences*, 38.

20. At Franklin, more Confederate soldiers charged than at Pickett's charge—eighteen brigades of infantry. See Connelly and McDonough, *Five Tragic Hours*, 92, 104.

21. Cunningham, *Reminiscences*, 38; Cox, *Battle of Franklin*, 155. Thomas Hay concluded that "never before had men been killed so fast" (p. 134). See Hay, *Hood's Tennessee Campaign*. Also see Connelly and McDonough, *Five Tragic Hours*, 125.

22. Cunningham, *Reminiscences*, 38; Cox, *Battle of Franklin*, 112, 118; Connelly, *Autumn of Glory*, 504; Hay, *Hood's Tennessee Campaign*, 122.

23. Cunningham, *Reminiscences*, 38. Bell Wiley noted that the color-bearers were typically courageous individuals because they often attracted enemy fire. He concluded that the "flag flying was a matter of inestimable pride, and its loss to the enemy was an incalculable disgrace" (p. 81). Reid Mitchell argues that the battle flag was the emblem of community—it linked soldiers with home (p. 19).

24. Cunningham, *Reminiscences*, 38–39. Also see Horn, *Army of Tennessee*, 400–405; Hay, *Hood's Tennessee Campaign*, 122–24; Connelly and McDonough, *Five Tragic Hours*, 84, 127, 132. Cunningham's recollection was printed in *Our Day* 1 (June 1883): 144.

25. Cunningham, *Reminiscences*, 39. Also see Richard M. McMurray, *John Bell Hood and the War for Southern Independence* (Lexington: University of Kentucky Press, 1982): 175.

26. Cunningham, *Reminiscences*, 40; Connelly and McDonough, *Five Tragic Hours*, 129; Cox, *Battle of Franklin*, 164. One veteran later recalled wandering across the field after the battle: "Then I beheld a scene, woeful and pathetic in the extreme. Side by side and stiff and stark in death, lay the forms of Brigadier-General Strahl and all of his staff. . . . The expression of their countenances indicated that death had come upon them quickly." See *New Orleans Times-Democrat*, 5 March 1893. Cunningham revered his commander. In the 1890s the Tennessean visited Strahl's sister in Kansas to reminisce about the Franklin experience. See Ridley, *Battles and Sketches*, 421–22.

27. See *Philadelphia Times*, 27 May 1882; Cox, *Battle of Franklin*, 164; Cunningham, *Reminiscences*, 38.

28. Cunningham's assumption was correct. Connelly and McDonough noted that Cheatham's headquarters was located on a rocky hill to the west of Columbia Pike. The rolling terrain blocked visibility of the field. Cheatham probably never did realize the slaughter that was taking place. See Connelly and McDonough, *Five Tragic Hours*, 126.

29. Watkins, *"Co. Aytch,"* 212–13. Also see Connelly and McDonough, *Five Tragic Hours*, 156.

30. I, *O.R.* 45: pt. 1: 667, 682, 707; Horn, *Decisive Battle of Nashville*, 9.

31. See *Nashville Daily American*, 2 December 1887; *CV* 1 (January 1893): 31; 12 (July 1904): 341; 18 (January 1910): 20; *SHSP* 29 (1897): 392; Hay, *Hood's Tennessee Campaign*, 122–25; Connelly, *Autumn of Glory*, 506.

32. Watkins, *"Co. Aytch,"* 212–13. Also see Connelly and McDonough, *Five Tragic Hours*, 156.

33. Horn, *Decisive Battle of Nashville*, 21–24; Connelly, *Autumn of Glory*, 507; Hay, *Hood's Tennessee Campaign*, 138.

34. Cunningham, *Reminiscences*, 40. Also see Horn, *Decisive Battle of Nashville*, 21–24, 74–93; Connelly, *Autumn of Glory*, 507–509; Hay, *Hood's Tennessee Campaign*, 138, 150–54; W. J. Worsham, *The Old Nineteenth Tennessee Regiment, C.S.A.* (Knoxville: Paragon Printing, 1902): 151.

35. Cunningham, *Reminiscences*, 41; *Nashville Daily American*, 19 December 1889.

36. Horn, *Decisive Battle of Nashville*, 108–11, 123; Hay, *Hood's Tennessee Campaign*, 155–56; *CV* 20 (November 1912): 522; Connelly, *Autumn of Glory*, 510; I, *O.R.* 45: pt. 1: 707. Worsham, *The Old Nineteenth*, 154. Strahl's old brigade actually formed the apex at the summit of Shy's Hill.

37. Cunningham, *Reminiscences*, 41; Horn, *Decisive Battle of Nashville*, 116, 123.

38. Tyler's brigade, the first to break, was located to the right of the 41st Tennessee. See I, *O.R.* 45: pt. 1: 707. Also see Cunningham, *Reminiscences*, 41; Horn, *Decisive Battle of Nashville*, 125–27; Hay, *Hood's Tennessee Campaign*, 160; Connelly, *Autumn of Glory*, 511.

39. *CV* 1 (May 1893): 146; Cunningham, *Reminiscences*, 42; *Nashville Daily American*, 19 December 1889. For more on the psychological impact of such an experience, see Linderman, *Embattled Courage*, 125.

40. Cunningham, *Reminiscences*, 42. A private in Company H, 1st Tennessee, noted that his regiment dwindled to twelve. See Watkins, *"Co. Aytch,"* 207; Bailey, *Tennessee's Confederate Generation*, 102.

41. Cunningham, *Reminiscences*, 42.

42. *CV* 1 (May 1893): 146.

43. Cunningham, *Reminiscences*, 43; *CV* 2 (June 1894): 176.

44. See Mitchell, "Perseverance of Soldiering," 127–30; Daniel, *Soldiering in Army of Tennessee*, 136.

45. See Ash, *Middle Tennessee Society*, 142, 167–69.

46. See Ella Lonn, *Desertion during the Civil War* (New York: Century, 1928); map insert; Goodpasture, *History of Tennessee*, 586.

47. For more on the Civil War as the defining memory, see Mitchell, *Civil War Soldiers*, 179.

48. *CV*, 12 (July 1904): 338; *Nashville Banner*, 22 December 1913. Also see Linderman, *Embattled Courage*, 18–23.

49. Many brave soldiers expressed dishonor over Confederate defeat. See James M. Foster, *Ghosts of the Confederacy: Defeat, the Lost Cause, and the Emergence of the New South, 1865–1913* (New York: Oxford University Press, 1987): 26.

## Chapter 9: Adjusting to Peacetime

1. Cunningham, *Reminiscences*, 43.

2. See *Nashville Daily American*, 18 January 1889.

3. Cunningham, *Reminiscences*, 43; *Confederate Archives*, roll 281. Also see Thomas B. Alexander, *Political Reconstruction in Tennessee* (New York: Russell and Russell, 1950): 24.

4. The terms *radical* and *conservative* were already in use in the March elections. See Alexander, *Political Reconstruction*, 39, 70, 114–27; Folmsbee, *Tennessee*, 356; Harold Hyman, *Era of the Oath: Northern Loyalty Tests during the Civil War and Reconstruction* (Philadelphia: University of Pennsylvania Press, 1954): 124. Congress refused to seat the delegates over loud Southern remonstrations. Instead, the Radical Republicans created the Joint Reconstruction Committee to decide individually on each Southern application for readmission. The Tennessee legislature adopted manhood suffrage on 5 February 1867. Also see Joseph H. Cartwright, *The Triumph of Jim Crow: Tennessee Race Relations in the 1880's* (Knoxville: University of Tennessee Press, 1976): 11.

5. Alexander, *Political Reconstruction*, 196–97; Folmsbee, *Tennessee*, 363.

6. Alexander, *Political Reconstruction*, 150. Also see *House Miscellaneous Documents, 41st Congress, 2nd Session, #53*, 24–35.

7. For more on the founding of the Ku Klux Klan, see Allen W. Trelease, *White Terror: The Ku Klux Klan Conspiracy and Southern Reconstruction* (New York: Harper & Row, 1971): 23; Rollin G. Osterweils, *Myth of the Lost Cause, 1865–1900* (Hamden, Conn.: Archen Books, 1973): 16–23. The Grand Cyclops was Dr. Eze-

kiel Y. Salmon. See "The KKK Organization—Bedford-Moore Area," *Bedford County Historical Quarterly* 5 (Fall 1981): 93.

8. See U.S. House of Representatives, *House Misc. Docs.*, *41st Cong.*, *2nd Sess.*, *#53*, 148–49; Alexander, *Political Reconstruction*, 191; Allan W. Trelease, *White Terror: The Ku Klux Klan Conspiracy and Southern Reconstruction* (New York: Harper & Row, 1971): 36, 177; *Shelbyville Times-Gazette*, 7 October 1969; Folmsbee, *Tennessee*, 364; Ash, *Middle Tennessee Society*, 203–4.

9. See *House Misc. Docs.*, *41st Cong.*, *2nd Sess.*, *#53*, 293. Also see *CV* 18 (June 1910): 282.

10. See *CV* 16 (November 1908): 590.

11. Many old-line Whigs initially ran the Conservative party but were now overpowered by a large ex-Confederate element. See Alexander, *Political Reconstruction*, 233–34; Folmsbee, *Tennessee*, 369–77; Roger L. Hart, *Redeemers, Bourbons and Populists: Tennessee, 1870–1896* (Baton Rouge: Louisana State University Press, 1975): 12. Brown defeated the Republican candidate, William Wisener of Shelbyville, by a two-to-one split. Conservatives also won eighty percent of the state senate seats (twenty) and legislature seats (sixty). They won six of Tennessee's eight congressional districts.

12. See *Bedford County, Register's Office, Tennessee Deed Book, Book EEE*. The 1870 census show that Mary Cunningham's real estate holdings and personal property still placed her in the "elite" category of the nineteenth civil district. See *9th Census, 1870*.

13. See *9th Census, 1870* and *CV* 9 (July 1901): 302; 22 (January 1914): 4. Catherine Clinton explains that Southern women taught lessons of culture through personal contact, or "modeling." See Clinton, *The Plantation Mistress*, 95.

14. Hart, *Redeemers, Bourbons and Populists*, 113, 233. Gaines Foster points out that the rise of urbanization, expansion of the market economy and town culture, and growth of the middle class contributed greatly to postwar tension and anxiety. In a contrasting argument, Stephen Ash states that, with the exception of Nashville, most towns in middle Tennessee did not experience any appreciable growth in the immediate postwar period. See Foster, *Ghosts of the Confederacy*, 80; Ash, *Middle Tennessee Society*, 228–30.

15. In the first year after the war, approximately one-third of the former slaveholding elite and yeoman class entered professions such as merchandising, journalism, law, medicine, and education. See Bailey, *Tennessee's Confederate Generation*, 127–28; Ash, *Middle Tennessee Society*, 236–37.

16. Between 1865 and 1867, Cunningham's partners included J. J. Reeves, a Mr. Russell, and G. Charles Freeman. See *R. G. Dun and Company Collection, Tennessee*, 2 vols., Baker Library, Harvard University School of Business Administration, Harvard University, Cambridge, 1:40; *Bedford County, Register's Office, Deed Book EEE*.

17. "A country store does not of necessity have to be in the country," explained Thomas Clark. "No southern town serving an agricultural trade is without its big general stores." See Thomas D. Clark, *Pills, Petticoats and Plows: The South-*

*ern Country Store* (New York: Bobbs-Merrill, 1944): 12. Also see the section on country stores in Roger Ransom and Richard Sutch, eds., *One Kind of Freedom* (Cambridge: Cambridge University Press, 1977); *Shelbyville Republican*, 24 September 1869; Ash, *Middle Tennessee Society*, 23.

18. R. G. *Dun and Co., Tennessee*, 1: 84.

19. Ibid., 1: 40. Also see *Nashville Banner*, 23 December 1913. *Shelbyville Republican*, 23 October 1868.

20. See *Shelbyville Republican*, 6 November 1868. In his classic study of Southern storekeepers, Clark noted that "working hard, living closely and paying all debts was ever a cardinal rule of economy with them. This whole philosophy of the credit system was one of strict control" (p. 53).

From 1867 to 1870, Cunningham's personal and real estate wealth rose to $9,000. The store inventory approached $2,500. See *9th Census, 1870; R. G. Dun and Co., Tennessee*, 1: 40.

21. Thomas D. Clark, *The Rural Press and the New South* (Baton Rouge: Louisiana State University Press, 1948): 2. Frank Mott states that journalism attracted men of character, and was viewed favorably as a profession. See Frank L. Mott, *American Journalism: A History, 1690–1960* (New York: Macmillan, 1962): 405. Also see Clark, *Rural Press*, 4.

22. Cyrus Cunningham continued to operate the store on the Shelbyville town square until his death in 1895. See *The Goodspeed Histories of Maury, Williamson, Rutherford, Wilson, Bedford and Marshall Counties of Tennessee* (Columbia, Tenn.: Woodward and Stinson Printing Co., 1971 reprint): 1141; *Bedford County, Register's Office, Trust Deeds and Chattel Mortgages, Book 1, 1868–1878; 10th Census, 1880; Shelbyville Times-Gazette*, 7 October 1969.

23. Few postwar Southern editors had a high school education. See *8th Census, 1860;* Clark, *Rural Press*, 3; Bedford *Bulletin*, 24 November 1871.

"Some [journalists] had little excuse for existence beyond the desire of their publishers to take a chance." See Philip M. Hamer, *Tennessee, A History, 1673–1932*, 2 vols. (New York: American Historical Society, 1933): 2: 794.

24. *Shelbyville Commercial*, 12 January 1872. Radical Reconstruction remained an important issue in the rural press. Clark said that "it appears that one question uppermost in the minds of every southern editor for three or four decades was the vital one of the degree of economic and social revolution which had occurred in the region during the Civil War and its immediate aftermath" (*Rural Press*, pp. 2–20, 80). Joseph C. Kiger expanded Clark's view to include eulogizing rural life in contrast to urban living, crime and punishment, and religion. Kiger, "Social Thought as Voiced in Rural Middle Tennessee Newspapers, 1878–1898," *Tennessee Historical Quarterly* 9 (June 1950): 131–54.

25. The Russ family had much newspaper experience in Shelbyville. They founded the Shelbyville *Expositor*, a Whig mouthpiece, in 1848. The newspaper reappeared in 1866 as the *Republican* with Robert C. Russ at the helm. The Russes were Cunningham's principal competition in the early 1870s. In one editorial, Cunningham attempted to link the established journalist with Republicanism.

For more on the Russ family, see *Shelbyville Times-Gazette*, 7 October 1969; *Centennial Celebration*, 29–30; *Shelbyville Republican*, 27 August 1869; *Shelbyville Commercial*, 12 January 1872; Trelease, *White Terror*, 22.

26. Readyprint played an important part in the progress of small town weeklies. With it, the rural press ran more stories on national politics, religion, mechanics, and regional patriotism and ran agricultural hints, fiction, and humor. See Clark, *Rural Press*, 6–7; Mott, *American Journalism*, 397.

27. See *CV* 1 (April 1893): 98. Later, his former commander, Col. James D. Tillman, used the *Reminiscences* as the main source in recounting the regimental history found in Lindsley's *Military Annals of Tennessee*. See *CV* 21 (January 1913): 5.

28. See Stuart McConnell, *Glorious Contentment: The Grand Army of the Republic, 1865–1900* (Chapel Hill: University of North Carolina Press, 1992): 172–81, 187; Shattuck, *A Shield and Hiding Place*, 116.

29. Cunningham, *Reminiscences*, introduction.

30. See S. A. Cunningham to John P. Nicholson, 25 April 1879, Samuel Brock Collection, Huntington Library, San Marino, Calif. Also see *CV* 1 (September 1893): 266.

31. *Bedford County, Clerk's Office, Circuit Court, Book 6.* Cunningham placed a large ad for Reeves and Cunningham in his newspaper. The ad indicated that the editor was still affiliated with the dry goods store in 1872, being a part-time journalist and a part-time merchant. See *Shelbyville Commercial*, 12 January 1872. For more on the Southern rural press as a victim of economic hard times, see Clark, *Rural Press*, 35–36.

32. See *Centennial Celebration*, 30.

33. *Shelbyville Commercial*, 23 January 1874. Also see *Shelbyville Times-Gazette*, 7 October 1969, 24. Although Cunningham continued his association with the dry goods firm, R. G. Dun Company agents reported that the business did not fare well. In fact, they strongly suspected that Cunningham was deeply in debt beginning in 1872. The agents concluded that "the press . . . is the best part of his business." See *R. G. Dun and Co., Tennessee*, 1: 84.

34. For a legal account of Cunningham's disastrous financial dealings between 1872 and 1875, see *Bedford County, Clerk's Office, Circuit Court, Book 6, 1868–1878; Bedford County, Register's Office, Trust Deeds and Chattel Mortgage, Book 1, 1868–1878; Book 2, 1878–1882; Bedford County, Register's Office, Deed Book, Book LLL, 1874–1878.* Cunningham's real estate holdings in Shelbyville were considerable, being estimated at three thousand to six thousand dollars. See *R. G. Dun and Co., Tennessee*, 1: 40–41, 84.

35. Infant Mary Cunningham died on 28 October 1875. See Helen Crawford Marsh and Timothy Richard Marsh, *Cemetery Records of Bedford County, Tennessee* (Shelbyville: Marsh Historical Publications, 1976): 206.

# Chapter 10: Fiasco in Chattanooga

1. *Our Day* 2 (October 1883): 50. Also see "Sumner A. Cunningham and the *Confederate Veteran* Magazine," *Southern Magazine* 34 (September 1934): 26, 49. Ben M. Hord was born on a cotton farm in Rutherford County in 1824. He attended college in Chapel Hill, North Carolina; served in the 1st North Carolina; and spent eighteen months in a prison camp. Hord founded the *Rural Sun* in 1874 and the *Spirit of the Farm* in 1885. He was appointed Commissioner of Agriculture for Tennessee in 1887. See *Nashville Daily American*, 12 February 1887.

2. *Shelbyville Rescue*, 29 November 1872.

3. See *Our Day* 1 (February 1883): 54; 2 (October 1883): 50.

4. Patten, a former Federal soldier who resided in Chattanooga, bought the troubled tabloid in 1874. Later he purchased Thedford's Black Draught and Mc-Elree's Wine of Cardui and consolidated them into the Chattanooga Medicine Company. See Charles D. McGuffey, *Standard History of Chattanooga, Tennessee, with Full Outline of the Early Settlement, Pioneer Life, Indian History and General and Particular History of the City to the Close of the Year 1910* (Knoxville: Crew and Dorey, 1911): 239–41. Also see, *CV* 21 (March 1913): 252.

5. *Chattanooga Times*, 1 July 1903. This twenty-fifth anniversary edition is found in the S. A. Cunningham biographical file, Chattanooga Bicentennial Library, Chattanooga, Tennessee. Also see recollection of S. A. Cunningham at a banquet honoring Adolph Ochs in Nashville on 14 July 1910. See McGuffey, *History of Chattanooga*, 241.

6. McGuffey, *History of Chattanooga*, 241; Gerald W. Johnson, *An Honorable Titan; A Biographical Study of Adolph S. Ochs* (New York: Harper & Brothers, 1956): 49.

7. Mary Cunningham registered the agreement with the county. See *Bedford County, Register's Office, Trust Deeds and Chattel Mortgage, Book 2, 1868–1878*; McGuffey, *History of Chattanooga*, 241; *Chattanooga Times*, 1 July 1903. Cunningham purchased a lot at the corner of East Terrace and James Street with a full view of Lookout Mountain. See *Nashville Daily American*, 6 December 1885.

8. Richard Hoe invented the hoe-stop cylinder press in 1832. It printed two thousand copies an hour on large single sheets of paper. It required strength to turn the hand crank. Many new mechanical devices that would improve printing were coming into use in the 1870s. Clearer and harder type, neater and more efficient presses, and better ink combined to make a more attractive finished product. Cunningham did not keep pace with the new technology. See Thomas D. Clark, *Pills, Petticoats and Plows: The Southern Country Store* (New York: Bobbs-Merrill, 1944): 4; Frank L. Mott, *American Journalism: A History: 1690–1960* (New York: Macmillan, 1962): 204, 294, 314, 400–402.

9. McGuffey, *History of Chattanooga*, 241; *Chattanooga Times*, 1 July 1903; Zella Armstrong, *The History of Hamilton County and Chattanooga, Tennessee*, 2 vols. (Chattanooga: Lookout Mountain Publishing Co., n.d.): 2: 138. For more on the partnership failures, see *Chattanooga Times*, 3 January 1877, 12 April 1877, 16 August 1877, 1 July 1903.

10. See *Chattanooga Times*, 1 October 1876, 11 October 1876, 21 October 1876, 31 October 1876. See McGuffey, *History of Chattanooga*, 241.

11. McGuffey, *History of Chattanooga*, 62, 241. This type of railroad expansion in Chattanooga was common throughout the South in the 1870s. See John A. Garraty, *The New Commonwealth, 1877–1890* (New York: Harper & Row, 1968): 78–127.

12. *Chattanooga Times*, 19 October 1876; 20 October 1876.

13. Ibid., 17 January 1877.

14. Ibid., 1 July 1903.

15. Reprinted in the *Chattanooga Times*, 6 February 1877. The *Atlanta Constitution* was rapidly acquiring a national reputation that started from a powerful regional footing. See Harold E. Davis, *Henry Grady's New South: Atlanta, A Brave and Beautiful City* (University: University of Alabama Press, 1990): 21.

16. *Chattanooga Times*, 9 March 1877; 29 April 1877. Cunningham managed to exchange news with the *Express* in Cartersville, Georgia.

17. Ibid., 4 May 1877.

18. Ibid., 9 August 1877.

19. Ibid., 21 April 1877, 26 February 1878, 1 July 1903.

20. Ibid., 10 May 1877. Also see R. Bruce Bickley, Jr., *Joel Chandler Harris* (Athens: University of Georgia Press, 1987 edition): 29–30; Davis, *Henry Grady*, 29–54.

21. *Chattanooga Times*, 12 March 1878; 1 July 1903. Also see *CV* 21 (March 1913): 252.

22. *Chattanooga Times*, 7 November 1876, 9 November 1876; See *CV* 1 (March 1893): 67. For more on the election of 1876, see Paul Haworth, *The Disputed Presidential Election of 1876* (Cleveland: Burrows Brothers, 1906); C. Vann Woodward, *Reunion and Reaction* (New York: Doubleday and Company, 1956); Paul H. Buck, *The Road to Reunion, 1865–1900* (Boston: Little, Brown, 1937); Keith Ian Polakoff, *The Politics of Inertia: The Election of 1876 and the End of Reconstruction* (Baton Rouge: Louisiana State University Press, 1973).

23. *Chattanooga Times*, 21 November 1876 through 3 March 1877.

24. Ibid., 5 April 1877.

25. Ibid., 11 April 1877.

26. Ibid., 8 February 1878. Although Cunningham's ideals were aligned with those of the Conservatives (Democrats) after 1865, it was not unusual for Southerners to hear his praise for the Republican president Hayes. After all, Hayes did liberate the South of an occupation army. "It was he who gave real peace and a sense of freedom to the Southern people," Cunningham remarked in later years. "It was not an infrequent remark that he was doing the South more good than Mr. Tilden could have done," *Our Day* 1 (February 1883): 35.

27. See Alexander, *Political Reconstruction*, 167–68; Folmsbee, Corlew, and Mitchell, *Tennessee*, 380.

28. *Chattanooga Times*, 27 January 1877.

29. *Our Day* 1 (April 1883).

30. *Chattanooga Times*, 18 January 1878.

31. The state credit wing peaked in 1875. When it declined in influence, forty-four men bolted to form the Sky Blue Democracy. Among the Sky Blues were Frank Cheatham, Duncan B. Cooper, and Adolph S. Ochs. See Hart, *Redeemers, Bourbons and Populists*, 23, 61–66; Folmsbee, *Tennessee*, 382; Cartwright, *Triumph of Jim Crow*, 42; *Nashville Daily American*, 7 July 1882, 18 September 1882.

32. *Chattanooga Times*, 27 January 1878.

33. Tennessee's agrarian revolt started in the early 1870s when the Grange organized more than a thousand chapters. They were followed by the inflationary Greenback party, Agricultural Wheel, and Southern Farmer's Alliance. The agrarian wing of the state Democratic party gained control in 1886. Afterward, Governor Robert Love Taylor did much to restore harmony to the faction-ridden party. See Folmsbee, *Tennessee*, 398–99; Cartwright, *Triumph of Jim Crow*, 43; Hart, *Redeemers, Bourbons and Populists*, 120; C. Vann Woodward, *Tom Watson, Agrarian Rebel* (New York: Oxford University Press, 1963).

34. *Chattanooga Times*, 16 February 1878.

35. See George Brown Tindall, *The Persistent Tradition in New South Politics* (Baton Rouge: Louisiana State University Press, 1975): 6; Daniel Walker Howe, *Victorian American* (Philadelphia: University of Pennsylvania Press, 1976).

36. *Chattanooga Times*, 13 March 1877.

37. Ibid., 30 May 1877. Cunningham later disavowed the Union holiday at the end of May in favor of 3 June, the birthdate of Jefferson Davis.

38. Ibid., 12 June 1877.

39. Ibid., 23 February 1877.

40. Ibid., 16 February 1877, 29 May 1877. Also see *Our Day* 1 (February 1883): 35; *CV* 1 (February 1893): 24, 49; 14 (June 1906): 256.

41. See *CV* 13 (December 1905): 578; Johnson, *An Honorable Titan*, 51; Clark, *Southern Country Store*, 248. McGuffey, *History of Chattanooga*, 241–42.


## Chapter 11: *Our Day*

1. *Chattanooga Weekly Commercial*, 30 June 1878; Lucy J. Cunyus, *The History of Bartow County* (Easley, S.C.: Tribune, 1971): 158. It was quite common for newspaper editors to move from job to job in the 1870s. See Louise Littleton Davis, *Frontier Tales of Tennessee* (Gretna, La.: Pelican, 1976): 158–62; *Atlanta Constitution*, 28 September 1878, 30 September 1878; Mott, *American Journalism*, 478.

2. See S. A. Cunningham to Albert S. Marks, 25 April 1879, Governor Albert S. Marks Papers, Manuscript Division, TSLA. For more on Cartersville, see Steven Hahn, *The Roots of Southern Populism: Yeoman Farmers and the Transformation of the Georgia Upcountry, 1850–1890* (New York: Oxford University Press, 1983): 206.

3. Hahn, *Roots of Southern Populism*, 143–51, 228; Woodward, *Tom Watson*, 52–83.

4. S. A. Cunningham to Albert S. Marks, 14 January 1879, Governor Albert S. Marks Papers, Manuscript Division, TSLA.

5. John Dollard, "A Method of Measuring Tension in Personal Documents," *Journal of Abnormal and Social Psychology* 42 (1947): 3–32.

6. S. A. Cunningham to Albert S. Marks, 21 January 1879, Governor Albert S. Marks Papers, Manuscript Division, TSLA.

7. See *Our Day* 1 (January 1883): 18.

8. Charles Henry Smith used the pen name Bill Arp. See Mott, *American Journalism*, 393. Also see *CV* 11 (October 1903): 436. For a recent biography, see David B. Parker, *Alias, Bill Arp: Charles Henry Smith and the South's "Goodly Heritage"* (Athens: University of Georgia Press, 1991).

9. Cunyus, *History of Bartow County*, 158. For more on issues that precipitated conflict between upcountry radicals and conservatives, see Hahn, *Roots of Southern Populism*, 227–47.

10. See *CV* 10 (December 1902): 543; *8th Census, 1880, Mortality Schedule, Monroe County, Georgia*.

11. *Nashville Banner*, 22 December 1913.

12. *CV* 10 (December 1902): 543.

13. Laura Davis Cunningham's grandfather, Thomas W. Davis, and great-uncle, Archibald Davis, are buried here. The author visited the graveyard in November 1992. Many graves in the cemetery are unmarked. It is located in a pine thicket along U.S. Route 83. See *Monroe County Georgia: A History* (Forsyth: Monroe County Historical Society, 1979): 650, 668; *Monroe County Cemeteries*, Miscellaneous files, Georgia Department of Archives and History, Atlanta, Georgia.

14. Paul Davis Cunningham resided in the Davis household until 1885. See *10th Census, 1880; CV* 9 (July 1901): 294; Zella Armstrong, *The History of Hamilton County and Chattanooga, Tennessee* (Chattanooga: Lookout Mountain Publishing, n.d.): 1, 149; S. A. Cunningham to Anson Nelson, 22 October 1881, 5 April 1882, 27 November 1885, Tennessee Historical Society Papers, Miscellaneous files, Manuscript Division, TSLA. The Society published *American Monthly*.

15. *Our Day* 1 (January 1883): 3, 32.

16. Ibid., 2.

17. Ibid.; Also see *Trow's New York City Directory for the Year Ending May 1, 1884* 97 (New York: Trow's City Directory Co., 1883): 363, 1296.

18. *Our Day* 1 (June 1883): 145–46.

19. Ibid., 1 (May 1883): 112.

20. Ibid., 1 (April 1883): 80.

21. See Ibid., 1 (January 1883).

22. See *Chattanooga Times*, 11 January 1877. For the challenge, see *Our Day* 1 (February 1883): 48.

23. *Our Day*, 1 (April 1883): 86.

24. Ibid.

25. Ibid., 1 (July 1883): 186.

26. See Ibid., 1 (January 1883): 10, 11; 1 (May 1883): 113; 1 (June 1883): 141; 1 (July 1883): 164.

27. Ibid., 1 (January 1883): 10.

28. See Ibid., 2 (March-April 1884): 133.

29. Ibid., 1 (April 1883): 185–86.

30. Ibid. Also see *Our Day* 2 (January-February 1884): 116; *CV* 19 (September 1911): 417; 21 (May 1913): 207.

31. *Our Day* 2 (October 1883): 57.

32. Ibid., 1 (February 1883): 64.

33. See Ibid., 1 (June 1883): 131.

34. Ibid., 2 (December 1883): 64–65.

35. Daniel Sutherland suggests that *Our Day* might have lasted longer had Cunningham not changed his tone from one of reconciliation to partisanship. However, Cunningham's style was always unwavering and cantankerous. For more on the shortcomings of *Our Day*, see Daniel E. Sutherland, *The Confederate Carpetbaggers* (Baton Rouge: Louisiana State University Press, 1988): 265–67.

36. Ibid.; Also see Ibid., 2 (March-April 1884): 140.

37. Ibid., 2 (July 1884): 142.

38. Cunningham donated his own personal set of *Our Day* to the Tennessee State Library on 27 August 1910. It is the only public file in existence today.

## Chapter 12: With the *Nashville American*

1. See *Nashville City Directory* 24 (Nashville: Marshall and Bruce Publishers, 1888).

2. For more on the shifting editor's and owner's position and the political views of the *American*, see *Our Day* 2 (December 1883): 91; Hart, *Redeemers, Bourbons and Populists*, 40–54; Cartwright, *Triumph of Jim Crow*, 43–47, 131–35, 174; William R. Majors, *Editorial Wild Oats: Edward Ward Carmack and Tennessee Politics* (Macon, Ga.: Mercer University Press, 1984).

3. Daniel Katz enumerated important factors that influence change in public and personal attitudes and concluded that most individuals search for political viewpoints that either support or reinforce one's own identity and self-image. See Katz, "The Functional Approach to the Study of Attitudes," *Public Opinion* 4 (1960): 163–204.

4. See *Nashville Daily American*, 3 October 1885. Cunningham's article discussed rebuilding efforts in Bellbuckle, a small town east of Shelbyville. Also see "Sumner A. Cunningham and the *Confederate Veteran* Magazine," *Southern Magazine* 34 (1934): 26.

5. See Majors, *Editorial Wild Oats*, 22–47. When Carmack became editor-in-chief in October 1888, the *American* expanded to eight columns. He left the *American* in 1892 to edit the *Memphis Daily Commercial*. Also see *Nashville Daily American*, 25 May 1887.

6. *Nashville Daily American*, 25 April 1886, 26 April 1886, 29 April 1886. For more on Sam Jones, see *Cartersville Centennial, 1872–1972* (Cartersville: Tribune

News Printing Co., 1972): 86–88; Fleurney Rivers Scrapbook, 40–41, Manuscript Division, TSLA.

7. *Nashville Daily American*, 25 April 1886, 26 April 1886, 29 April 1886.

8. For examples, see *Nashville Daily American*, 8–27 May 1886, 22 November 1887, 22 October 1888, 25 May 1891.

9. For more on the trend toward associationalism, see Peter L. Decker, *Fortunes and Failures: White-Collar Mobility in Nineteenth-Century San Francisco* (Cambridge: Harvard University Press, 1978).

10. See *Nashville Daily American*, 14 April 1887, 12 May 1887, 13 February 1889.

11. See ibid., 23 April 1887, 3 September 1887, 14 December 1890. Also see issues for 19 October 1890, 11 December 1890, 19 December 1890, 5 July 1891.

12. For a list of Cunningham's reports, see ibid., 1 May 1887 (St. Charles Hotel, New Orleans), 20 May 1888 (Wagoner's Hotel, Nashville), 18 March 1888 (Linck's Hotel, Nashville), 1 April 1888 (Maxwell House, Nashville), 22 April 1888 (Nicholson Hotel, Nashville), 18 July 1887 (Monte Sano Hotel, Huntsville, Alabama), 27 May 1888 (Morehead City Hotel, Tennessee), 29 August 1888 (Roan Mountain Hotel, East Tennessee), 9 April 1890 (East Brook Springs, Tennessee), 13 May 1890 (Mammoth Caves, Kentucky), 1 July 1890 (Monteagle, Tennessee), 2 July 1890 (Hot Springs, North Carolina), 22 July 1890 (Tate Epsom Springs, Tennessee).

13. For a sampling, see ibid., 4 May 1886, 18 July 1886, 24 November 1886, 21 January 1887, 9 February 1887, 18 July 1887, 6 August 1887, 16 August 1887, 17 October 1887, 5 January 1890, 8 May 1892, 3 February 1886, 18 February 1886, 21 February 1886, 21 March 1886, 18 April 1886, 4 September 1887, 1 November 1887, 18 December 1887, 26 February 1888, 24 June 1888, 9 June 1889, 15 August 1889, 25 August 1889, 28 August 1889, 9 September 1889, 21 September 1890, 10 December 1890, 12 February 1892.

14. Ibid., 24 May 1888.

15. Ibid., 11 February 1887.

16. See ibid., 17 November 1888, 28 November 1888, 7 December 1888, 18 January 1889, 30 January 1889, 5 February 1889, 25 March 1889.

17. Comments from the *Liberty Herald* in Tennessee reprinted in *Nashville Daily American*, 9 February 1889.

18. Comments from the *Columbia Herald* in Tennessee reprinted in *Nashville Daily American*, 23 November 1888.

19. Bickley, *Joel Chandler Harris*, 30.

20. Folmsbee, *Tennessee*, 425; Paul E. Isaac, *Prohibition and Politics: Turbulent Decades in Tennessee, 1885–1920* (Knoxville: University of Tennessee Press, 1965): 10–11, 29–35.

21. *Chattanooga Times*, 15 April 1877.

22. See *Our Day* 1 (January 1883): 21; 1 (February 1883): 49.

23. S. A. Cunningham to Anson Nelson, 27 November 1885, Tennessee Historical Society, Miscellaneous files, Manuscript Division, TSLA. For additional

information on the views Cunningham shared with Nelson on temperance, see *Our Day* 2 (October 1883): 52.

24. Ironically, Carmack reversed his position on prohibition in 1906 when he ran for the U.S. Senate. In the campaign, he defended temperance vehemently. His defeat and subsequent assassination in 1908 were both tied to liquor interests. His death provided new impetus to the cause of prohibition. Legislation was passed in 1909 prohibiting the manufacture of liquor in Tennessee. The new law also fragmented the Democratic party. See Isaac, *Prohibition and Politics*, 106–9, 157–59; Folmsbee, *Tennessee*, 438–39.

25. Cartwright, *Triumph of Jim Crow*, 214.

26. See *Our Day* 1 (February 1883): 49. Catherine Clinton argues that one component of race agitation in the postwar era was caused by the fear of white males regarding their own virility. See Clinton, *The Plantation Mistress*, 222.

## Chapter 13: Associational Ties

1. William W. White believes that the "tone and pitch of the whole veteran movement had been revealed" shortly after the Civil War. According to White, most ex-Confederates 1) were tired of war; 2) were not interested in politics; 3) believed defeat came as a result of superior numbers; 4) accepted military defeat; 5) desired to honor the dead; 6) had no fraternal feelings toward Northern veterans but would work for a stronger Union; and 7) regretted only that they had lost. See White, *The Confederate Veteran* (Tuscaloosa, Ala.: Confederate Publishing Co., 1962): 10–11. Also see Benjamin Kendrick and Alex M. Arnett, *The South Looks At Its Past* (Chapel Hill: University of North Carolina Press, 1935): 107–8; Waler L. Fleming, *Documentary History of Reconstruction*, 2 vols. (Cleveland: Bobbs-Merrill, 1906): 1: 59.

2. *Nashville Daily American*, 24 October 1889; *CV* 18 (April 1910): 14.

3. *Nashville Daily American*, 24 October 1889.

4. Ibid., 23 August 1890; *CV* 6 (September 1899): 395.

5. *Memphis Commercial-Appeal*, 30 May 1911. Also see White, *Confederate Veteran*, 14.

6. *The Confederate Gray Book: Frank Cheatham Bivouac, United Confederate Veterans* (Nashville: n.d.): 1; *Frank Cheatham Bivouac Papers, Minute Book, 1887–1905*, 16 December 1887, 6 January 1888, Manuscript Division, TSLA; *Confederate Gray Book*, 1; *Nashville Daily American*, 7 September 1889.

7. See Foster, *Ghosts of the Confederacy*, 107–12, appendix 2. The G.A.R. reflected similar statistics in middle class dominance. See McConnell, *Glorious Contentment*, 81–83.

8. Frank Cheatham Bivouac represented almost twenty percent of all Tennesseans affiliated with the United Confederate Veterans Association in 1892. For the figures, see *Minutes of the Fifth Annual Meeting of the Association of Confeder-*

ate Soldiers, Tennessee Division (Nashville: Foster and Webb Printers, 1892): 14 (*Minutes* hereafter cited in notes to this chapter as *Tenn. UCV Reunion*); *Frank Cheatham Minute Book*, 1888–1892; *Nashville Banner*, 7 May 1910, 8 October, 1910; McConnell, *Glorious Contentment*, 53.

9. Hon. Peter Turney, *The South Justified, An Address Delivered before Frank Cheatham Bivouac #1 of the Association of Confederate Soldiers, Tennessee Division, Saturday, August 18, 1888* (Nashville: Tavel Printers, 1888).

10. Ibid., p. 25.

11. The statement about Cunningham was offered after his death by a colleague who knew the journalist well. See *Nashville Tennessean*, 21 December 1913.

12. For example, Cunningham reported on dedication ceremonies in Hopkinsville and Lexington, Kentucky; New Orleans; and Nashville. See *Nashville Daily American*, 11 April 1887, 22 May 1887, 19 November 1887, 2 December 1887.

13. For reprints, see *Nashville Union; New Orleans Times-Democrat; Louisville Courier-Journal; New Orleans Times-Picayune; New York Evangelist,* and other newspapers. Cunningham's account turned up in a London newspaper complete with editorial comment. See *Nashville Daily American*, 17 November 1889. "Battles and Leaders" first appeared in 1884 and signaled a "new journalistic homage" that promoted sectional reconciliation through soldiers' reminiscences. See Foster, *Ghosts of the Confederacy*, 69; Osterweis, *Myth of the Lost Cause*, 44, 66–91.

14. Cunningham, *Reminiscences*, 40.

15. *SHSP* 34 (1896): 192.

16. A new moon appeared at 1:48 a.m. on 29 November 1864, and the battle of Franklin was fought under a moonless sky. See *Blum's Farmers' and Planters' Almanac For the Year 1864* (Salem, N.C.: L. V. and E. T. Blum, 1864): 13. Also see Thomas B. Hay, *Hood's Tennessee Campaign* (Dayton, Ohio: Morningside Press, 1976): 134; *CV* 12 (July 1904): 341; 18 (January 1910): 20.

17. See *Nashville Daily American*, 10 March 1890. For his feature on Camp Morton, see ibid., 14 September 1891.

18. See C. D. Elliot, *A Plea for the Tennessee Confederate Memorial and Historical Association* (Nashville: C. R. and H. H. Hatch Printers, 1886). Also see *9th Tenn. UCV Reunion*, 28–29, 30–34; *CV* 22 (January 1913): 5. See *Nashville Tennessean* and *Nashville American*, 4 November 1911. Cheatham Bivouac copied much of the state constitution for its local use.

19. See White, *Confederate Veteran*, 19–22; Herman Hattaway, *General Stephen D. Lee* (Jackson: University Press of Mississippi, 1976): 194. For more on the origins of the ex-Confederate societies in Virginia, see Thomas L. Connelly, *The Marble Man: Robert E. Lee and His Image in American Society* (Baton Rouge: Louisiana State University Press, 1977); Foster, *Ghosts of the Confederacy;* William Garrett Piston, *Lee's Tarnished Lieutenant* (Athens: University of Georgia Press, 1987); *Proceedings of the Great Reunion of the Veterans of the Confederate States Cavalry, Held in the City of New Orleans on February 13, 1888* (New Orleans: Hopkins Press, 1888); John A. Simpson, "The Cult of the 'Lost

Cause': The *Confederate Veteran* Magazine, 1893–1913" (M.A. thesis, University of Arkansas, 1974): 17–53; Hattaway, *S.D. Lee*, 194; *1st Tenn. UCV Reunion*, 7; *Nashville Daily American*, 26 February 1886. Seven members of Cheatham Bivouac attended the second meeting, in 1889.

20. Article by Jastremski printed in *CV* 12 (September 1904): 425. For more on Jastremski, see Edward Pinkowski, *Pills, Pens and Politics: The Story of General Leon Jastremski, 1843–1907* (Wilmington, Del.: Captain Stanislaus Mlotowski Memorial Brigade Society, 1974). For the article by J. F. Shipp, see *CV* 3 (May 1895): 145; 3 (October 1895): 292. Actually, a group of touring veterans from both armies commissioned H. V. Boynton in 1888 to prepare a brochure on the Chickamauga park project. See Gilbert E. Govan and James W. Livingood, *The Chattanooga Country, 1540–1962* (Chapel Hill: University of North Carolina Press, 1963): 365–69; *CV* 5 (April 1897): 120.

21. On 19 August 1890 President Benjamin Harrison signed a bill establishing Chickamauga as the first national military park. See Govan and Livingood, *Chattanooga Country*, 369; *CV* 21 (April 1913): 209–11; H. V. Boynton, "The National Military Park," *Century* 27 (1895): 703–8; Paul H. Buck, *The Road to Reunion, 1865–1900* (Boston: Little, Brown, 1937): 260; *Arkansas Gazette*, 18 September 1895; *Memphis Commercial-Appeal*, 21 September 1895; *Harper's Weekly* 34 (1895): 585.

22. Francis Trevelyn Miller, ed., *The Photographic History of the Civil War in Ten Volumes* (New York: Review of Reviews, 1911): 10: 296–300.

23. Fred S. Washington presided over and represented three organizations: the Army of Northern Virginia, Louisiana Division; the Army of Tennessee, Louisiana Division; and the Veteran Confederate States Cavalry Association. For more on his famous circular, see *New Orleans Times-Picayune*, 10 June 1889; *Arkansas Gazette*, 16 May 1911; *CV* 3 (May 1895): 145; 12 (September 1904): 425; *Proceedings of the Convention for Organization and Adoption of the Constitution of the United Confederate Veterans Association* (New Orleans: Hopkins Press, 1891): 3; Foster, *Ghosts of the Confederacy*, 105–9; Osterweis, *Myth of the Lost Cause*, 92–93.

24. Hattaway, *S.D. Lee*, 195; *New Orleans Times-Picayune*, 12 June 1889.

25. See *CV* 1 (January 1893): 11.

26. *New Orleans Times-Picayune*, 12 June 1889.

27. For a copy of the UCV constitution, see *CV* 2 (October 1894): 296–303; Robert C. Wood, *Confederate Handbook* (New Orleans: Graham Press, 1903). The UCV was structured into three departments headed by a lieutenant general, who was its administrator. The mid-level was called the division and commanded by a major general. The lowest level was the local camp. Herman Hattaway claims that the UCV hierarchy was emphatically nonmilitary despite the military facade. The main objectives were always social, literary, historical, and benevolent. William White asserts, rightly so, that the UCV had an overweight bureaucracy. See White, *Confederate Veteran*, 31; Hattaway, *S. D. Lee*, 196–97; *CV* 12 (September 1904): 425; *Proceedings of Adoption of UCV Constitution*, 8; *New Orleans Times-Picayune*, 11 June 1889; John A. Simpson, "John B. Gordon

and the United Confederate Veterans," *Atlanta Historical Bulletin* 21 (Fall 1977): 42–52. The UCV hierarchy included:

| | |
|---|---|
| Commander: | John B. Gordon, 1889–1904 |
| | Stephen D. Lee, 1904–1907 |
| | Clement A. Evans, 1907–1910 |
| | George W. Gordon, 1910–1911 |
| | C. Irvine Walker, 1911–1912 (temporary) |
| | Bennett H. Young, 1912–1915 |
| Adj. Gen. | George Moorman, 1889–1903 |
| | William E. Mickle, 1903–1913 |
| Chaplain | J. William Jones, 1889–1903 |
| Quartermaster General | J. F. Shipp, 1889–1910 |

The G.A.R. also utilized a quasimilitary structure, as did many other late nineteenth-century fraternal groups. For a comparative examination of the founding of the G.A.R., see McConnell, *Glorious Contentment*, 24–52.

28. *CV* 1 (April 1893): 114; 2 (April 1894): front cover.

## Chapter 14: General Agent Cunningham

1. See White, *Confederate Veteran*, 34; *CV* 11 (August 1903): 348; 17 (July 1909): 307; Miller, *Photographic History of the Civil War*, 10: 298; *9th Tenn. UCV Reunion*, 24–25. For a breakdown of memberships by state, on a percentage basis, see Adjutant General William Mickle's report printed in *CV* 15 (August 1907): 341.

2. *Nashville Daily American*, 7 December 1889, 8 December 1889. See William R. Majors, *Editorial Wild Oats; Edward Ward Carmack and Tennessee Politics* (Macon, Ga.: Mercer University Press, 1984), 32–47.

3. *Nashville Daily American*, 16 December 1889, 10 December 1889, 21 December 1889.

4. Ibid., 7 December 1889. For typical press responses to the monument scheme, see *Memphis Commercial-Appeal*, 7 December 1889; *New Orleans Times-Picayune*, 7 December 1889. *Nashville Daily American*, 9 December 1889, 13 December 1889; *New Orleans Times-Picayune*, 13 December 1889. Also see *CV* 1 (January 1893): 33; 13 (January 1905): 8; 19 (November 1911): 560.

5. *Nashville Daily American*, 18 December 1889. Cheatham Bivouac in Nashville eagerly appointed a committee to solicit contributions and began turning funds over to Childress. See *Nashville Daily American*, 11 January 1890; 17 May 1891; 18 June 1891; *Minutes of the Second Annual Meeting and Reunion of the United Confederate Veterans, Held in the City of Jackson, Miss., on June 2, 1891* (New Orleans: Hopkins Press, 1891): 8; *CV* 1 (January 1893): 26–27. For more on the planned activities of the bivouac, see *Nashville Daily American*, 9 June 1891.

6. Unaddressed letter from J. W. Childress, 1 July 1891, S. A. Cunningham

Papers, Southern Historical Collection, Wilson Library, University of North Carolina, Chapel Hill, N.C.

7. Cunningham's handwritten application form is located in the *Frank Cheatham Bivouac Papers*, 1 May 1891, Manuscript Division, TSLA.

8. Ibid. Also see *4th Tenn. UCV Reunion*, 40; *CV* 2 (February 1894): 38; *Nashville Daily American*, 21 June 1888, 26 February 1889.

9. See John Dollard, "A Method of Measuring Tension in Personal Documents," *Journal of Abnormal and Social Psychology* 42 (1947): 3–32. Also examine the content analysis of verbatim explanations technique devised by Martin E. P. Seligman. Robert J. Trotter explains Seligman's theory on how humans rationalize unfortunate events in their lives. See Robert J. Trotter, "Stop Blaming Yourself," *Psychology Today* 21 (February 1987): 31–38.

10. *Frank Cheatham Bivouac Papers*, 1 May 1891, p. 16. Cunningham probably supported a resolution to admit veterans to the bivouac who had fought only up to the battle of Nashville. The measure was defeated twice. See *Frank Cheatham Bivouac Papers*, 7 August 1891, 2 December 1898.

11. *Frank Cheatham Bivouac Papers*, 1 May 1891.

12. See Bailey, *Tennessee's Confederate Generation*, 100.

13. V. Y. Cook to Edith Pope, 14 February 1921, Confederate Collection, Tennessee Historical Society Papers, Manuscript Division, TSLA.

14. *Nashville Daily American*, 5 July 1891. At a bivouac meeting on 3 July 1891, the members "resolved, that it is the sense of this Bivouac that the appointment of Comrade S. A. Cunningham to be the General agent [*sic*] of the Davis monumental fund is eminently proper and judicious and highly gratifying to his comrades of the bivouac." See *Frank Cheatham Bivouac Papers*, 3 July 1891.

15. See *Frank Cheatham Bivouac Papers*, 4 November 1898. Also see entries on 2 October 1891, 3 March 1893, 1 September 1898; *6th Tenn. UCV Reunion*, 6; *Frank Cheatham Bivouac Papers*, 3 November 1899.

For examples of Cunningham's participation in the bivouac, see *Frank Cheatham Bivouac Papers*, 3 April 1897, 3 September 1897, 7 January 1898, 4 February 1898, 1 April 1898, 3 June 1898, 5 August 1898, 6 January 1899, 7 March 1902, 1 August 1902, 1 May 1903, 3 July 1903, 1 August 1903, 1 July 1904, 10 March 1905, 5 May 1905.

16. *Nashville Daily American*, 3 October 1891; 16 April 1892. Also see *Nashville Banner*, 22 December 1913.

17. *CV* 1 (January 1893): 9. Also see *Nashville Daily American*, 5 July 1891, 9 November 1891, 23 December 1891.

18. See *CV* 1 (January 1893): 17; *Nashville Daily American*, 21 January 1890, 6 February 1890, 11 March 1890, 7 December 1890, 19 October 1891, 23 November 1891.

19. *Nashville Daily American*, 29 February 1892, 4 April 1892.

20. Varina Howell Davis to S. A. Cunningham, 5 July 1892, 26 August 1906, Davis Collection, Manuscript Division, TSLA. Also see *CV* 6 (September 1898): 401; Varina Howell Davis to S. A. Cunningham, 12 February 1895, Margaret

Howell Davis to S. A. Cunningham, 4 November 1890, 5 July 1892, 26 August 1906, Davis Collection, Manuscript Division, TSLA.

21. Varina Howell Davis to S. A. Cunningham, 13 February 1905, Davis Collection, Manuscript Division, TSLA.

22. At the memorial service for Varina Davis, held at St. Paul's Church in Richmond, Cunningham escorted the remains to the cemetery as an honorary pallbearer. See *CV* 14 (November 1906): 485.

23. One newspaper noted, "Jefferson Davis is gone, followed to the grave, we doubt not, by more affection and gratitude on the part of the South, and on more respectful and just appreciation on the part of the North, than were always his portion during his life." See *Arkansas Gazette*, 7 December 1889. For other honors, see *Memphis Commercial-Appeal*, 21 May 1893, 28 May 1893, 30 May 1893; *Arkansas Gazette* 21 May 1893, 30 May 1893; "Honors to Jefferson Davis," *American Monthly Review of Reviews* 8 (1893): 6; *CV* 1 (June 1893): 176.

24. See *Minutes of 1st UCV Reunion*, 4.

25. *Minutes of 3rd UCV Reunion*, 172.

26. Ibid.; *CV* 1 (March 1893): 69; 1 (May 1893), 132.

27. Cunningham's future nemesis, John C. Underwood, represented Kentucky on the UCV committee. The selection was reasonable. Underwood not only had a solid reputation as a fund-raiser; he was also a friend of Commander Gordon. See *Minutes of 3rd UCV Reunion*, 172; *Minutes of 4th UCV Reunion*, 11.

28. See *CV* 1 (April 1893), 120.

29. See *Richmond Times*, 2 July 1896, in C. Vann Woodward, *Origins of the New South, 1877–1913* (Baton Rouge: Louisiana State University Press, 1971 reprint): 156. Also see *Arkansas Gazette*, 3 July 1896; *Minutes of 6th UCV Reunion*, 191; *CV* 4 (November 1896): 360.

30. *CV* 4 (August 1896): 256; 4 (November 1896): 360.

31. *Minutes of 9th UCV Reunion*, 105, 133–34. Also see *CV* 7 (June 1899): 253; 7 (December 1899), 534; 15 (July 1907): 294; M. Louise Benton Graham, Daisy M. L. Hodgson, and Virginia Frazer Boyle, eds., *History of the Confederate Memorial Associations of the South* (New Orleans: Graham Press, 1904). Also see *New Orleans Times-Picayune*, 10 May 1900.

32. *Minutes of 17th UCV Reunion*, 118–56; *CV* 11 (July 1907): 294–95, 299–301.


## Chapter 15: The *Confederate Veteran*

1. *Nashville Daily American*, 4 February 1892. Also see *Nashville Banner*, 22 December 1913; *CV* 1 (January 1893): 1.

2. *CV* 1 (January 1893): 1.

3. *CV* 13 (January 1905): 8; 19 (December 1911): 560.

4. Havron's *Confederate Veteran* replaced the defunct *Southern Bivouac*. Its tone was harsh, and it dwelled on political themes. See *The Confederate Veteran Magazine: A Medium of Inter-Communication for Confederate Soldiers* 1 (January–July 1890).

5. See *Bedford County, Clerk's Office, Wills, Book 1, 1890;* "Bedford County, Will Book 1," *Bedford County Historical Quarterly* 7 (Spring 1983): 27; Helen Crawford Marsh and Timothy Richard Marsh, *Newspaper Vital Records of Bedford County, Tennessee* (Shelbyville, Tenn.: Marsh Historical Publications, 1984): 19.

6. *CV* 1 (October 1893): 290; 6 (December 1898): 560.

7. *CV* 1 (January 1893): 1. Also see Osterweis, *Myth of the Lost Cause*, 94.

8. *CV* 13 (January 1905): 8.

9. *CV* 6 (March 1898): 98.

10. Varina Howell Davis to S. A. Cunningham, 23 September 1894, Davis Collection, Manuscript Division, TSLA; *CV* 1 (April 1893): 108.

11. *CV* 2 (November 1894): 341. Not all veterans shared excitement about the *Veteran*, however. One critic said that Virginians "naturally feel slighted when they find most of your reading matter referring to the men and movements of the Tennessee army. I feel assured that you could get voluntary contributions from a dozen or more such writers as Dr. J. William Jones." See *CV* 1 (July 1893): 197. Cunningham struck a fairer balance between both theaters of war in later years. In this regard he did a more credible job than Jones did in the *Southern Historical Society Papers*. For more on the conspiratorial animosity between Virginians and non-Virginians, see Piston, *Lee's Tarnished Lieutenant*, 117–121.

12. See *CV* 2 (May 1894): 155; *Frank Cheatham Bivouac Papers*, 15 January 1904.

13. See *CV* 1 (July 1893): 197; 1 (October 1893): 304.

14. The objective of the new publication was laid out in its first issue: "The full history of the Confederacy has not hitherto been written. We have bits and hints and outlines and colorings here and there; but of the real inner history—the mainspring, the motive, the incident of that vast uprising of the South—how little comparatively has been given to the world! The *demanded* history will be given in the CONFEDERATE WAR JOURNAL." See *Confederate War Journal Illustrated* 1 (April 1893): 1. Hereafter cited as *CWJI*.

15. Ibid., 1 (December 1893): 134. The *CWJI* attempted a Southern version of the pictorial works of *Harper's* and Frank Leslie.

16. For instance, Wright sat at the dignitaries' stand at the 7th UCV reunion (1897) and was tendered a resolution of thanks at the 12th UCV reunion (1902) for his services in the preservation of Confederate history. Wright worked for the U.S. War Department collecting records pertinent to the Civil War. *CWJI* 1 (December 1893): 142.

17. See *CV* 1 (April 1893): 98; 1 (June 1893): 162; 1 (November 1893): 377–78; 2 (April 1894): 123–24; 2 (February 1894): 48–49; 7 (June 1899): 297.

18. *CV* 1 (May 1893): 130.

19. See *CV* 1 (July 1893): 199–200; 1 (August 1893): 228; 1 (December 1893): 369; 2 (February 1894): 48–49; 2 (April 1894): 123–24. LaBree possessed outstanding credentials as an editor and author of Confederate military history. See George G. Fetter, *Notable Men of Kentucky At the Beginning of the 20th Century* (Louisville: Fetter Printers, 1902): 195.

20. *CV* 6 (April 1899): 159. Also see *CV* 7 (July 1899): 297. It is ironic that Ben LaBree contributed an earlier article to the *Veteran*. See *CV* 4 (December 1896): 432. LaBree, a member of the Kentucky Historical Society, continued to publish *The Lost Cause* until 1904. See *Register of the Kentucky Historical Society* 14 (January 1916): 40.

21. See *CV* 7 (September 1899): 448. A UDC chapter in Mississippi took LaBree's name while he still lived, "the first man to be so honored." See *Press Reference Book of Prominent Kentuckians* (Louisville: Standard Company, n.d.): 175.

22. See S. A. Cunningham to George Moorman, 11 February 1898, Adjutant General's Letter Box, United Confederate Veterans Association Papers, University Library, Louisiana State University.

23. *CV* 1 (July 1893): 194.

24. See *Frank Cheatham Bivouac Papers*, 4 August 1893.

25. The souvenir idea was so successful that Cunningham printed special reunion editions and sold them at future conventions. For a representative sample, see *CV* 2 (April 1894).

26. *CV* 2 (April 1894): 125; 2 (May 1894): 133–36, 155–56. Cunningham printed Underwood's lengthy speech in full. See ibid., 2 (October 1894): 304.

27. In 1895 the membership defeated Underwood's revisions. See *CV* 2 (November 1894): 325; 3 (July 1895): 170.

28. *CV* 2 (May 1894): 136; *Memphis Appeal-Avalanche*, 23 April 1894.

29. See B. H. Teague to S. A. Cunningham, 15 October 1899, S. A. Cunningham Papers, Southern Historical Collection, Wilson Library, University of North Carolina, Chapel Hill, N.C.

30. *CV* 2 (May 1894): 155. The UCV did not award a publishing contract to anyone, but the new constitution certified that only the commander could distribute information relative to the organization. See ibid., 133–34; 2 (August 1894): 226.

31. *CV* 5 (July 1897): 392; *Minutes of 6th UCV Reunion*, 110; *Report of the United Confederate Veterans' Historical Committee* (New Orleans, 1895), 11; S. A. Cunningham to Emilie Todd Helm, 26 February 1898, Helm Collection, Kentucky Historical Society, Frankfort, Ky.; S. A. Cunningham to James W. Eldridge, 26 January 1899, Samuel Brock Collection, Huntington Library, San Marino, Calif.

32. See *CV* 1 (January 1893): 1; 1 (August 1893): 240; 5 (March 1897): 132; Mott, *American Journalism*, 394.

33. See *CV* 2 (July 1894): 193; 3 (November 1895): 321.

34. *CV* 12 (December 1904): 576.

35. *CV* 1 (May 1893): 129.

36. *CV* 2 (April 1894): 97.

37. *CV* 5 (September 1897): 464.

38. *CV* 2 (January 1894): 3, 16; 1 (December 1893): 353; 2 (August 1894): 240; 21 (October 1913): 471.

39. *CV* 2 (July 1894): 220; 4 (June 1896): ad; 5 (August 1897): 416.

40. For examples, see *CV* 1 (January 1893); 2 (April 1894); 3 (November 1895);

4 (December 1896); 6 (October 1898); 4 (December 1896): 404.

41. See *CV* 2 (April 1894); 5 (June 1897); 22 (June 1904).

42. *CV* 1 (November 1893): 336; 1 (December 1893): 354; 2 (January 1894): 3; 2 (August 1894): 240.

43. *CV* 3 (March 1895): 80.

44. *CV* 2 (December 1894): 368; 16 (April 1907): 152; *Nashville City Directory* (1913) 69; *CV* 3 (January 1895): 1–32. Clearer type and a brand new press were installed in 1895. See *CV* 2 (December 1894): 368; 3 (March 1895): 80.

45. For statistics, see the letterhead on the following correspondence: S. A. Cunningham to Emilie Todd Helm, 8 January 1896, Helm Collection, Kentucky Historical Society, Frankfort, Ky.; S. A. Cunningham to Joseph Jones, 15 February 1894, Joseph Jones Papers, Louisiana Historical Association Collection, Howard-Tilton Memorial Library, Tulane University, New Orleans, La. Southern addresses received ninety-one percent of all copies of the *Veteran* that were mailed. For the figures see *CV* 8 (March 1900): 126–28; 10 (December 1902): 540.

46. John Meriwether, *The History of Literary and Intellectual Life in the Southern States*, in *The South in the Building of the Nation*, 12 vols. (Richmond: Southern Historical Publication Society, 1909): 10:516; *CV* 5 (March 1897): 112; 16 (January 1908): 1; 18 (January 1910): 8.

47. S. A. Cunningham to Jefferson Davis Monument Association, no date, Confederate Collection, Tennessee Historical Society Papers, Manuscript Division, TSLA. Judging by the content, the letter was written in mid-1892.

48. Ibid.

49. *CV* 10 (May 1902): 207; 12 (February 1904): 83; 15 (July 1907): 303.


## Chapter 16: Patron and Critic

1. See *Frank Cheatham Bivouac Papers*, 1 September 1893. Also see entry for 5 May 1899; *Nashville Tennessean*, 6 June 1908; *Nashville Banner*, 5 June 1909; *Minutes of 20th UCV Reunion*, appendix, 2; *Minutes of 22nd UCV Reunion*, appendix, 1. In his first recorded remarks, Cunningham welcomed General John M. Schofield to the 1895 reunion. The editor traveled to the convention in Schofield's private railroad car. See *Minutes of 5th UCV Reunion*, 55; *CV* 3 (September 1895): 274.

2. See C. Irvine Walker's speech in *Minutes of 22nd UCV Reunion*, 91. Commander Stephen D. Lee voiced similar comments in 1905: "We come together because we love the past, because our lives have been linked together by a great experience—by the richest, deepest experience that has come to any generation of Americans; by a common story so rich in heroism, in sacrifice, in patriotism, that everything else we remember grows cheap when we think of the Confederacy." See *CV* 13 (July 1905): 294; White, *Confederate Veteran*, 40.

3. *CV* 1 (September 1893): 272.

4. *CV* 3 (July 1895): 208.

5. S. A. Cunningham to William L. DeRossett, 25 August 1896, William L. DeRossett Collection, William R. Perkins Library, Duke University, Durham, N.C.

6. *CV* 3 (June 1895): 180.

7. See *CV* 4 (August 1896): 241; 20 (May 1912): 195.

8. For example, see *CV* 6 (August 1898): 354–55, 394. Gaines Foster notes correctly that attention shifted away from the veterans at reunions and toward the upper-class hierarchy, visiting dignitaries, and upper-middle-class men who came to be seen. This development, he felt, "trivialized" the Confederate tradition. See Foster, *Ghosts of the Confederacy*, 169–78; McConnell, *Glorious Contentment*, 31–39.

9. *CV* 10 (February 1902): 52.

10. *CV* 4 (August 1896): 242. Cunningham was accurate in his charge. The UCV hierarchy did monopolize convention time and control the decision-making process. See Howard Dore, "Rhetoric of the UCV," in Waldo W. Braden, ed., *Oratory of the New South* (Baton Rouge: Louisiana State University Press, 1970): 143–73.

11. Paul H. Buck, *The Road to Reunion, 1865–1900* (Boston: Little, Brown, 1937): 259.

12. Preconvention costs forced many planning committees to devise innovative fund-raisers. In 1901 Memphis organized an exhibition baseball game between two Southern League teams to help defray the cost of hosting the reunion. This was one of the first charitable contests in professional baseball history. See *Arkansas Gazette*, 21 April 1901.

13. See *CV* 5 (July 1897): 339.

14. See *CV* 13 (July 1905): 300; 12 (June 1904): 261; 12 (May 1904): 220.

15. *CV* 12 (June 1904): 261.

16. *CV* 12 (April 1904): 149; 12 (July 1904): 323.

17. *CV* 2 (August 1894): 225. Also see ibid., 19 (February 1911): 61–64.

18. *CV* 17 (April 1909): 161.

19. *CV* 10 (September 1902): 392.

20. Many sponsors and maids were unmarried women from prominent families. They dressed in white (symbolic of virginity) and reinforced the traditional image of Southern womanhood. The presence of these ladies at Confederate reunions indirectly reaffirmed the veterans' manhood. See Foster, *Ghosts of the Confederacy*, 136–37. Also see Annie E. Cody, *History of the Tennessee Division, United Daughters of the Confederacy* (Nashville: Cullom and Ghertner, 1945).

21. *Frank Cheatham Bivouac Papers*, 7 May 1897, 6 August 1897; *CV* 5 (May 1897): 194.

22. *Nashville Banner*, 22 December 1913.

23. *CV* 19 (January 1911): 37. Also see *CV* 8 (August 1900): 344; 16 (February 1908): 56; 18 (December 1910): 552.

24. *CV* 13 (December 1905): 536–38, 540; 20 (September 1912): 403; 21 (May 1913): 171.

25. See *CV* 16 (June 1908), xxxviii; 18 (November 1910): 506. Cunningham is

pictured with the youth organization beside the Confederate monument in Centennial Park.

26. Knauss had attempted to hold a memorial service in 1896, but there was no response. A large crowd did attend on 5 June 1897. See *CV* 5 (September 1897): 455–58.

27. *CV* 5 (December 1897): 595–98.

28. *CV* 6 (April 1898): 160. Also see ibid., 6 (August 1898): 363, 401–3; 9 (August 1901): 351–52; 11 (June 1903): 351; 9 (June 1901): 259; 12 (March 1904): 102.

29. *CV* 6 (May 1898): 147.

30. McKinley delivered the speech on 14 December 1898. See *Speeches and Addresses of William McKinley* (New York: Doubleday and McClure, 1900): 159. Also see *CV* 6 (December 1898): 546; 9 (September 1901): 395.

31. *CV* 6 (December 1898): 546.

32. For examples of the issue of federal appropriations for Confederate gravesites, see *CV* 8 (August 1900): 371; 9 (May 1901): 246; 10 (June 1902): 319–20; 11 (February 1903): 54; 11 (April 1903): 199; 12 (March 1904): 102; *Arkansas Gazette*, 11 May 1899, 8 May 1901; *Minutes of 9th UCV Reunion*, 34–35, 137, 158; *Memphis Commercial-Appeal*, 12 May 1899, 30 May 1901; *CV* 9 (June 1901): 259; 12 (March 1904): 102.

33. *CV* 2 (May 1894): 144.

34. *CV* 3 (April 1895): 112.

35. The flag issue entered the presidential campaign in 1888. The lyrics to one street song went: "And Grover C. will sorry be, and sorely rue the day / He undertook to give the rebel flags away / And Grover C. and Allen T. will find, as all men do, / How vain it is to 'buck agin' the boys who wore the blue." See Mary R. Dearing, *Veterans in Politics; The Story of the GAR* (Baton Rouge: Louisiana State University Press, 1952): 382–83. For a complete analysis of the flag controversy, see ibid., 342–83; Allan Nevins, *Grover Cleveland; A Study in Courage* (New York: Dodd, Mead, 1932). Nevins concluded that Cleveland had usurped his constitutional authority in offering to return the flags.

36. *CV* 6 (June 1898): 245, 252–55. For a similar statement, see *New Orleans Times-Picayune*, 31 May 1898; *CV* 6 (June 1898): 245; 13 (November 1905): 551. Also see *Arkansas Gazette*, 4 June 1905, 17 June 1905; *The Flags of the Confederate Armies* (St. Louis: Ware, 1905). As late as 1962 Northern depositories were releasing Confederate battle flags. In that year, Governor Matthew E. Walsh of Indiana returned two flags to Arkansas Governor Orval Faubus. See *Arkansas Gazette*, 2 June 1962.

37. See Buck, *Road to Reunion*, 256–57; *Arkansas Gazette*, 4 October 1890.

38. See *CV* 7 (May 1899): 233; 7 (July 1899): 335; 7 (October 1899): 439; 8 (July 1900): 297; 10 (December 1902): 547; 12 (August 1904): 373; 12 (October 1904): 502; 19 (September 1911): 453.

39. *CV* 3 (October 1895): 289; *New Orleans Times-Picayune*, 27 June 1890, 25 June 1897; *CV* 7 (March 1899): 99; 9 (April 1901): 133; *Minutes of 10th UCV Reunion*, 82–83.

40. *CV* 6 (April 1898): 146.

41. *CV* 8 (June 1900): 266.

42. See *Minutes of 10th UCV Reunion*, 111–13; *Memphis Commercial-Appeal*, 2 June 1900.

43. See *CV* 8 (July 1900): 297; Dearing, *Veterans in Politics*, 495. Also see *CV* 12 (October 1904): 502; 17 (June 1909): 298; 21 (February 1913): 54; 21 (October 1913): 472; 21 (November 1913): 521.

44. *CV* 19 (September 1911): 414–15; 19 (October 1911): 709; "Fighting the Civil War Over Again," *Outlook* 98 (1911): 709.

45. *CV* 19 (September 1911): 459; *CV* 20 (November 1912): 509; 21 (April 1913): 201–3; 21 (June 1913): 280; Report of the Pennsylvania Commission, *Fiftieth Anniversary of the Battle of Gettysburg* (Harrisburg, Pa.: State Printing Office, 1914): 6.

46. *CV* 21 (February 1913): 54–55; 21 (October 1913): 472; 21 (November 1913): 521; 21 (December 1913): 556.

47. See *Fiftieth Anniversary of Battle of Gettysburg*, 59; *Memphis Commercial-Appeal*, 3 July 1913.

48. *CV* 21 (September 1913): 429; *Fiftieth Anniversary of Battle of Gettysburg*: 218–19.

49. Reported in ibid., 216.

50. *CV* 21 (October 1913): 472.

51. *CV* 21 (August 1913): 377.

52. *CV* 21 (November 1913): 521. Also see supporting comments by the Reverend James H. McNeilly on page 556.

53. See *CV* 19 (February 1911): 56.

54. The church was located at 200 17th Avenue South. See *Nashville City Directory* (1913), 65; *Nashville Banner*, 23 December 1913. See James I. Vance Collection, Scrapbook no. 1, 91–92, Manuscript Division, TSLA; *Minutes of the General Assembly of the Presbyterian Church in the U.S.A.* (Philadelphia: Office of the General Assembly, 1906): 30; *Minutes of the General Assembly of the Presbyterian Church in the U.S.A.* (Philadelphia: Office of the General Assembly, 1907): 877; *Minutes of the General Assembly of the Presbyterian Church in the U.S.A.* (Philadelphia: Office of the General Assembly, 1908): 843; *Minutes of the General Assembly of the Presbyterian Church* (1909): 847.

55. The property sold for $16,500 to the Ancient and Accepted Scottish Rite of the Valley, a Masonic organization. See *Davidson County, Tennessee, Deed Book, Register's Office*, Book 436. First Church was led by the famous theologian Dr. James I. Vance. He was one of the most powerful religious figures in Nashville. See James I. Vance Collection, Scrapbook no. 1, pp. 91–92; Don H. Doyle, *Nashville: In the New South, 1880–1930* (Knoxville: University of Tennessee Press, 1985): 123; E. C. Scott, *Ministerial Directory of the Presbyterian Church U.S., 1861–1941* (Austin, Tex.: Von Boeckmann-Jones Co., 1942): 733.

56. *CV* 16 (May 1908): 208.

57. *Tennessee Historical Society, Minute Book, 1875–1882*, folder 16, entry for 13 April 1880, Manuscript Division, TSLA. Also see Doyle, *Nashville*, 4; *CV* 15

(April 1907): 152; 3 (September 1895): 272; 18 (May 1910): 216; 15 (April 1907): 152; 17 (February 1909): 53.

58. *CV* 14 (August 1906): 341; 15 (September 1907): 419; 17 (January 1909): 15.

59. See *CV* 20 (November 1912): 512; 21 (January 1913): 5; *Nashville Tennessean and Nashville American*, 3 October 1912, 4 October 1912; *Nashville Banner*, 1 October 1912, 3 October 1912.

60. *Nashville Banner*, 3 October 1912. Comments from other Tennessee papers are found within this issue.

61. The prestigious Hermitage Club was founded in 1882. Much information is lacking on the fraternity. Some of the information presented in the text is based on conversations with Genella Olker, the knowledgeable reference librarian at the Tennessee State Library and Archive, on 11 July 1984; other information is from Doyle, *Nashville*, 68–69. Doyle described the Hermitage Club as the most prominent downtown men's club in Nashville.

62. See *Frank Cheatham Bivouac Papers*, 27 June 1902. This committee was organized after four thousand Nashvillians gathered to discuss world peace proposals voiced by the tsar of Russia. Two close friends of Cunningham's, S. A. Champion (a lawyer) and the theologian Dr. James I. Vance, also served on the committee. Both men played a significant role late in Cunningham's life.

63. *CV* 22 (February 1914): 53.


## Chapter 17: "Proper Histories"

1. *CV* 1 (May 1893): 144. For similar thoughts, see Parker, *Alias, Bill Arp*, 86–98.

2. See *CV* 10 (December 1902): 537; 18 (September 1910): 408; 20 (October 1912): 456.

3. See *CV* 14 (January 1906): 5.

4. *CV* 8 (September 1900): 395. Also see *CV* 19 (July 1911): 327. In Arp's words: "Conquered, but not convinced, we have accepted the situation." See Parker, *Alias, Bill Arp*, 70.

5. *CV* 1 (July 1893): 210.

6. *CV* 17 (July 1909): 313.

7. *CV* 8 (March 1900): 104.

8. *CV* 6 (April 1898): 146.

9. See *CV* 6 (July 1898): 304.

10. *CV* 6 (November 1898): 512.

11. *CV* 2 (March 1894): 336; 11 (March 1903): 108.

12. *CV* 8 (November 1900): 480; 9 (November 1901): 496.

13. *CV* 10 (October 1902): 437.

14. *CV* 11 (January 1903): 4.

15. *CV* 13 (September 1905): 421.

16. *CV* 15 (January 1907): 8.

17. See Governor Albert S. Marks Papers, Benton McMillan Papers, J. B. Frazier Papers, John I. Cox Papers, Malcolm R. Patterson Papers, and Ben W. Hooper Papers, Manuscript Division, TSLA.

18. *CV* 13 (October 1905): 472–73; 13 (November 1905): 520.

19. For exceptions, see *CV* 1 (February 1893): 48; 1 (March 1893): 67; 20 (August 1912): front cover; 2 (July 1894): 209.

20. *CV* 8 (December 1900): 519.

21. *CV* 8 (November 1905): 488–90. At Tuskegee Institute, Roosevelt delivered a speech in which he encouraged obedience to Jim Crow legislation. Cunningham printed the entire speech. See 17 (April 1909): 151.

22. *CV* 17 (February 1909): 54.

23. See annual reports of History Committee, printed in *CV* following the annual reunions. Also see the remarks of the Reverend J.H. McNeilly, Dr. Hunter McGuire, and Lucius O. Wilson in *CV* 2 (April 1894): 128; 7 (November 1899): 500–509; 8 (March 1900): 103. For G.A.R. involvement in the "blue-penciled" histories controversy, see McConnell, *Glorious Contentment*, 224–28.

24. See S. G. French in ibid., 4 (May 1896): 151.

25. Hattaway, *S. D. Lee*, 210.

26. See *CV* 3 (June 1895): 164.

27. *CV* 5 (September 1897): 451.

28. *CV* 5 (July 1897): 391.

29. See *CV* 2 (April 1894): back cover; 8 (September 1905): 427. Books approved by the history committee and made available by Cunningham included *The Justification of the South in Secession* by J. L. M. Curry, *The South as a Factor in the Territorial Advancement of the United States* by W. R. Garrett, *Political History of the Confederacy* by Clement A. Evans, *The South since the War* by S. D. Lee, *Naval History* by J. H. Parker, and *Morale of the Confederate Armies* by J. W. Jones. See *CV* 7 (June 1899): 244–55. Also see *CV* 6 (March 1898): 138; Clement A. Evans to S. A. Cunningham, 30 July 1899, S. A. Cunningham Papers, Southern Historical Collection, Wilson Library, University of North Carolina, Chapel Hill, N.C.; Clement A. Evans, ed., *Confederate Military History: Tennessee*, 8 vols. (Atlanta: Confederate Publishing Company, 1899): 7: 137.

30. See *Minutes of 5th Tenn. UCV Reunion*, 53; *Frank Cheatham Bivouac Papers*, 7 September 1894.

31. *CV* 3 (June 1895): 168. For this key history committee report see ibid., 6 (October 1898): 475–78.

32. *CV* 10 (January 1902): 5.

33. *CV* 8 (November 1900): 503. In 1897 the UCV promoted the establishment of a historical archive in each Southern state. Alabama led the way in 1901, and Tennessee followed in 1905. See *CV* 13 (February 1905): 54. Also see *CV* 3 (August 1895): 254; 5 (May 1897): 225; 5 (June 1897): 307–36; 5 (September 1897): 488; 9 (December 1901): 563; *Minutes of 9th UCV Reunion*, 147; 5 (December 1897): inside front cover; 13 (May 1905): 227–28.

34. *CV* 3 (October 1895): 316; 10 (September 1902): 387. Also see *CV* 6 (July 1898): 350; 21 (January 1913): 24; Osterweis, *Myth of the Lost Cause*, 111.

35. *CV* 19 (April 1911): 148. The controversy began when Sarah Moffett, a student at Roanoke College, refused to attend history class as a protest against the Elson book. See *CV* 19 (August 1911): 365.

36. *CV* 19 (May 1911): 194–96; 19 (July 1911): 318.

37. *CV* 19 (June 1911): 275.

38. Ibid.

39. *CV* 19 (July 1911): 320.

40. *CV* 19 (August 1911): 365. Ironically, the college president earlier had offered Elson a teaching position, which he declined. See Foster, *Ghosts of the Confederacy*, 190.

41. For a compilation of UDC and UCV condemnations of the Elson book, see *CV* 19 (November 1911). George Thornburgh sent a report from the Little Rock UCV to Cunningham on the usage of Elson's book in Arkansas. See George Thornburgh to S. A. Cunningham, 17 September 1912, Confederate Collection, Tennessee Historical Society Papers, Manuscript Division, TSLA.

## Chapter 18: The Confederate Memorial Institute

1. *CV* 4 (February 1896): 48. Also see Matthew Josephson, *The Politico's, 1865–1896* (New York: Harcourt, Brace, 1938): 434; Mary R. Dearing, *Veterans in Politics: The Story of the GAR* (Baton Rouge: Louisiana State University Press, 1952): 393–95; S. A. Cunningham to William L. DeRossett, 13 August 1896, William L. DeRossett Collection, William R. Perkins Library, Duke University, Durham, N.C.

2. For other contemporary Southern views on the pension system, see *Arkansas Gazette*, 3 May 1895, 16 May 1895; *Memphis Commercial-Appeal*, 24 June 1896; *New Orleans Times-Picayune*, 12 November 1897; William H. Glasson, "The South and Service Pension Laws," *South Atlantic Quarterly* 1 (1902): 360.
For examples printed in the *Veteran* throughout its history, see. *CV* 6 (January 1898): 38; 6 (September 1898): 411–13; 6 (December 1898): 555; 12 (November 1904): 548; 16 (February 1908): 81; 20 (May 1912): 227–29.

3. *CV* 7 (January 1899): 27. Tennessee remained the lowest state in pension relief ten years later. Some states budgeted less than fifteen dollars a month for each patient. See *Nashville Banner*, 2 January 1909; 3 April 1895, p. 108.

4. *CV* 16 (October 1908): 485–86. Actually, the Florida legislature first proposed to standardize pension requirements throughout the South. The UCV endorsed the plan in 1899. See *Minutes of 9th UCV Reunion*, 108–9.

5. *CV* 5 (March 1895): 100; *Nashville Tennessean and Nashville American*, 4 March 1911.

6. See *Nashville Banner*, 2 January 1909.

7. This action was in compliance with a directive of the Tennessee 46th General Assembly. See *Minutes of 2nd Tenn. UCV*, 5.

8. See Annie E. Cody, *History of the Tennessee Division, United Daughters of the Confederacy* (Nashville: Cullom and Ghertner, 1945): 10–11; *Minutes of*

*8th Tenn. UCV Reunion*, 27; Cunningham, *Reminiscences*, 40; *CV* 17 (February 1909): 138.

9. See *CV* 11 (April 1903): 151; 16 (November 1908): 573–74, 596; 16 (October 1908): 485–86.

10. *CV* 1 (January 1893): 16.

11. See *Frank Cheatham Bivouac Papers*, 4 May 1900, 5 May 1905; *Nashville Tennessean*, 4 March 1911.

12. *CV* 5 (February 1897): 64. The first veteran described in "The Last Roll" was General J. O. Shelby. Recent indexing of the *Veteran* makes "The Last Roll" a valuable tool for researchers.

13. *CV* 16 (February 1908): 56; 11 (August 1903): 348; 15 (August 1907): 341; 17 (July 1909): 307; *Nashville Tennessean*, 26 October 1912.

14. *CV* 15 (September 1907): 392. Also see *CV* 1 (March 1893): 84, 163; 4 (August 1896): 276; 8 (September 1900): 407. For more opinions on the importance of Decoration Day to Southerners, see *CV* 16 (May 1908): 120; *Memphis Commercial-Appeal*, 25 May 1895, 28 May 1901, 4 June 1905, 3 June 1908; *Memphis Appeal-Avalanche*, 21 May 1892; *Arkansas Gazette*, 15 May 1895, 25 May 1895.

15. See *CV* 10 (May 1902): 207.

16. *CV* 17 (August 1909): 392.

17. See *CV* 12 (February 1904): 78.

18. Cunningham used the same masthead for many years. See *CV* 2 (March 1894): 65.

19. About sixty percent of all Confederate monuments were erected between 1900 and 1912. See Foster, *Ghosts of the Confederacy*, 40, 129, 158. Little Rock, Arkansas, offered a typical example of local enthusiasm. See *Arkansas Gazette*, 30 May 1897, 9 October 1901, 16 May 1903, 4 June 1905.

20. See *Circular Letter Number Seven*, United Confederate Veterans, 1 March 1894. For positive comments from Cunningham, see *CV* 1 (January 1893): 23; 1 (May 1893): 155–57.

21. For a full account of the Oakwood preparations and ceremony, see *CV* 1 (May 1893): 156–57; *Arkansas Gazette*, 27 April 1894, 29 May 1895, 2 June 1895. For the most part, Northern coverage was moderate.

22. *CV* 3 (May 1895): 145; 3 (June 1895): 145, 161.

23. *CV* 1 (June 1895). Also see *New Orleans Times-Picayune*, 28 May 1895, 31 May 1895; *Arkansas Gazette*, 31 May 1895.

24. Folmsbee, *Tennessee*, 430. Also see *CV* 5 (June 1897): 158.

25. For more on Nashville's monument to the private soldier, see *CV* 17 (July 1909): 311.

26. See *CV* 7 (October 1899): 496–99.

27. *CV* 1 (January 1893): 3; 1 (December 1893): 361.

28. Rouss was a shrewd businessman. His prices—cost plus five percent—undercut even Sears and Montgomery Ward. See Sutherland, *Confederate Carpetbaggers*, 157–60, 292. For more on Rouss, see Larry A. Mullin, *The Napoleon of Gotham: A Study of the Life of Charles Broadway Rouss* (Winchester, Va., 1974).

29. Confederate Memorial Association, *The South's Battle Abbey* (Atlanta:

Respess Co., n.d.): 2–3. *Arkansas Gazette*, 21 April 1896, 3 July 1896; *CV* 4 (March 1896): 66.

30. Confederate Memorial Association, *The South's Battle Abbey* (Atlanta: Respess Company, n.d.): 3.

31. Sutherland, *Confederate Carpetbaggers*, 160.

32. Cunningham ran a photograph of the Tennessee officers—President P. P. Pickard, Co-Vice-Presidents General W. H. Jackson and R. Lin Cave, Secretary John P. Hickman, and Treasurer George F. Hager. Cave and Hickman were close friends. See *CV* 3 (January 1895): 8.

33. Confederate Memorial Association, *The South's Battle Abbey*, 4; *Minutes of 15th UCV Reunion*, 56; *CV* 3 (September 1895): 276.

34. *CV* 3 (November 1895): front cover. Besides Chipley, Evans, and Cabell, the members of the executive committee, organized in 1896, included George H. Stuart (Maryland), J. R. McIntosh (Mississippi), George D. Johnston (Alabama), J. B. Cary (Virginia), J. A. Chalaron (Louisiana), W. R. Garrett (Tennessee), John O. Casler (Indian Territory), J. C. Cravens (Missouri), John H. Carter (Kentucky), Howard Williams (Georgia), W. C. Radcliffe (Arkansas), Thomas W. Goree (Texas), R. F. Hoke (North Carolina), John M. Hickey (Washington D.C.), C. S. White (West Virginia). Rouss was personally represented on the committee by A. G. Dickinson. It did not include a representative of every state that had fought for the Confederacy. See Confederate Memorial Association, *The South's Battle Abbey*, 5–7.

35. See General Order #150, 5 October 1895, printed in Confederate Memorial Association, *The South's Battle Abbey*, 6; *CV* 3 (November 1895): 339–41.

36. *Frank Cheatham Bivouac Papers*, 1 February 1895; 16 September 1895.

37. *CV* 3 (October 1895): 313.

38. *Frank Cheatham Bivouac Papers*, 1 November 1895; 5 December 1895.

39. Ibid.

40. See *CV* 3 (September 1895): 276; Confederate Memorial Association, *The South's Battle Abbey*, 6–7. Also see *CV* 5 (May 1897): 198. Varina Howell Davis said, with sarcasm, that if Rouss had his way the Abbey would probably be built in Boston. See *Arkansas Gazette*, 3 July 1896.

41. See *CV* 3 (November 1895): 339–41. Also see Confederate Memorial Association, *The South's Battle Abbey*, 6–7.

42. See *Frank Cheatham Bivouac Papers*, 13 March 1896.

43. See *CV* 4 (June 1896): 176–77. Other Southern cities held similar medieval festivals—the forerunners of today's "Renaissance festivals." See *Memphis Commercial-Appeal*, 3 May 1896.

44. See *CV* 4 (July 1896): 199. For earlier comments on the same subject, see *CV* 4 (March 1896): 68.

45. See *CV* 4 (November 1896): 372; 4 (December 1896): 404; *Minutes of 7th UCV Reunion*, 62–64.

46. See *CV* 71 (August 1899): 346.

47. See Confederate Memorial Association, *The South's Battle Abbey*, 6–7. For a copy of the charter, see *Minutes of 6th UCV Reunion*, 97–100.

48. See *Minutes of 7th UCV Reunion*, 65. Chalaron was no newcomer to the Confederate association. In the 1880s he assisted in organizing the Association of the Army of Tennessee and the UCV. In 1900 he headed the New Orleans Confederate Museum. See Foster, *Ghosts of the Confederacy*, 164.

49. In a letter dated 23 November 1895, President W. D. Chipley told Cunningham that "Rouss is all right but has bad advisors. So now that we are inclined to have confidence in the man himself, we shall keep an eye on the 'advisors.'" See *CV* 7 (September 1899): 393.

50. *Minutes of 7th UCV Reunion*, 65; *CV* 5 (May 1897): 197–99.

51. *Minutes of 7th UCV Reunion*, 62–64.

52. *CV* 5 (June 1897): 389.

53. *Frank Cheatham Bivouac Papers*, 3 December 1897.

54. Ibid., 4 March 1898.

55. *CV* 6 (June 1898): 278.

56. Ibid.

57. See J. A. Chalaron to S. A. Cunningham, 10 August 1899, S. A. Cunningham Papers, Southern Historical Collection, Wilson Library, University of North Carolina, Chapel Hill, N.C.

58. *Minutes of 8th UCV Reunion*, 53–59.

59. See *Frank Cheatham Bivouac Papers*, 5 August 1898; *CV* 6 (August 1898): 354–55.


## Chapter 19: Battle over the Battle Abbey

1. *CV* 7 (August 1899): 346. Cunningham's personal secretary, Edith Pope, described Underwood in similar terms in the 1940s. See F. H. Sweet to Edith Pope, 6 February 1943, S. A. Cunningham Papers, Southern Historical Collection, Wilson Library, University of North Carolina, Chapel Hill, N.C.

2. *CV* 7 (August 1899): 371.

3. *CV* 6 (April 1899): 160.

4. *CV* 7 (June 1899): 257–58; *Minutes of 19th UCV Reunion*, 1 et al.

5. *CV* 172–74.

6. See J. A. Chalaron to S. A. Cunningham, undated letter in 1899, S. A. Cunningham Papers. Also see *CV* 7 (June 1899): 258. The relationship between Evans and Cunningham soured at the Nashville reunion in 1897. At that gathering the Tennessee delegtion alienated Evans when it voted as a bloc against Atlanta as the site of the next reunion. Cunningham publicly endorsed Louisville. See *Minutes of 7th UCV Reunion*.

7. "I was nauseated by General Gordon's gush over him [Underwood]," fumed Chalaron, "and it is an insult almost to the body of the UCV's intelligence to have him carry on in that way." J. A. Chalaron to S. A. Cunningham, 10 August 1899, S. A. Cunningham Papers.

8. Cunningham used the *Veteran* to campaign for Nashville. He felt that such

lobbying was unnecessary, because the city deserved the prize because of the amount of hard cash it had on deposit. See *CV* 7 (June 1899): 258.

9. *CV* 7 (July 1899): 296; 7 (August 1899): 346, 351.

10. *CV* 7 (August 1899): 345.

11. *CV* 7 (August 1899): 346.

12. *CV* 7 (November 1899): 489.

13. S. A. Champion had impeccable credentials. He read law under John C. Brown and represented Henry County in the state legislature. He moved to Nashville in 1884, where he earned a reputation for being a conscientious and candid advisor and advocate of progressive reforms in the Tennessee Bar. He sat on the state executive committee for the Democratic party. His associational activities included memberships in McKendree Methodist Church and on the Nashville Park Commission. This highly respected member of the community died on 25 April 1906. See *Proceedings of the 25th Annual Meeting of the Bar Association of Tennessee* (n.p.: 1906), 26–29.

14. Underwood sued Cunningham and the Southwest Methodist-Episcopal Publishing House for fifty thousand dollars each. See *Underwood v. Cunningham, United States Circuit Court of Appeals, Sixth Circuit Court, Nashville* (Louisville: Courier-Journal Printing Co., 1901), Special Collections, Vanderbilt University Library.

15. *CV* 7 (August 1899): 347.

16. Ibid.

17. J. A. Chalaron to S. A. Cunningham, 16 August 1899, S. A. Cunningham Papers. Also see S. A. Cunningham to J. A. Chalaron, 10 August 1899.

18. *CV* 7 (June 1899): 257; 7 (August 1899): 345–52, 371–72; 7 (October 1899); 466–70; 7 (November 1899): 488–89.

19. See *CV* 7 (October 1899): 466–70.

20. E. E. Stickley to S. A. Cunningham, 10 October 1899, S. A. Cunningham Papers. For similar letters, see I. M. Shirer to S. A. Cunningham, 16 October 1899; George H. Cole to S. A. Cunningham, undated.

21. *CV* 7 (September 1899): 396.

22. Frierson Bivouac (Shelbyville) and Wilson Camp (Savannah, Ga.) also sent supportive resolutions to Cunningham. See *CV* 7 (November 1899): 489; *Frank Cheatham Bivouac Papers*, 21 September 1899, 4 August 1899.

23. The *Dallas News* article is reprinted in the *Veteran*. See *CV* 7 (October 1899): 466.

24. B. H. Teague to S. A. Cunningham, 15 October 1899, S. A. Cunningham Papers.

25. Ibid.

26. Ibid.

27. Ibid.

28. Ibid.

29. See *CV* 10 (March 1902): 105; *Underwood v. Cunningham*, p. 27. For a detailed account of Cunningham's complaints, see pp. 1–73.

30. *Underwood v. Cunningham,* 33–37, 136.

31. Ibid., 58–60; *CV* 7 (November 1899): 488.

32. F. C. Chadwell to *Nashville American,* undated letter in 1899. See S. A. Cunningham Papers.

33. See *CV* 10 (March 1902): 105.

34. *Frank Cheatham Bivouac Papers,* 7 July 1899.

35. The Tennessee contributions disappeared without a trace. See *Minutes of 15th UCV Reunion,* 30. Also see *Frank Cheatham Bivouac Papers,* 7 July 1899, 6 April 1900, 6 July 1900, 3 August 1900, 7 September 1900, 7 December 1900.

36. *CV* 8 (April 1900): 156.

37. *Frank Cheatham Bivouac Papers,* 4 May 1900; *CV* 8 (April 1900): 156.

38. See William P. Tolley to S. A. Cunningham, 21 July 1900, S. A. Cunningham Papers.

39. Ibid.

40. *Minutes of 10th UCV Reunion,* 74–75.

41. *CV* 8 (October 1900), 454.

42. *CV* 8 (August 1900): 344.

43. Lewis Tillman to S. A. Cunningham, 21 September 1900, S. A. Cunningham Papers. Tillman (1845–1938) had been a lifelong friend of Cunningham's. See Tillman, *Tillman Genealogy,* 7.

44. S. A. Champion to S. A. Cunningham, 5 February 1901, S. A. Cunningham Papers. Also see *Underwood v. Cunningham,* 98; *CV* 9 (February 1901): 56; 9 (April 1901): 150.

45. Malcolm McNeil to S. A. Cunningham, 23 January 1901, S. A. Cunningham Papers.

46. J. A. Chalaron to S. A. Cunningham, 16 August 1899, S. A. Cunningham Papers.

47. Wood resided in Louisiana, and Chalaron knew him. See J. A. Chalaron to S. A. Cunningham, 23 February 1901, S. A. Cunningham Papers.

48. Prior to the libel suit, Meek left Nashville for another publishing position in Cleveland. See S. W. Meek to S. A. Champion, 16 July 1901, S. A. Cunningham Papers. S. A. Cunningham to J. A. Chalaron, 21 July 1901, Administrative Papers, 1870–1960, Louisiana Historical Association Collection, Howard-Tilton Memorial Library, Tulane University, New Orleans, Louisiana.

49. *Underwood v. Cunningham,* 90, 122–24, 137. Also see Malcolm McNeil to S. A. Cunningham, 3 May 1901, S. A. Cunningham Papers.

50. *Underwood v. Cunningham,* 121, 127–34; *CV* 9 (April 1901): 150.

51. *Underwood v. Cunningham,* 96, 101; *CV* 9 (June 1901): 252.

52. See *CV* 9 (July 1901): 295. Cunningham admitted that "her religious teachings was a great and permanent force in his life." See *CV* 6 (August 1898): 395; 8 (April 1900): 179–80; 8 (July 1900): 332; 9 (May 1901): 231. Also see Clinton, *The Plantation Mistress,* 90, 95.

53. *CV* 9 (May 1901): 231. For a complete account of Paul's tragic death, see *CV* 9 (July 1901): 294–302; *Nashville Tennessean,* 23 December 1913.

54. See Mrs. W. R. Lyman to Edith Pope, 21 April 1912, Confederate Collec-

tion, Tennessee Historical Society Papers, Manuscript Division, TSLA. *CV* 9 (July 1901): 294. It is possible that the body was never recovered. There is no grave for Paul in the Cunningham section of Willow Mount Cemetery in Shelbyville or in the Davis family graveyard near Forsyth, Georgia.

55. See *Frank Cheatham Bivouac Papers*, 2 August 1901; George Reese to S. A. Cunningham, 14 August 1901, S. A. Cunningham Papers. Varina Howell Davis to S. A. Cunningham, undated, Davis Collection, Manuscript Division, TSLA.

56. *CV* 9 (August 1901): 342; *Monroe County (Forsyth) Advertiser*, 30 August 1901.

57. *CV* 9 (December 1901): 514.


## Chapter 20: Desperate Times

1. Clement A. Evans to S. A. Cunningham, 5 June 1901, S. A. Cunningham Papers, Southern Historical Collection, Wilson Library, University of North Carolina, Chapel Hill, N.C. Also see *Underwood v. Cunningham*, 96; Malcolm McNeil to S. A. Cunningham, 3 May 1901, and George Reese to S. A. Cunningham, 19 June 1901, S. A. Cunningham Papers.

2. For a sampling of the veterans' indifference to the Battle Abbey project, see George Reese to S. A. Cunningham, 22 January 1902, S. A. Cunningham Papers.

3. C. B. Rouss to S. A. Cunningham, 23 May 1901, reprinted in *CV* 10 (March 1902): 105. Rouss was known to be abrasive, vulgar, brash, ambitious, and blunt. See Sutherland, *Confederate Carpetbaggers*, 157.

4. Cunningham's lawyer proved that Section 4559 of *Shannon's Code*, chapter 126 of the *Acts of the General Assembly of 1871*, had been violated in the first trial. The *Code* clearly showed that codefendants had the right to request separate trials. See *Underwood v. Cunningham*, 147. Also see *CV* 9 (July 1901): 303; George Reese to S. A. Cunningham, 19 June 1901, S. A. Cunningham Papers.

5. George Reese to S. A. Cunningham, 19 June 1901, S. A. Cunningham Papers.

6. Ibid., 18 March 1902. Also see V. Y. Cook to S. A. Cunningham, 2 April 1902, S. A. Cunningham Papers.

7. See *CV* 9 (October 1901): 339–40; 10 (October 1902): 463.

8. S. A. Cunningham to J. A. Chalaron, 21 July 1901, Adminsitrative Papers, 1887–1960, Louisiana Historical Association Collection, Howard-Tilton Memorial Library, Tulane University, New Orleans, La.

9. *Minutes of 11th UCV Reunion*, 47–51.

10. *CV* 9 (June 1901): 252. George Reese accurately forecast this event in a letter to Cunningham, saying, "I am satisfied that if this matter is brought up in the Convention, it will create trouble in our grand organization." See George Reese to S. A. Cunningham, 29 April 1901, S. A. Cunningham Papers; *CV* 9 (June 1901): 252–54. The financial statement of the Executive Committee was printed in full. Also see *CV* 10 (April 1902): 151.

11. For all points on which the judge agreed with the defense lawyers, see *Underwood v. Cunningham*, 100–34.

12. See *CV* 10 (June 1902): 249–53; 10 (December 1902): 540. Cunningham did win a suit against attorney John A. Pitts, who had written a brief for Judge Clark in the second trial. It was decided that Pitts's comments had "injuriously reflected" on Cunningham's case. See *CV* 9 (July 1901): 303; 10 (October 1902): 448.

13. *CV* 8 (June 1902): 299.

14. See ibid., 10 (April 1902): 150. The legislatures in Tennessee and Texas favored the plan along with the UDC. See *CV* 10 (July 1902): 312; 12 (April 1904): 176.

15. George Reese to S. A. Cunningham, 26 March 1902 and 14 April 1902, S. A. Cunningham Papers.

16. *CV* 10 (April 1902): 151.

17. Clement A. Evans to S. A. Cunningham, 7 April 1902, S. A. Cunningham Papers.

18. Clement A. Evans to S. A. Cunningham, 5 May 1902, S. A. Cunningham Papers. Also see *CV* 10 (April 1902): 151.

19. *Minutes of 12th UCV Reunion*, 67–69.

20. *Frank Cheatham Bivouac Papers*, 2 May 1902.

21. The CMA hired the firm of Weeks, Battle and Marshall. As for Jones's appointment, he was given a salary of $125 per month with no commission. See *Minutes of 13th UCV Reunion*, 77–78. Also see *Arkansas Gazette*, 14 June 1904; *CV* 12 (October 1904): 481. Later Jones offered his own personal bound set of the *Veteran* as a gift to the Battle Abbey library. See *CV* 14 (April 1906): 160.

22. See *Minutes of 14th UCV Reunion*, 30; *CV* 12 (October 1904): 481; *CV* 13 (August 1905): 376–77; *Minutes of 17th UCV Reunion*, 65–66; *Minutes of 15th UCV Reunion*, 36–39; *CV* 14 (November 1906): 488.

23. In 1910 the new chairman of the Executive Board, J. Taylor Ellyson, announced that the financial goal for the Battle Abbey had been reached. Construction began two years later and Julian S. Carr officiated at the dedication in 1921. For more details on the final phase of the Battle Abbey project, see *Minutes of 17th UCV Reunion*, 15; *Minutes of 18th UCV Reunion*, 102–3; *Minutes of 19th UCV Reunion*, 53–54; *Minutes of 20th UCV Reunion*, 111–14; *Minutes of 21st UCV Reunion*, 124; *CV* 15 (April 1907): 151; 19 (March 1911): 106–7; 19 (May 1911): 215–16; 21 (July 1913): 354–55; 29 (June 1921): 204.

Foster concluded that "the Battle Abbey scheme became less a monument to Southern valor than an object lesson in how Virginians could dominate the Confederate past." Surely the role of one stubborn Tennessean cannot be overlooked. See Foster, *Ghosts of the Confederacy*, 112.


## Chapter 21: Crowning Glories

1. *CV* 2 (May 1894): 152.

2. J. B. Killebrew, ex-commissioner of agriculture for Tennessee, wrote a three-column sketch on Sam Davis in 1871. But the story was not well known until Cunningham popularized it twenty-four years later. See *Nashville Union and Ameri-*

can, 30 June 1871, 4 July 1871. Also see *CV* 5 (February 1897): 84. For the most complete account of the Sam Davis story, see S. A. Cunningham, "Sam Davis," *American Historical Magazine* 24 (July 1899): 194–209. Also see Osterweis, *Myth of the Lost Cause*, 100.

3. *CV* 3 (May 1895): 149.

4. *CV* 3 (July 1895): 203.

5. *CV* 3 (August 1895).

6. See McConnell, *Glorious Contentment*, 107.

7. *CV* 3 (July 1895): 203.

8. *CV* 4 (August 1895): 240.

9. *CV* 3 (September 1895); 3 (November 1895): 336; 4 (January 1896): 16. Owen N. Meredith, "The Sam Davis Home," *Tennessee Historical Quarterly* 24 (1965): 303–20. Cunningham simplified the process by providing a pledge form in his magazine.

10. See published names and addresses of contributors in *CV* 3 (December 1895): 370; 4 (May 1896): 143; 8 (March 1900): 100; Memphis *Commercial-Appeal*, 30 April 1909.

11. *CV* 4 (March 1896): 80.

12. *CV* 4 (May 1896): 142; *Frank Cheatham Bivouac Papers*, 1 May 1896.

13. Cunningham, "Sam Davis," *American Historical Magazine* (July 1899): 194–204; *CV* 7 (December 1899): 538–42; 16 (October 1908): 522–28.

14. See Cunningham, *Sam Davis, The Story of an Old-Fashioned Boy* (Nashville: Confederate Veteran, 1914).

15. See *CV* 5 (July 1897): 358–59. The Confederate overcoat was pictured herein.

16. Cunningham, "Sam Davis," 205.

17. *CV* 5 (July 1897): 358.

18. S. A. Cunningham to James W. Eldridge, 21 December 1897, Samuel Brock Collection, Huntington Library, San Marino, Calif.

19. S. A. Cunningham to James W. Eldridge, 30 April 1898, Samuel Brock Collection.

20. See Cunningham, "Sam Davis," 203; *CV* 5 (April 1897): 181–82. Today Mrs. Davis's letter is displayed in the museum at the Sam Davis home near Smyrna.

21. *CV* 11 (November 1903): 492.

22. *CV* 8 (January 1900): 3.

23. *CV* 8 (March 1900): 99.

24. See *CV* 14 (May 1906): 200; 15 (November 1907): 488; 16 (August 1908): 375; 16 (November 1908): 560; 17 (June 1909): 280; *Nashville Tennessean*, 9 February 1908.

25. *CV* 21 (July 1913): 323. Also see 17 (May 1909): 200; 17 (June 1909): 280; James I. Vance Collection, Scrapbook #1, 1899–1917, Manuscript Division, TSLA.

26. *CV* 14 (November 1906). Sample topics included Camp Morton, Camp Douglas, Camp Chase, and Johnson's Island Prison. J. William Jones contributed an earlier article entitled "The Treatment of Prisoners During the War." See *CV* 13 (September 1905): 401–5.

27. *CV* 14 (September 1906): 394. Cunningham found nothing improper in building a monument to Wirz. For more, see *CV* 14 (October 1906): 446–48.

28. See *CV* 15 (May 1907): 202–3; 21 (July 1913): 323; Cunningham, *Col. Richard Owen; The Good Samaritan of Camp Morton* (Nashville: Confederate Veteran, 1914).

29. *CV* 7.

30. See *CV* 19 (April 1911): 150–51; 19 (July 1911): 320; Cunningham, *The Good Samaritan*, 3, 31.

31. For a discussion of financial problems, see *CV* 21 (June 1913): 278–79. See Miscellaneous Items, Confederate Collection, Tennessee Historical Society Papers, Manuscript Division, TSLA.

32. *CV* 20 (April 1912): 150.

33. Cunningham, *The Good Samaritan*, 11.

34. Ibid., 4, 11. For more on Cunningham's feelings about the Owen memorial tablet, see *Nashville Tennessean*, 18 May 1913; Unknown to Edith D. Pope, 21 March 1914, Confederate Collection.

35. Cunningham, *The Good Samaritan*, 4. H. M. Hamill completed the article after Cunningham's death. He also read Cunningham's keynote address at the dedication ceremony to the Tennessee Historical Society.

36. Cunningham, *Sam Davis*, 35. One significant difference was that the Davises owned five times as many slaves as did the Cunninghams.

37. Ibid., 35–36.

38. Ibid., 37.

39. *CV* 3 (September 1895): front cover; 8 (November 1900): 478. Southerners routinely made reference to Christianity when explaining their history. Piston asserts that many turn-of-the-century "historians" saw James Longstreet as a Judas figure. See Piston, *Lee's Tarnished Lieutenant*, 112. For more on the notion of civil religion, see Charles R. Wilson, *Baptized in Blood: The Religion of the Lost Cause, 1865–1920* (Athens: University of Georgia Press, 1980).

40. Cunningham, *Sam Davis*, 44.

41. Charles Venable, a wartime aid to Lee, claims that the Confederate commander uttered the exact same phrase shortly before the surrender at Appomattox on 9 April 1865. See Connelly, *The Marble Man*, 51.

42. See George P. Morrill, "The Soldier Who Wouldn't Tell," *Read Magazine* 35 (March 1986): 20–26.

43. On a less auspicious note, the Sam Davis statue in Pulaski was the rally point for a KKK demonstration in 1989. See *Sunday (Portland) Oregonian*, 8 October 1989.


Chapter 22: "Having Done What He Could"

1. See *Nashville City Directory* (1912 and 1913); also see *Nashville Banner*, 8 January 1910; *CV* 16 (October 1898): 490; 13 (August 1905); Will T. Hale and

Dixon L. Merritt, *A History of Tennessee and Tennesseans*, 4 vols. (Chicago: Lewis Publishing Co., 1913): 4:863.

2. A report filed by V. Y. Cook estimated that fourteen percent of all surviving Confederate veterans died each year beginning in 1907. See unaddressed letter from V. Y. Cook, William Alexander Smith Papers, William R. Perkins Library, Duke University, Durham, N.C.

3. *CV* 19 (July 1901): 354. Also see July issues for 1903 and 1911.

4. *CV* 18 (July 1910): 312.

5. *CV* 17 (September 1909): 440; 17 (October 1909): 488.

6. See *Nashville Tennessean*, 7 December 1912.

7. Cook was a merchant and planter from Batesville, Arkansas. He had been commander of the local UCV camp and an aide to commanders John B. Gordon, Lee, Evans, G. W. Gordon, and Young. Cook's associational activities included president of the Arkansas Historical Association and trustee of the University of Arkansas. See William E. Mickle, *Well-Known Confederate Veterans and Their War Records* (New Orleans: Mickle Publishing Co., 1915): 25.

8. See *Davidson County, County Clerk's Office, Wills, 1909.*

9. Ibid.

10. The board of trustees included Cook, R. H. Dudley, Bennett H. Young, K. Van Zandt, Edith Pope, Clement A. Evans, and Clarence M. Owens. See *Davidson County, County Clerk's Office, Wills, 1909; CV* 22 (January 1914): 1.

11. See Rebecca Cameron to Professor J. G. de Roulhac Hamilton, 28 June 1911, J. G. de Roulhac Hamilton Papers, Southern Historical Collection, Wilson Library, University of North Carolina, Chapel Hill, N.C.

12. *CV* 20 (August 1912): 360.

13. *CV* 20 (December 1912): 552.

14. See *CV* 21 (April 1913): 153–55; *Nashville Banner*, 22 December 1913. For an account of the long-standing friendship between Cunningham and Dan Emmett, see John A. Simpson, "Shall We Change the Words to 'Dixie'?," *Southern Folklore Quarterly* 45 (1981): 19–40. Emmett's handwritten reproduction of "Dixie," which he prepared especially for Cunningham, is in the Confederate Collection, Tennessee Historical Society Papers, Manuscript Division, TSLA.

15. He died in St. Thomas Hospital, Nashville, at 6:38 P.M. on Saturday, 20 December 1913. See *Nashville Tennessean*, 21 December 1913; *Shelbyville Gazette*, 25 December 1913. Also see *Nashville Banner*, 18, 19, 20 December 1913; *Nashville Tennessean*, 18, 21 December 1913; James I. Vance Collection, Scrapbook no. 1, 1899–1917, Manuscript Division, TSLA.

16. *CV* 19 (December 1911): 557; 22 (January 1914): 13; 23 (September 1915): 392. *Nashville Banner*, 22 December 1913. Also see *Nashville Tennessean*, 25 December 1913. The thirty-member committee, composed mostly of Nashville ladies, met irregularly.

17. See *CV* 23 (August 1915): 344; 28 (August 1920): 123; 29 (November–December 1921): 403–7. For more on the planning of the monument, see G. Moretti to Edith D. Pope, 2 September 1919, 23 January 1920, 23 March 1920, in Confed-

erate Collection, Tennessee Historical Society Papers. For the words that appear on the sides of the monument, see Marsh and Marsh, *Cemetery Records of Bedford County*, 206.

18. See Reda C. Goff, "The Confederate Veteran Magazine," *Tennessee Historical Quarterly* 31 (1972): 59; *Who Was Who, 1897–1942*, 2 vols. (New York: Century, 1942): 1:284.

19. For minutes of trustee meetings from 1914 to 1917, see Confederate Collection, Tennessee Historical Society Papers; *CV* 22 (February 1914): 64.

20. See Foster, *Ghosts of the Confederacy*, 196.

21. *Arkansas Gazette*, 25 December 1932.

22. *CV* 2 (April 1894): 128. Edith D. Pope was born to William Campbell Pope and Mary Caroline Drake Pope of Thompson Station, Williamson County, Tennessee. She had two sisters and a brother, and was educated at the Tennessee Female College in Franklin.

23. Edith D. Pope to Mrs. W. J. Behan, 9 January 1914, Memorial Association Papers, 1866–1958, Louisiana Historical Association Collection, Howard-Tilton Memorial Library, Tulane University, New Orleans, La.

24. For more on the Sweet-Pope correspondence, see Edith D. Pope to F. G. Sweet, 25 August 1934; Forest H. Sweet to Edith Pope, 25 August 1934; Forest H. Sweet to Edith Pope, 10 August 1935; F. H. Sweet to Edith Pope, 6 February 1943, S. A. Cunningham Papers, Southern Historical Collection, Wilson Library, University of North Carolina, Chapel Hill, N.C.

F. G. and F. H. Sweet operated a Battle Creek firm known as the American Historical Material, Autographs, Books and Prints Bought and Sold. When Parke-Bernet Galleries of New York City auctioned his private collection in 1963, it contained no Cunningham-Pope documents. See Forest H. Sweet, *Directory of Collectors of books, autographs, prints and other historical material relating to Abraham Lincoln* (Battle Creek: F. H. Sweet, 1946, 1949); Parke-Bernet Galleries, *Inventory of Forest H. Sweet Collection Sold in Auction, September 24, 1962, #2205*.

25. See *Nashville Banner*, 1 September 1944; *Nashville Tennessean*, 26 January 1947; *Nashville Review Appeal*, 30 January 1947.


## Epilogue

1. See *CV* 22 (January 1914): 6–7.

2. *CV* 21 (December 1913): 568. People like Cunningham who advocated the Lost Cause philosophy were not simplistic or romantic. Rather, the values he championed actually helped Southerners adjust to a new order. See Foster, *Ghosts of the Confederacy*, 6–8.

3. See *Confederate Patriot Index, 1924–1978*, Tennessee Division, United Daughters of the Confederacy, 2 vols. (Columbia, Tenn.: P-Vine Press, 1978): 2: 132; *United Daughters of the Confederacy, Tennessee Division, Registrar's Book*, Manuscript Division, TSLA, 49: 107–10.

4. See *Nashville Tennessean*, 20 March 1985; interview with Annette McNeil, Librarian, *Nashville Tennessean* Archive, 15 July 1985; Patricia L. Faust, ed., *Historical Times Illustrated Encyclopedia of the Civil War* (New York: Harper & Row, 1986): 157; S. A. Cunningham File, United Daughters of the Confederacy Library, Richmond, Va.

5. William Faulkner, *Intruder in the Dust* (New York: Vintage Books, 1948 reprint), 194–95.

# Bibliography

## Primary Sources

PUBLIC RECORDS

*Bedford County, Tennessee. Circuit Court, County Clerk's Office*, 1865–1879.
*Bedford County, Tennessee. County Clerk's Office, Tax Lists*, 1812–1875.
*Bedford County, Tennessee. Deed Book, Register's Office*, 1834–1877.
*Bedford County, Tennessee, Trust Deeds and Chattel Mortgages*, 1868–1878.
*Bedford County, Tennessee. Wills, County Clerk's Office*, 1890.
*Chattanooga City Directory*, 1880–1882.
*Civil War Questionnaires*, 22 vols. Nashville: Tennessee Historical Commission, 1922.
Confederate War Records Division. *Compiled Service Records of Soldiers Who Served in Organizations from the State of Tennessee, 41st Infantry, A-C*, roll 281. Washington, D.C.: National Archives, 1959.
——— . Record Group 241. *Consolidated Index to Compiled Service Records of Confederate Soldiers, M253, Cumm-Currles*, roll 111. Washington, D.C.: National Archives, 1959.
*Davidson County, Tennessee. Deed Book, Register's Office*, 1909.
*Davidson County, Tennessee. Tax Books*, 1886–1914.
*Davidson County, Tennessee. Wills, County Clerk's Office*, 1909.
*List of Military Organizations and Officers from Tennessee in Both the Confederate and Union Armies*. New York: Williamsburg Press, 1908.
*Marriage Records, Tennessee*. Microfiche Collection, Church Library, Church of Jesus Christ of Latter-Day Saints, Eugene, Oregon.
*Minutes of the Twenty-seventh General Assembly of the Cumberland Presbyterian Church in the United States*. St. Louis: Republican, 1857.
*Monroe County, Georgia. Marriage Records, Court of the Ordinary*, 1834–1867.
*Nashville City Directory*, 1885–1914.
Report of the Pennsylvania Commission. *Fiftieth Anniversary of the Battle of Gettysburg*. Harrisburg: State Printing Office, 1914.

*Selected Records of the War Department Relating to Confederate Prisoners of War, 1861–1865*, roll 102. Washington, D.C.: National Archives, 1959.

*Trow's New York City Directory for the Year Ending May 1, 1884*, 97. New York: Trow City Directory Co., 1883.

*Underwood v. Cunningham, United States Circuit Court of Appeals, Sixth Circuit Court, Nashville*. Louisville: Courier-Journal Printing Company, 1901.

*United States Circuit Court of Appeals, Sixth District, Nashville*. LIII. Rochester, N.Y.: Lawyers' Cooperative Publishing Company, 1903.

U.S. Census, *Agricultural Schedule, Bedford County, Tennessee*, 1830–1860.

———, *Population, Bedford County, Tennessee*, 1830–1860.

———, *Population, Davidson County, Tennessee*, 1880–1910.

———, *Population, Monroe County, Georgia*, 1880.

———, *Slave Abstracts, Bedford County, Tennessee*, 1830–1860.

———, *White Population, Bedford County, Tennessee*, 1830–1860.

U.S. Congress. House Committee on Veterans Affairs. *Historical Statistics of the Veteran Population, 1865–1960; A Compendium of Facts About Veterans*. House Committee Report no. 69, 87th Congress, 1st session, 1961.

U.S. Department of Commerce. Bureau of the Census. *Negro Population, 1790–1915*. Washington, D.C.: Government Printing Office, 1918.

U.S. Department of Commerce. Bureau of the Census. *White Population, 1840–1910*.

U.S. House of Representatives. *House Miscellaneous Documents, no. 53*, 41st Congress, 2nd session.

*War of the Rebellion: A Compilation of the Official Records of the Union and Confederate Armies*. 128 vols. Washington, D.C.: Government Printing Office, 1880–1901.


PROCEEDINGS

*Minutes of the Annual Association of Confederate Soldiers, Tennessee*, 1888–1913.

*Minutes of the Annual United Confederate Veterans Association*, 1891–1914.

*Minutes of the General Assembly of the Presbyterian Church in the U.S.A.*, 1906–1909.

*Proceedings of the Convention for the Organization and Adoption of the Constitution of the United Confederate Veterans Association*. New Orleans: Hopkins Press, 1891.

*Proceedings of the Great Reunion of the Veterans of the Confederate States Cavalry, Held in the City of New Orleans on February 13, 1888*. New Orleans: Hopkins Press, 1888.

*Proceedings of the 25th Annual Meeting of the Bar Association of Tennessee*, 1906.

United Confederate Veterans. *Circular Letter Number Seven*, 1 March 1894.

NEWSPAPERS AND PERIODICALS

*Arkansas Gazette*, 1889–1913.
*Chattanooga Times*, 1876–1879.
*Chattanooga Times*, Twenty-fifth Anniversary edition, 1 July 1903. In S. A. Cunningham biographical file, Chattanooga Bicentennial Library, Chattanooga, Tennessee.
*Chattanooga Weekly Commercial*, 1878.
*The Confederate Veteran Magazine: A Medium of Intercommunication for Confederate Soldiers*, January–July 1890.
*Confederate Veteran*, 1893–1921.
*Confederate War Journal Illustrated*, 1893–1894.
*Indianapolis Daily Journal*, February–September 1862.
*Memphis Appeal-Avalanche*, 1891–1894.
*Memphis Commercial-Appeal*, 1894–1913.
*Memphis Daily-Appeal*, 1889–1890.
*Nashville Banner*, 1909–1912.
*Nashville Daily American*, 1885–1914.
*Nashville Tennessean*, 1911–1914.
*Nashville Tennessean and Nashville American*, 1912.
*New Orleans Times-Democrat*, March 1893.
*New Orleans Times-Picayune*, 1889–1902.
*Shelbyville Commercial*, 1818–1884
*Shelbyville Expositor*
*Shelbyville Republican*
*Shelbyville Times-Gazette*, Sesqui-Centennial Historical Edition, October 7, 1969.
*Shelbyville Whig*, 1818–


MANUSCRIPTS

Baker Library, Harvard University Graduate School of Business Administration, Cambridge, Massachusetts.
R. G. Dun and Company Collection, Tennessee, 2 vols.
Bedford County Library, History Room, Shelbyville, Tennessee.
Lucille Frizzel Jacobs, "Duck River Valley in Tennessee and Its Pioneers."
Gilly Stevens, "Early Church History of Bedford County."
Rose Tate Stewart, "Pioneer Schools of Bedford County and Their Masters."
Chattanooga Bicentennial Library, Chattanooga, Tennessee.
S. A. Cunningham biographical file.
Georgia Department of Archives and History, Atlanta, Georgia.
Monroe County Cemeteries. Miscellaneous file.
Howard-Tilton Memorial Library, Manuscript Division, Tulane University, New Orleans, Louisiana.
Louisiana Historical Association, Memorial Association Papers, 1866–1958.

Huntington Library, San Marino, California.
  Samuel Brock Collection.
Kentucky Historical Society, Frankfort, Kentucky.
  Emilie Todd Helm Collection.
Louisiana State University Library, Baton Rouge, Louisiana.
  Adjutant-General's Correspondence, United Confederate Veterans Association.
William R. Perkins Library, Duke University, Durham, North Carolina.
  William Alexander Smith Papers.
  C. Clay Papers.
  Confederate Veteran Papers.
  William L. DeRossett Papers.
  Paul H. Hayne Papers.
Tennessee State Library and Archives, Manuscript Division, Nashville, Tennessee.
  Frank Cheatham Bivouac Papers, Minute Book, 1887–1906.
  Correspondence of the Governor's Office of Tennessee (CGO).
    William B. Bate, 1883–1887.
    John C. Brown, 1871–1875.
    John P. Buchanan, 1891–1893.
    John Cox, 1905–1907.
    James Frazier, 1903–1905.
    Ben Hooper, 1911–1915.
    Robert L. Love, 1887–1891, 1897–1899.
    Benton McMillan, 1899–1903.
    Albert S. Marks, 1879–1883.
    Malcolm Patterson, 1907–1911.
    James D. Porter, 1875–1879.
    Peter Turney, 1893–1897.
    S. A. Cunningham biographical sketch.
    Varina Howell Davis Papers.
    Robert Farquaharson biographical sketch.
    Margaret Howell Davis Hayes Papers.
    William Henry McRaven Papers.
    Methodist Publishing Company Archive, S. A. Cunningham file.
    Fleurney Rivers Scrapbook, no. 1.
    Tennessee Historical Society Minute Book, 1875–1882.
    Tennessee Historical Society, Miscellaneous file.
    United Daughters of the Confederacy, Tennessee Division, Register's Book, 49.
    James I. Vance Collection.
United Daughters of the Confederacy Library, Richmond, Virginia.
  S. A. Cunningham file.
Virginia Historical Society, Richmond, Virginia.
  Kate Mason Rowland Collection.

Wilson Library, Southern Historical Collection, University of North Carolina, Chapel Hill, North Carolina.
   S. A. Cunningham Papers.

## ARTICLES

"At Gettysburg." *Outlook* 104 (1913): 541.

Boynton, H. V. "The Chickamauga National Park." *Harper's Weekly* 34 (1895): 584–85.

——. "The National Military Park." *Century* 43 (1895): 703–8.

Carnahan, James. "Treatment of Prisoners at Camp Morton." *Century* 42 (1891): 757–75.

Cunningham, S. A. "Sam Davis." *American Historical Review* 24 (1899): 194–209.

"Fighting the Civil War Over Again." *Outlook* 98 (1911): 707.

"Gettysburg Fifty Years After." *American Monthly Review of Reviews* 48 (1913): 177–83.

Glasson, William H. "The South and Service Pension Laws." *South Atlantic Quarterly* 1 (1902): 351–60.

"Honors to Jefferson Davis." *American Monthly Review of Reviews* 8 (1893): 6–7.

Miles, Nelson A. "My Treatment of Jefferson Davis." *Independent* 58 (1905): 413–17.

"The South's Care for Her Confederate Veterans." *American Monthly Review of Reviews* 36 (1907): 40–47.

## BOOKS AND PAMPHLETS

Beers, D. G. and Company. *Map of Bedford County, Tennessee.* Philadelphia: D. G. Beers, 1878.

*Bibliography of State Participation in the Civil War.* Washington, D.C.: Government Printing Office, 1913.

*Blum's Farmers' and Planters' Almanac For the Year 1864.* Salem, N.C.: L.V. and E.T. Blum, 1864.

*Centennial Celebration, 4th of July, 1876. At Shelbyville, Bedford County, Tennessee.* Chattanooga: Crandall, 1877.

Cisco, Jay Guy. *Tennessee Authors, Short Biographical Sketches of All Authors, Past and Present Who Have Made Their Homes in Tennessee.* Nashville: Cisco, 1907.

*Confederate Gray Book: Frank Cheatham Bivouac, United Confederate Veterans.* Nashville, n.d.

Confederate Memorial Association. *The South's Battle Abbey.* Atlanta: Respess Co., n.d.

Cox, Jacob D. *The Battle of Franklin, November 30, 1864.* New York: Scribner's, 1897.

Cunningham, Sumner A. *Col. Richard Owen: The Good Samaritan of Camp Morton.* Nashville: Confederate Veteran, 1914.

——. *Reminiscences of the 41st Tennessee Regiment.* Shelbyville: Commercial Press, 1872.

——. *Sam Davis: The Story of An Old-Fashioned Boy.* Nashville: Confederate Veteran, 1914.

Davidson, W. J. "Diary of Private W.J. Davidson, Company C, Forty-first Tennessee Regiment." In Drake, Edwin L., ed., *The Annals of the Army of Tennessee and Early Western History.* Nashville: A. D. Haynes, 1878.

Drake, E. L., ed. *The Annals of the Army of Tennessee and Early Western History.* Nashville: A.D. Haynes, 1878.

Elliott, C. D. *A Plea for the Tennessee Confederate Memorial and Historical Association.* Nashville: C. R. and H. H. Hatch Printers, 1886.

Evans, Clement A., ed. *Confederate Military History: Tennessee,* 8 vols. Atlanta: Confederate Publishing Co., 1899.

Fetter, George G. *Notable Men of Kentucky at the Beginning of the 20th Century.* Louisville: Fetter Printers, 1902.

*Flags of the Confederate Armies.* St. Louis: Ware Publishers, 1905.

Fleming, Walter L. *Documentary History of Reconstruction,* 2 vols. Cleveland: Bobbs-Merrill, 1906.

Fox, William F. *Regimental Losses in the American Civil War 1861–1865.* Albany, N.Y.: Albany Publishing Co., 1889.

Gielow, Martha S. *An Evening of Song and Stories of the South: In Aid of the Sam Davis Monument.* Nashville: Brandon, 1901.

Goodpasture, A. V. *A History of Tennessee.* Nashville: Goodspeed, 1886.

*The Goodspeed Histories of Maury, Williamson, Rutherford, Wilson, Bedford, and Marshall Counties of Tennessee.* Columbia, Tenn.: Woodward and Stinson Printing Co., 1971.

Graham, M. Louise Benton, Daisy M. L. Hodgson, and Virginia Frazer Boyle, eds. *History of the Confederated Memorial Associations of the South.* New Orleans: Graham Press, 1904.

Haworth, Paul. *The Disputed Presidential Election of 1876.* Cleveland: Burrows Brothers, 1906.

Hood, John Bell. *Advance and Retreat: Personal Experiences in the United States and Confederate Armies.* New Orleans: 1880.

Johnson, Robert Underwood, and Clarence C. Buel, eds. *Battles and Leaders of the Civil War,* 4 vols. New York: Century, 1887.

Johnston, Joseph E. *Narrative of Military Operations, Directed in the Late War between the States.* Bloomington: Indiana University Press, 1959.

Jones, J. William, ed. *Southern Historical Society Papers, 1876–1907.* Richmond, Va.: Southern Historical Society Press.

Lindsley, J. M., ed. *The Military Annals of Tennessee: A Review of Military Operations with Regimental Histories and Memorial Rolls.* Nashville: Lindsley Publishers, 1886.

Lists of Military Organizations and Officers from Tennessee in Both the Confederate and Union Armies. New York: Williamsburg Press, 1908.

Livermore, Thomas L. Numbers and Losses in the Civil War in America, 1861–1865. New York: Houghton, Mifflin, 1901.

McGuffey, Charles D. Standard History of Chattanooga, Tennessee, With Full Outline of the Early Settlement, Pioneer Life, Indian History and General and Particular History of the City to the Close of the Year 1910. Knoxville: Crew and Dorey, 1911.

Meriwether, John. The History of Literary and Intellectual Life in the Southern States. Vol. 10 in The South in the Building of the Nation. 12 vols. Richmond: Southern Historical Publication Society, 1909.

Mickle, William E. Well-Known Confederate Veterans And Their War Records. New Orleans: Mickle Publishing Co., 1915.

Miller, Francis Trevelyn, ed. The Photographic History of the Civil War In Ten Volumes. Vols. 1 and 10. New York: Review of Reviews, 1911.

Register of the Kentucky Historical Society, 1902–1916.

Ridley, Bromfield L. Battles and Sketches of the Army of Tennessee. Mexico, Mo.: Missouri Printing Co., 1906.

Speeches and Addresses of William McKinley. New York: Doubleday and McClure, 1900.

Temple, Oliver P. Notable Men of Tennessee: From 1833 to 1875. New York: Cosmopolitan Press, 1912.

Tillman, George Newton. Tillman Genealogy. Nashville: McQuiddy Printing, 1905.

Turney, Peter. The South Justified, an Address Delivered Before Frank Cheatham Bivouac #1 of the Association of Confederate Soldiers, Tennessee Division, Saturday, August 18, 1888. Nashville: Tavel Printers, 1888.

Watkins, Sam R. "Co. Aytch," Maury Grays, First Tennessee Regiment: or, A Side Show of the Big Show. Chattanooga: Times Press, 1900.

Who's Who in Tennessee: A Biographical Reference Book of Notable Tennesseans of Today. Memphis: Paul and Douglass Co., 1911.

Wood, Robert C. Confederate Handbook. New Orleans: Graham Press, 1903.

Worsham, W. J. The Old Nineteenth Tennessee Regiment, C.S.A. Knoxville: Paragon Printing, 1902.

Wright, Marcus J. Tennessee in the War, 1861–1865: Lists of Military Organizations and Officers from Tennessee in both the Confederate and Union Armies. New York: Williamsbridge Press, 1908.

## Secondary Sources

### ARTICLES

Alexander, Thomas B. "Neither Peace Nor War: Conditions in Tennessee in 1865." East Tennessee Historical Society Papers, no. 21 (1949): 33–51.

Barton, Michael. "Other Voices: Evidence on the Moral Socialization of American Children in 1864 and its Psychodynamics." *American Journal of Psychoanalysis* 37 (1977): 235–39.

"Bedford County Tax List, 1836." *Bedford County Historical Quarterly* 3 (1979).

"Bedford County, Will Book I." *Bedford County Historical Quarterly* 3 (1979).

Breeden, James O. "A Medical History of the Later Stages of the Atlanta Campaign." *Journal of Southern History* 35 (1969): 31–59.

Crawford, W. T. "The Mystery of Spring Hill." *Civil War History* 1 (1955): 101–26.

Crownover, Sims. "The Battle of Franklin." *Tennessee Historical Quarterly* 14 (1955): 291–322.

Cummings, Charles M. "Otho French Strahl: 'Choicest Spirit to Embrace the South.'" *Tennessee Historical Quarterly* 24 (1965): 341–55.

———. "Richard Owen, Teacher in Tennessee." *Tennessee Historical Quarterly* 28 (1969): 273–96.

Dollard, John. "A Method of Measuring Tension in Personal Documents." *Journal of Abnormal and Social Psychology* 42 (1947): 3–32.

Donald, David. "The Confederate Soldier as a Fighting Man." *Journal of Southern History* 25 (1959): 178–93.

Goff, Reda C. "The Confederate Veteran Magazine." *Tennessee Historical Quarterly* 31 (1972): 45–60.

Hay, Thomas R. "The Battle of Chattanooga." *Georgia Historical Quarterly* 8 (1924): 121–41.

———. "The Davis-Hood-Johnston Controversy of 1864." *Mississippi Valley Historical Review* 11 (1924): 54–84.

Hoffman, Martin L. "Childrearing Practices: Generalizations From Empirical Research." *Child Development* 34 (1963): 259–318.

Katz, Daniel. "The Functional Approach to the Study of Attitudes." *Public Opinion* 4 (1960): 163–204.

Kiger, Joseph C. "Social Thought as Voiced in Rural Middle Tennessee Newspapers, 1878–1898." *Tennessee Historical Quarterly* 9 (1950): 131–54.

"The K.K.K. Organization—Bedford-Moore Area." *Bedford County Historical Quarterly* 5 (1981).

Lash, Jeffrey N. "Joseph E. Johnston's Grenada Blunder: A Failure in Command." *Civil War History* 23 (1977): 114–28.

McGrew, Amie Caldwell. "Bedford County Communities." *Bedford County Historical Quarterly* 1 (1977).

McMurray, Richard M. "The Atlanta Campaign of 1864: A New Look." *Civil War History* 22 (1976): 5–15.

———. "Confederate Morale in the Atlanta Campaign of 1864." *Georgia Historical Quarterly* 54 (1970): 226–43.

McNeil, William J. "A Survey of Confederate Soldier Morale During Sherman's Campaign Through Georgia and the Carolinas." *Georgia Historical Quarterly* 55 (1971): 1–26.

Maslowski, Pete. "A Study of Morale in Civil War Soldiers." *Military Affairs* 34 (1970): 120–26.

Meredith, Owen N. "The Sam Davis Home." *Tennessee Historical Quarterly* 24 (1965): 303–20.

Morrill, George P. "The Soldier Who Wouldn't Tell." *Read Magazine* 35 (March 1986): 20–26.

Norton, Herman. "Revivalism in the Confederate Armies." *Civil War History* 6 (1960): 410–24.

Patterson, R. L. "Richmond." *Bedford County Historical Quarterly* 3 (1979).

Prim, G. Clinton, Jr. "Born Again in the Trenches: Revivals in the Army of Tennessee." *Tennessee Historical Quarterly* 43 (1984): 250–72.

Rosen, G. "Nostalgia: A Forgotten Nervous Disorder." *Psychological Medicine* 4 (1974): 340–51.

Simpson, John A. "The Cult of the 'Lost Cause.'" *Tennessee Historical Quarterly* 34 (1975): 350–61.

———. "John B. Gordon and the United Confederate Veterans." *Atlanta Historical Bulletin* 21 (1977): 44–52.

———. "Shall We Change the Words to *Dixie?*" *Southern Folklore Quarterly* 45 (1981): 19–40.

"Sumner A. Cunningham and the *Confederate Veteran* Magazine." *Southern Magazine* 34 (1934): 26, 49.

Thomas, Eugene W. "Prisoners of War Exchange During the American Civil War." Ph.D. dissertation, Auburn University, 1976.

"Thomas Rawlings Myers' Memoirs, March 28, 1916." *Bedford County Historical Quarterly* 5 (1981).

Trotter, Robert J. "Stop Blaming Yourself." *Psychology Today* 21 (February 1987): 31–38.

Walker, Peter Franklin. "Building a Tennessee Army, Autumn, 1861." *Tennessee Historical Quarterly* 16 (1957): 99–116.

BOOKS AND PAMPHLETS

Alexander, Thomas B. *Political Reconstruction in Tennessee*. New York: Russell and Russell, 1950.

Amann, William F. *Personnel of the Civil War*. 2 vols. New York: Yoseloff, 1961.

Armstrong, Zella. *The History of Hamilton County and Chattanooga, Tennessee*. 2 vols. Chattanooga: Lookout Mountain Publishing Co., n.d.

Ash, Stephen V. *Middle Tennessee Society Transformed, 1860–1870: War and Peace in the Upper South* (Baton Rouge: Louisiana State University Press, 1988).

Bailey, Fred Arthur. *Class and Tennessee's Confederate Generation*. Chapel Hill: University of North Carolina Press, 1987.

Bearrs, Edwin C., and Warren Grabau. *The Battle of Jackson, May 14, 1863*. Baltimore: Gateway Press, 1981.

Beers, Henry. *Guide to the Archives of the Government of the Confederate States of America.* Washington, D.C.: General Services Administration, 1968.

————, ed. *Regimental Publications and Personal Narratives of the Civil War.* 3 vols. New York: New York Public Library, 1961–1971.

Beringer, Richard E., Herman Hattaway, Archer Jones, and William N. Still, Jr. *Why the South Lost the Civil War.* Athens: University of Georgia Press, 1986.

Bickley, R. Bruce, Jr. *Joel Chandler Harris.* Athens: University of Georgia Press, 1987.

Boritt, Gabor S., ed. *Why the Confederacy Lost.* New York: Oxford University Press, 1992.

Braden, Waldo W., ed. *Oratory of the New South.* Baton Rouge: Louisiana State University Press, 1970.

Brooks, Stewart. *Civil War Medicine.* Springfield, Ill.: Charles C. Thomas Publishers, 1968.

Brown, Richard D. *Modernization: The Transformation of American Life, 1600–1865.* New York: Hill and Wang, 1976.

Buck, Paul H. *The Road to Reunion, 1865–1900.* Boston: Little, Brown, 1937.

Burnham, W. Dean. *Presidential Ballots, 1832–1896.* Baltimore: Johns Hopkins University Press, 1955.

Carter, Samuel. *The Final Fortress: The Campaign for Vicksburg, 1862–1863.* New York: St. Martin's Press, 1980.

————. *The Siege of Atlanta, 1864.* New York: St. Martin's Press, 1973.

*Cartersville Centennial, 1872–1972.* Cartersville: Tribune News Printing Co., 1972.

Cartwright, Joseph H. *The Triumph of Jim Crow: Tennessee Race Relations in the 1880's.* Knoxville: University of Tennessee Press, 1976.

Cash, W. J. *The Mind of the South.* New York: Knopf, 1941.

Clark, Blanche Henry. *The Tennessee Yeoman, 1840–1860.* Nashville: Vanderbilt University Press, 1942.

Clark, Thomas D. *Pills, Petticoats and Plows; The Southern Country Store.* N.Y.: Bobbs-Merrill Co., 1944.

————. *The Rural Press and the New South.* Baton Rouge: Louisiana State University Press, 1948.

Clinton, Catherine. *The Plantation Mistress: Woman's World in the Old South.* N.Y.: Pantheon Books, 1982.

Cody, Annie E. *Histories of Chapters of Tennessee Division, United Daughters of the Confederacy.* N.p., 1945.

————. *History of the Tennessee Division, United Daughters of the Confederacy.* Nashville: Cullom and Ghertner Co., 1945.

Commager, Henry Steele. *The American Mind: An Interpretation of American Thought and Character Since the 1880's.* New Haven: Yale University Press, 1950.

*Confederate Patriot Index, 1924–1978, Tennessee Division, United Daughters of the Confederacy.* 2 vols. Columbia, Tenn.: P-Vine Press, 1978.

*Congressional Quarterly's Guide to U.S. Elections.* Washington, D.C.: Congressional Quarterly, 1975.

Connelly, Thomas L. *The Army of the Heartland: The Army of Tennessee, 1861–1862.* Baton Rouge: Louisiana State University Press, 1967.

———. *Autumn of Glory: The Army of Tennessee, 1862–1865.* Baton Rouge: Louisiana State University Press, 1971.

———. *Civil War Tennessee: Battles and Leaders.* Knoxville: University of Tennessee Press, 1979.

———. *The Marble Man: Robert E. Lee and His Image in American Society.* Baton Rouge: Louisiana State University Press, 1977.

Connelly, Thomas L., and Archer Jones. *The Politics of Command: Factions and Ideas in Confederate Strategy.* Baton Rouge: Louisiana State University Press, 1973.

Connelly, Thomas L., and James Lee McDonough. *Five Tragic Hours: The Battle of Franklin.* Knoxville: University of Tennessee Press, 1983.

*Constitution and by-Laws, Tennessee Division, United Daughters of the Confederacy.* N.p., 1961.

Cook, Jerry W. *Obituaries of Our Ancestors As Transcribed from the Shelbyville Gazette, Bedford County, Tennessee.* Wartrace, Tenn.: 1990.

Cooling, Benjamin Franklin. *Forts Henry and Donelson: The Key to the Confederate Heartland.* Knoxville: University of Tennessee Press, 1987.

Craig, Tracy Linton, ed. *Directory of Historical Societies and Agencies in the United States and Canada.* Nashville: American Association for State and Local History, 1982.

Cummings, Charles M. *Yankee Quaker, Confederate General: The Curious Career of Bushrod Johnson.* Rutherford, N.J.: Fairleigh Dickinson University Press, 1971.

Cunningham, Edward. *The Port Hudson Campaign, 1862–1863.* Baton Rouge: Louisiana State University Press, 1963.

Cunyus, Lucy J. *The History of Bartow County.* Easley, S.C.: Tribune Publishing Co., 1971.

Daniel, Larry J. *Soldiering in the Army of Tennessee: A Portrait of Life in a Confederate Army.* Chapel Hill: University of North Carolina Press, 1991.

Davis, Harold E. *Henry Grady's New South: Atlanta, a Brave and Beautiful City.* University: University of Alabama Press, 1990.

Davis, Louise Littleton. *Frontier Tales of Tennessee.* Gretna, La.: Pelican, 1976.

Davis, Robert Scott, Jr. *Research in Georgia.* Easley, S.C.: Southern Historical Press, 1981.

Dearing, Mary R. *Veterans In Politics: The Story of the GAR.* Baton Rouge: Louisiana State University Press, 1952.

Decker, Peter. *Fortunes and Failures: White-Collar Mobility in Nineteenth-Century San Francisco.* Cambridge: Harvard University Press, 1978.

DeSantis, Vincent. *Republicans Face the Southern Question.* Baltimore: Johns Hopkins University Press, 1959.

Dodd, Donald B., and Wynette S. Dodd, eds. *Historical Statistics of the South, 1790–1970*. University: University of Alabama Press, 1973.

Downey, Fairfax. *Storming the Gateway: Chattanooga, 1863*. New York: McKay, 1960.

Doyle, Don H. *Nashville: In the New South, 1880–1930*. Knoxville: University of Tennessee Press, 1985.

Dyer, Frederick. *A Compendium of the War of the Rebellion*. 3 vols. New York: Yoseloff, 1959.

Dyer, John P. *The Gallant Hood*. Indianapolis: Bobbs-Merrill, 1950.

Esposito, Vincent J. *The West Point Atlas of American Wars*. Vol. 1. New York: Praequer, 1959.

Faulkner, Harold U. *Politics, Reform, and Expansion: 1890–1900*. Baton Rouge: Louisiana State University Press, 1959.

Faulkner, William. *Intruder in the Dust*. New York: Random House, 1948 reprint.

Faust, Patricia L., ed. *Historical Times Illustrated Encyclopedia of the Civil War*. New York: Harper & Row, 1986.

Folmsbee, Stanley J., Robert E. Corlew, and Enoch L. Mitchell. *Tennessee: A Short History*. Knoxville: University of Tennessee Press, 1969.

Foote, Shelby. *The Civil War*. 3 vols. New York: Random House, 1974.

*Forsyth, Monroe County, Georgia: Sesqui-Centennial. 1823–1973*. N.p., n.d.

Foster, Austin P. *Counties of Tennessee*. Nashville: Department of Education Office, 1923.

Foster, Gaines M. *Ghosts of the Confederacy: Defeat, the Lost Cause, and the Emergence of the New South, 1865–1913*. New York: Oxford University Press, 1987.

Fuller, Claud E., and Richard E. Steuart. *Firearms of the Confederacy*. Huntington, W.Va.: Standard Publications, 1944.

Garraty, John A. *The New Commonwealth, 1877–1890*. New York: Harper & Row, 1968.

Gaston, Paul M. *The New South Creed: A Study in Southern Mythmaking*. New York: Knopf, 1970.

Govan, Gilbert E., and James W. Livingood. *The Chattanooga Country, 1540–1962*. Chapel Hill: University of North Carolina Press, 1963.

———. *A Different Valor: The Story of General Joseph E. Johnston, C.S.A.* New York: Bobbs-Merrill, 1956.

Grantham, Dewey, ed. *The South and the Sectional Image*. New York: Harper & Row, 1967.

Hahn, Steven. *The Roots of Southern Populism: Yeomen Farmers and the Transformation of the Georgian Upcountry, 1850–1890*. New York: Oxford University Press, 1983.

Hale, Will T., and Dixon L. Merritt. *A History of Tennessee and Tennesseans*. Vol. 4. Chicago: Lewis Publishing Co., 1913.

Hamer, Philip M. *Tennessee: A History, 1673–1932*. Vol. 2. New York: American Historical Society, 1933.

Hamilton, James J. *The Battle of Fort Donelson*. South Brunswick, N.J.: Yoseloff, 1968.

Hart, Roger L. *Redeemers, Bourbons and Populists: Tennessee, 1870–1896*. Baton Rouge: Louisiana State University Press, 1975.

Hattaway, Herman. *General Stephen D. Lee*. Jackson: University Press of Mississippi, 1976.

Hay, Thomas B. *Hood's Tennessee Campaign*. Dayton, Ohio: Morningside Press, 1976 reprint.

Hershon, Stanley P. *Farewell to the Bloody Shirt*. Bloomington: Indiana University Press, 1962.

Hesseltine, William B. *Civil War Prisons*. Iowa City: State University of Iowa Press, 1962.

———. *Confederate Leaders in the New South*. Baton Rouge: Louisiana State University Press, 1950.

Horn, Stanley. *The Army of Tennessee: A Military History*. New York: Bobbs-Merrill, 1941.

———. *The Decisive Battle of Nashville*. Baton Rouge: Louisiana State University Press, 1956.

———. *Invisible Empire: The Story of the Ku Klux Klan*. Boston: Houghton Mifflin, 1939.

Howe, Daniel Walker. *Victorian America*. Philadelphia: University of Pennsylvania Press, 1976.

Hughes, Nathaniel C. *General William J. Hardee: Old Reliable*. Baton Rouge: Louisiana State University Press, 1965.

Hutson, J. L. *Old Times in Bedford County*. Shelbyville, Tenn.: Shelbyville Lions Club, n.d.

Hyman, Harold. *Era of the Oath: Northern Loyalty Tests during the Civil War and Reconstruction*. Philadelphia: University of Pennsylvania Press, 1954.

Isaac, Paul E. *Prohibition and Politics: Turbulent Decades in Tennessee, 1885–1920*. Knoxville: University of Tennessee Press, 1965.

Jennings, Thelma. *The Nashville Convention: Southern Movement for Unity, 1848–1851*. Memphis: Memphis State University Press, 1980.

Johnson, Gerald W. *An Honorable Titan: A Biographical Study of Adolph S. Ochs*. New York: Harper & Brothers, 1956.

Jones, Archer. *Confederate Strategy from Shiloh to Vicksburg*. Baton Rouge: Louisiana State University Press, 1961.

Josephson, Matthew. *The Politicos, 1865–1896*. New York: Harcourt, Brace, 1938.

Kendrick, Benjamin, and Alex M. Arnett. *The South Looks at Its Past*. Chapel Hill: University of North Carolina Press, 1935.

Kilpatrick, James J., and Louis D. Rubin, eds. *The Lasting South: Fourteen Southerners Look at Their Home*. Chicago: Regnery Co., 1957.

Linderman, Gerald. *Embattled Courage: The Experience of Combat in the American Civil War*. New York: Free Press, 1987.

Lipset, Seymour M., and Reinhard Bendix, eds. *Class, Status, and Power:*

*Social Stratification in Comparative Perspectives*. New York: Free Press, 1966.

Lonn, Ella. *Desertion during the Civil War*. New York: Century, 1928.

Losson, Christopher. *Tennessee's Forgotten Warriors: Frank Cheatham and His Confederate Division*. Knoxville: University of Tennessee Press, 1989.

Lucas, Silas Emmett, Jr., ed. *Some Georgia County Records: Being Some of the Legal Records of Bibbs, Butts, Fayette, Henry, Monroe and Newton Counties, Georgia*. Easley, S.C.: Southern Historical Press, 1977.

McConnell, Stuart. *Glorious Contentment: The Grand Army of the Republic, 1865–1900*. Chapel Hill: University of North Carolina Press, 1992.

McDonough, James Lee. *Chattanooga: A Death Grip on the Confederacy*. Knoxville: University of Tennessee Press, 1984.

McMurray, Richard M. *John Bell Hood and the War for Southern Independence*. Lexington: University of Kentucky Press, 1982.

———. *Two Great Rebel Armies: An Essay in Confederate Military History*. Chapel Hill: University of North Carolina Press, 1989.

McWhiney, Grady, and Perry D. Jamieson. *Attack and Die: Civil War Military Tactics and the Southern Heritage*. University: University of Alabama Press, 1982.

Maddox, Joseph T. *Some Mid-1800 People: Monroe County, Georgia*. N.p., n.d.

Majors, William R. *Editorial Wild Oats: Edward Ward Carmack and Tennessee Politics*. Macon, Ga.: Mercer University Press, 1984.

Marsh, Helen Crawford, and Timothy Richard Marsh. *Bedford County, Tennessee: Bible Records*. Vol. 1. Shelbyville: Marsh Historical Publications, 1977.

———. *Cemetery Records of Bedford County, Tennessee*. Shelbyville: Marsh Historical Publications, 1976.

———. *Newspaper Vital Records of Bedford County, Tennessee*. Shelbyville: Marsh Historical Publications, 1984.

Maslowski, Peter. *Treason Must Be Made Odious: Military Occupation and Wartime Reconstruction in Nashville, Tennessee, 1862–1865*. Millwood, N.Y.: KTO Press, 1978.

Meyer, D. H. *The Instructed Conscience: The Shaping of the American National Ethic*. Philadelphia: University of Pennsylvania Press, 1972.

Millis, Walter. *The Martial Spirit*. Cambridge: Riverside Press, 1931.

Mitchell, Reid. *Civil War Soldiers: Their Expectations and Their Experiences*. New York: Touchstone, 1988.

*Monroe County, Georgia: A History*. Forsyth, Ga.: Monroe County Historical Society, 1979.

Mooney, Chase C. *Slavery in Tennessee*. Bloomington: Indiana University Press, 1957.

Morgan, H. Wayne. *From Hayes to McKinley: National Party Politics, 1877–1896*. Syracuse, N.Y.: Syracuse University Press, 1969.

Morris, Richard B. *Encyclopedia of American History*. New York: Harper & Row, 1970.

Mott, Frank L. *American Journalism: A History, 1690–1960*. New York: Macmillan Co., 1962.

———. *A History of American Magazines, 1885–1905*. Cambridge: Harvard University Press, 1957.

Mullin, Larry A. *The Napoleon of Gotham: A Study of the Life of Charles Broadway Rouss*. Winchester, Va., 1974.

Nevins, Allan. *Grover Cleveland: A Study In Courage*. New York: Dodd, Mead, 1932.

*Newspapers in Microform: United States, 1948–1972*. Washington, D.C.: Library of Congress, 1973.

Nolan, Alan T. *Lee Considered: General Robert E. Lee and Civil War History*. Chapel Hill: University of North Carolina Press, 1991.

Osterweis, Rollin G. *The Myth of the Lost Cause, 1865–1900*. Hamden, Conn.: Archon Books, 1973.

Parker, David B. *Alias, Bill Arp: Charles Henry Smith and the South's "Goodly Heritage."* Athens: University of Georgia Press, 1991.

Parke-Bernet Galleries. *Inventory of Forest H. Sweet Collection Sold in Auction, September 24, 1962, #2205*.

Patton, James W. *Unionism and Reconstruction in Tennessee, 1860–1869*. Chapel Hill: University of North Carolina Press, 1934.

Petersen, Svend. *A Statistical History of the American Presidential Elections*. New York: Frederick Ungar, 1963.

Pinkowski, Edward. *Pills, Pens and Politics: The Story of General Leon Jastremski: 1843–1907*. Wilmington, Del.: Captain Stanislaus Mlotowski Memorial Brigade Society, 1974.

Piston, William Garrett. *Lee's Tarnished Lieutenant: James Longstreet and His Place in Southern History*. Athens: University of Georgia Press, 1987.

Polakoff, Keith Ian. *The Politics of Inertia: The Election of 1876 and the End of Reconstruction*. Baton Rouge: Louisiana State University Press, 1973.

*Prominent Reference Book of Prominent Kentuckians*. Louisville: Standard, n.d.

Purdue, Howell, and Elizabeth Purdue. *Pat Cleburne, Confederate General*. Hillsboro, Tex.: Hill Junior College Press, 1973.

Ransom, Roger, and Richard Sutch, eds. *One Kind of Freedom*. Cambridge: Cambridge University Press, 1977.

Robartson, James I., ed. *An Index-Guide to the Southern Historical Society Papers, 1876–1959*. Millwood, N.Y.: Kraus International Publications, 1980.

Roffalovich, George. *An Historical Sketch of Monroe County*. N.p., n.d.

Roland, Charles P. *Albert Sidney Johnston, Soldier of Three Republics*. Austin: University of Texas Press, 1964.

Ross, Ishbel. *First Lady of the South*. New York: Harper & Brothers, 1958.

Rowland, Dunbar. *Jefferson Davis, Constitutionalist: His Letters, Papers, and Speeches*. Jackson: Mississippi State Department of Archives and History, 1923.

Scott, E. C. *Ministerial Directory of the Presbyterian Church U.S., 1861–1941*. Austin, Tex.: Von Boeckmann-Jones, 1942.

Shattuck, Gardiner H. *A Shield and Hiding Place: The Religious Life of the Civil War Armies*. Macon, Ga.: Mercer University Press, 1987.

Steiner, Paul E. *Disease in the Civil War: Natural Biological Warfare in 1861–1865*. Springfield, Ill.: Charles C. Thomas, 1968.

———. *Medical-Military Portraits of Union and Confederate Generals*. Philadelphia: Whitmore Publishing Co., 1968.

Stickles, Arndt M. *Simon B. Buckner, Borderland Knight*. Chapel Hill: University of North Carolina Press, 1940.

Strode, Hudson. *Jefferson Davis: Private Letters, 1823–1889*. New York: Harcourt, Brace and World, 1966.

———. *Jefferson Davis: Tragic Hero*. 3 vols. New York: Harcourt, Brace and World, 1964.

Sutherland, Daniel E. *The Confederate Carpetbaggers*. Baton Rouge: Louisiana State University Press, 1988.

Sweet, Forest. *Directory of Collectors of Books, Autographs, Prints and Other Historical Material Relating to Abraham Lincoln*. Battle Creek, Mich.: F. H. Sweet, 1946, 1949.

Taylor, William R. *Cavalier and Yankee: The Old South and the American National Character*. New York: George Braziller, 1961.

*Tennessee, Bedford Quadrangle* (U.S. Geological Survey Map).

*Tennesseans in the Civil War: A Military History of Confederate and Union Units with Available Rosters of Personnel*. 2 vols. Nashville: Civil War Centennial Commission, 1964.

*Tennessee Records of Bedford County. General Index to Deeds, 1808–1840*. Vol. 1. Nashville: Historical Records Survey, Works Progress Administration, 1940.

Thomas, Eugene W. "Prisoners of War Exchange During the American Civil War." Ph.D. dissertation, Auburn University, 1976.

Tindall, George Brown. *The Persistent Tradition in New South Politics*. Baton Rouge: Louisiana State University Press, 1975.

Trelease, Allan W. *White Terror: The Ku Klux Klan Conspiracy and Southern Reconstruction*. New York: Harper & Row, 1971.

Warner, Ezra J. *Generals in Gray: Lives of the Confederate Commanders*. Baton Rouge: Louisiana State University Press, 1959.

Weaver, Richard. *The Southern Tradition At Bay: A History of Post-Bellum Thought*. New Rochelle, N.Y.: Arlington House, 1968.

White, William W. *The Confederate Veteran*. Tuscaloosa, Ala.: Confederate Publishing Co., 1962.

Wiley, Bell I. *The Life of Johnny Reb: The Common Soldier of the Confederacy*. Baton Rouge: Louisiana State University Press, 1978.

Williams, T. Harry. *P.G.T. Beauregard: Napoleon in Gray*. Baton Rouge: Louisiana State University Press, 1955.

Wilson, Charles R. *Baptized in Blood: The Religion of the Lost Cause, 1865–1920*. Athens: University of Georgia Press, 1980.

Wilson, Edmund. *Patriotic Gore: Studies in the Literature of the American Civil War*. New York: Oxford University Press, 1962.

Winslow, Hattie L., and Joseph R. H. Moore. *Camp Morton, 1861–1865*. Indianapolis: Indiana Historical Society, 1940.

Woodward, C. Vann. *The Burden of Southern History*. Baton Rouge: Louisiana State University Press, 1968.

―――. *Origins of the New South, 1877–1913*. Baton Rouge: Louisiana State University Press, 1971.

―――. *Reunion and Reaction*. New York: Doubleday & Company, 1956.

―――. *The Strange Career of Jim Crow*. New York: Oxford University Press, 1966.

―――. *Thinking Back: The Perils of Writing History*. Baton Rouge: Louisiana State University Press, 1987.

―――. *Tom Watson: Agrarian Rebel*. New York: Oxford University Press, 1963.

Wright, Gavin. *The Political Economy of the Cotton South: Households, Markets and Wealth in the Nineteenth Century*. New York: Norton, 1978.

Wyatt-Brown, Bertram. *Southern Honor: Ethics and Behavior in the Old South*. New York: Oxford University Press, 1982.

# Index

"Cassville incident," 37
Centennial Park, 123–24, 158
*Century Magazine*, 78
Chalaron, J. A., 106; in the Battle
    Abbey feud, 128, 130, 131, 132, 138,
    142, 143
Champion, S. A., 133, 136, 141–42
*Charm* (steamboat), 23
Chattanooga, Tennessee: yellow fever
    epidemic in, 65
Chattanooga campaign, 30–31
*Chattanooga Dispatch*, 60
Chattanooga Railroad, 58
*Chattanooga Times*: Cunningham's
    editorship/ownership of, 57–64, 67;
    "Cincinnati's hatred of the South"
    editorial, 58–59
*Chattanooga Weekly Commercial*, 65
Cheatham, Benjamin F., 36
Cheatham Bivouac. *See* Frank B.
    Cheatham Bivouac #1
Chicago, monument building in, 123
Chickamauga: battle of, 29–30;
    proposed military park at, 63
Childress, John W., 72, 77, 82–83
Chipley, W. D., 126, 129
*Christian Advocate*, 67
*The Clansman* (Dixon), 118
Colleges, Southern, 117–19
Columbia Pike, 43, 44
Colyar, A. S., 72, 74
Company B, 41st Tennessee Infantry
    Regiment: Richmond Gentry's
    assignment to, 10; Cunningham's
    enlistment and assignment to, 10–
    11; military life of, at Camp
    Trousdale, 11, 12–13; in battle for
    Fort Donelson, 13–16; at Camp
    Morton, 17–21; reassemblage in
    Clinton, Mississippi, 22; at Port
    Hudson, Louisiana, 23–24;
    desertions from, 24, 27, 28, 34, 37,
    38, 40, 48; in battle of Raymond,
    Mississippi, 25–26; reassignment to
    Georgia division, 27; in battle of

Chickamauga, 29–30; in
    Chattanooga campaign, 30–31;
    religious revivalism in, 35–36; in
    Atlanta campaign, 36–40; at Spring
    Hill, 42–43; in battle of Franklin,
    43–46; at Shy's Hill, 47; first reunion
    of the, 62–63. See also
    *Reminiscences of the 41st Tennessee
    Regiment* (Cunningham, S.A.)
Confederate graves, care of, 105
Confederate history, interpretations
    of, 115–19
Confederate Memorial Association:
    and the Battle Abbey feud, 126–45
    passim
Confederate Memorial Institute,
    120–30
*Confederate Military History* (Evans,
    C.A.), 117
Confederate pensions, 120–21
Confederate regiments in Tennessee,
    10–11
Confederate reunions, 78. *See also*
    Reunions
*Confederate Veteran*, 1, 89;
    Cunningham's editorship/ownership
    of, 90–100; quest for official
    endorsement of the *Confederate
    Veteran* by the UCV, 91–95, 99–100;
    coverage of UDC activities, 103–4;
    editorial on secession, 113; Elson
    controversy in the, 118–19; "The
    Last Roll" series in, 122; "A
    Confederate Westminster" in, 125;
    in the Underwood-Cunningham
    lawsuit over the Battle Abbey, 131–
    33, 134, 136, 138–39, 142, 143; "How
    Shall Sam Davis Be Honored"
    editorial in, 148; disposition of the,
    156; Edith Pope as editor of the, 156,
    158–60; last issue of the, 159; rebirth
    of the, 161
Confederate veterans organizations,
    76–81
*Confederate War Journal Illustrated*, 92

Randolph, Janet, 104, 106
Raymond, Mississippi, battle of, 25–26
*Red Rock: A Chronicle of Reconstruction* (Page), 118
Reese, George, 142, 143–44
Reeves and Cunningham Dry Goods Store, 53, 55
Regimental histories, preparation of, 117
Regimental reunions, 62–63
*Reminiscences of the 41st Tennessee Regiment* (Cunningham, S. A.), 54–55, 78
Reunions: Blue-Gray, 106–9; regimental, 62–63; Confederate, 78; state, 100; UCV, 101–9, 110; Gettysburg, 108–9
R. G. Dun and Co., 53
Richmond Gentrys: Cunningham's enlistment in, 10–11
*Rise and Fall of the Confederate Government* (Davis, J.), 117
Robinson, Sarah Buchanan (cousin), 3
Rodeffer, J. D., 118
Roosevelt, Theodore, 114, 115
Root, Elihu, 121
Rose, D. G., 20
Rouss, Charles Broadway, 125–26, 128, 136–37, 143
Russ, Robert, 55
Rutherford, Mildred Lewis, 104

S. A. Cunningham Camp of the United Son's of Confederate Veterans, 124
S. A. Cunningham Junior Sons of Confederate Veterans (boys club), 105
St. Thomas Hospital, 2
Secession, Cunningham's defense of, 113
Senter, DeWitt C., 52
Shaw, Albert D., 107
Shaw, H. B., 152
Shelbyville, Tennessee, 4, 18, 52, 110;

Cunningham's funeral in, 3, 157–58; Ku Klux Klan in, 55; erection of Confederate monument in, 124–25; Cunningham monument in, 157–58
*Shelbyville Bulletin*, 53
*Shelbyville Commercial*: Cunningham's editorship/ownership of, 53–56
*Shelbyville Rescue*, 53, 54
Sherman, William T., 23, 63
Shipp, J. F., 80
Shook, Isaac, 5
Shy's Hill, 47
60th Indiana, 18
"Solid South," race issue and the, 114–15
Southern colleges, 117–19
*Southern Historical Society Papers*, 62, 78–79
Southern loyalty: Cunningham on the subject of, 113
Southern Press Association, 82–83, 87, 97
Southwest Methodist-Episcopal Publishing House, 96–97, 133, 138
Spanish-American War, 105, 107
Spencer, William W., 150
Spring Hill, 42–43
State reunions, 100
Strahl, Otho F., 38, 42, 44, 45, 78, 147

Taft, William Howard, 107, 115
Tanner, Joseph, 71
Taylor, Robert Love, 115
Teague, B. H., 93–94, 134–35
Tennessee: military campaign of 1864 in, 41–49; politics and political restoration in, 50–52; race relations in, 51, 75; state debt issue in, 61–62; prohibition movement in, 74–75; pension system in, 120–21
Tennessee Bourbonism, 60, 61
Tennessee Centennial Exposition, 127, 129

Tennessee Coal, Iron and Railroad Company, 74
Tennessee Historical Society, 67, 72, 73, 75, 79, 110, 148
Tennessee State Library, 54
30th Louisiana, 23
Tilden, Samuel B., 60
Tillman, James D., 30, 31, 38, 63, 155
Tillman, Lewis, 138
Tolley, William P., 137
Toney, Marcus, 127
Turley, Thomas B., 124
Turney, Peter, 77–78

Underwood, John C., 87–88, 94, 97–98, 123; as superintendent and secretary for the Battle Abbey, 128, 129; and lawsuit with Cunningham over the Battle Abbey, 131–45
United Confederate Veterans Association (UCV), 1, 81, 105, 158; and Jefferson Davis monument project, 82, 83, 84, 86, 87–88; Cunningham's quest for official endorsement of the *Confederate Veteran* by the, 91–95, 99–100; and Cunningham's criticisms of reunion management, 101–9; history committee, 116–19; committee on charities, 121; in the Battle Abbey feud, 132, 142, 143. *See also* S. A. Cunningham Camp of the United Son's of Confederate Veterans
United Daughters of the Confederacy (UDC), 1, 158; and construction of the Jefferson Davis monument, 88; coverage in *Confederate Veteran* of

activities by, 103–5; and special service medal to Cunningham, 105; and the Samuel Davis monument project, 149; and Cunningham Memorial Scholarship, 161. *See also* S. A. Cunningham Junior Sons of Confederate Veterans (boys club)
Universal manhood suffrage, 51

Vance, James I., 2, 161
Vicksburg, Mississippi, 20, 22, 27, 28

Wakefield, Mrs. Thomas (Addie), 156
Walker, Susie, 104
Walker, W. H. T., 27
*War Journal*, 92–93
Washington, Booker T., 114
Washington, Fred S., 80, 81
Willard, Frances E., 75
Willow Mount Cemetery (Shelbyville, Tennessee), 3, 124
Wilson, Woodrow, 108–9
Wirz, Henry, 149–50
*Woman's Health Journal*, 67
Women's Christian Temperance Union, 75
Wood, Robert C., 126, 128, 138
Wright, Marcus J., 54, 92, 121

Yazoo City, Mississippi, 27–28
Yeoman radicalism, 65, 66
Young, Bennett H., 3, 103, 116
Young, James, 148
Young Men's Democratic Club, 86

Zolnay, George Julian, 148–49